MOLLIE FANCHER,

THE BROOKLYN ENIGMA.

An authentic statement Fa...

...ife of Mary J. Fancher...

Unimpeachable Testimony of Many Witnesses.

By ABRAM...

BROOKLYN, N. Y.

"MAD" MOLLIE
BROOKLYN'S SUPERNATURAL "SAINT"

One Woman's Bout With Possession, Clairvoyance, Multiple Personalities And Uncanny Predictions!

Early works about Mad Mollie were snapped up by a curious public.

Brooklyn was a bustling borough of New York City during the time that Mollie Fancher lived there.

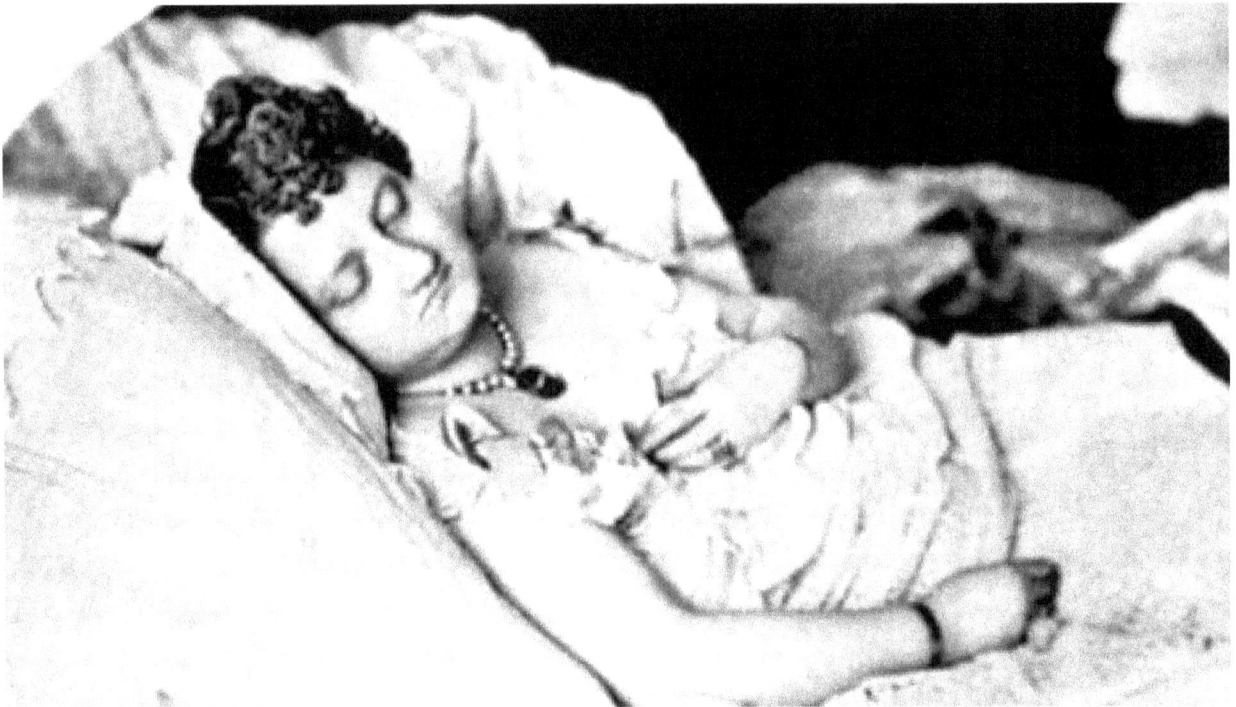

For a good part of half a century, Mollie just closed her eyes and slept her life away.

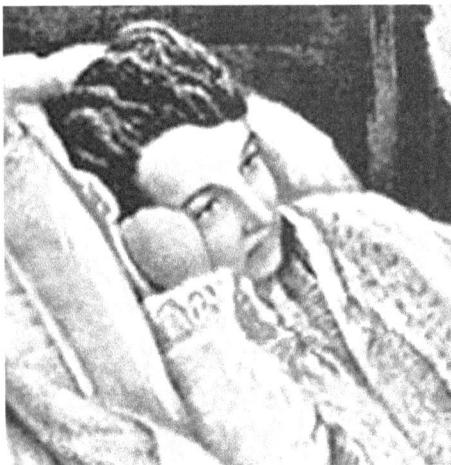

Skeptics abounded when it came to her fasting, claiming that she was receiving food surreptitiously.

Despite her long periods of sleep, Mollie did have an array of visitors — some of high social standing.

"MAD" MOLLIE

MOLLIE FANCHER, THE BROOKLYN ENIGMA

An Authentic Statement of Facts In The Life of Mary J. Fancher

The Psychological Marvel of the Nineteenth Century

Sean Casteel and Timothy Green Beckley

"MAD" MOLLIE

Sean Casteel
and
Timothy Green Beckley

Revised Edition

Published in the United States of America By
Global Communications/Conspiracy Journal
Box 753 · New Brunswick, NJ 08903

Staff Members
Timothy G. Beckley, Publisher
Carol Ann Rodriguez, Assistant to the Publisher
Sean Casteel, General Associate Editor
Tim R. Swartz, Graphics and Editorial Consultant
William Kern, Editorial and Art Consultant

Sign Up On The Web For Our Free Weekly Newsletter
and Mail Order Version of Conspiracy Journal
and Bizarre Bazaar
www.ConspiracyJournal.com

Order Hot Line: 1-732-602-3407
PayPal: MrUFO8@hotmail.com

POST OFFICE BOX 753
NEW BRUNSWICK, NJ 08903

TABLE OF CONTENTS

GOOD GOLLY MISS MOLLIE

By Timothy Green Beckley

There is no doubt but that Mollie Fancher was a very strange person, thus her entry into our very apropos-named book series. Though probably pretty much forgotten now, in her heyday Mollie received quite a bit of attention in the New York City press as "the Brooklyn Enigma."

Why was she considered such a public spectacle? What was it about Mollie that drew local and international attention and caused the public to line up to visit her at her bedside?

** – It is said she fasted for just around half a century.

** – She slept like a log for days at a time and never got up even to walk around the room.

** – It was claimed that she had lost a good percentage of her senses – that of smell, taste and sight.

** – Despite this she could accurately tell time just by listening to the tick tock of a clock that was out of normal hearing range.

** – She created elaborate embroidered pieces though she apparently lacked mobility, and certainly had no weaving device at her disposal.

** – She sustained herself financially by creating wax flowers which some say materialized out of thin air because no one observed her making them. In fact, it was said that she was pretty much paralyzed.

** – She could see into the future and make predictions which her followers said were mostly accurate.

** – She was oblivious to the sensation of pain inflicted on her by experimenters.

** — She was said to be able to read a book or the paper simply by holding it in her hands although her vision was so poor she was legally considered blind.

And, as author Sean Casteel informs us, Mollie was not just your ordinary run-of- the-mill paranormal oddity but had multiple personalities, was possessed by demonic forces (or so it seems) and had various skills which should have been outside of the realm of what she could accomplish due to her infirmities.

But, as this book will reveal, Mollie was not the only woman seized with weird, supernatural abilities that made her "stand out" from the rest of the populace during roughly the same time period. Sean writes of the other "fasting girls" who seem to have garnered a cult following of at least the curious if not the downright devoted. Were the ladies deep in a religious fervor? Were they merely hysterical ("mad" by common standards)? Or did they possess what we might consider to be paranormal qualities? Was the Lord behind their "fits of fancy," or did the devil have them by the tail?

We can pretty much say with certainty that if these woman had lived just a hundred or so years previous, they might have been condemned by the church and suffered the consequences of being a witch. Their piety would not have shielded them against the wrath of the maniacal clergy, a religious establishment determined to prevent the penitents from influencing their faithful that God Almighty, though invisible, was commanding miracles that would demonstrate that His omnipotent influence could still be felt all around us on an everyday basis.

Sean writes of others – mostly women – some modern, a few historical, who seem to tip the paranormal scales in a positive direction.

He writes of the first recorded stigmata in the case of Saint Francis of Assisi and how, over a century later, Saint Catherine of Siena, Italy, received a "sensation" stigmata as she prayed over her deceased father.

And of an illiterate Italian woman named Natuzzo Evolo, whose blood from her stigmatic wounds would form images and words in Hebrew and Aramaic on a bandage or cloth. Some claimed to have received miraculous healings and other graces from Natuzzo up until her death in 2009.

Not to be outdone, a young Croatian priest says his stigmata caused him to greatly fear God, and he claims to also have been given the powers of levitation, prophecy and bilocation – the ability to be in two places at once.

But our research into this unsettling arena of supernatural traits is by no means over. The truth is, we could continue to review the lives of many individuals going back throughout history. We could include figures like Joan of Arc, who claimed to have spoken with God and been instructed by Him to go into battle. Was Joan an example of spirit possession? Or simple self-delusion? Or was she a real conduit of the Almighty?

SISTERS UNDER THE SKIN

Not all of the manifestations reported around the same time as Mad Mollie made news were of a miraculous nature, as if under the tutelage of God. The spiritualist movement was in full swing during the last half of the nineteenth century thanks to two young girls from just outside of Rochester, New York.

On the last day of March 1848, just before midnight, a mysterious racket of knocking and thumping were heard throughout the house. Fifteen-year-old Maggie and eleven-year-old Katy huddled under their blankets in raw fear as they were encircled by hellish sounds coming from the dark recesses of the small rural home they resided in along with their parents.

As the evening progressed, it seemed to all those present as if the sounds were coming from an intelligent source and were not just the creaking of the floorboards or the wind whistling down the chimney. The girls devised a little game in which they tried to communicate with whomever or whatever was creating this clatter. Snapping their fingers and clapping their hands loudly, they asked the presumed spirit to respond accordingly. It replied with a series of knocking sounds that came from the wall just above their bed, which was now illuminated by candlelight supplied by the matriarchal woman of the household.

A rather jaded site on the internet, History.Net, continued the account of this historic event by stating that this is what happened next, as if they had been in the room: "Taking pity upon her terrified mother, Katy then offered a hint of explanation for the sounds. 'O, mother, I know what it is. Tomorrow is April-fool day and it's somebody trying to fool us,' she began. But Mrs. Fox apparently refused to consider the suggestion of a prank. The ghost, she believed, was real and, terrified though she was, she decided to test it herself. Initially, she asked the ghost to count to 10. After it responded appropriately, she asked other questions, among them, the number of children she had borne. Seven raps came back. How many were still living? Six raps. Their ages? Each was rapped out correctly. As Mrs. Fox later related, she then demanded, If it was an injured spirit, make two raps. Promptly two knocks were returned. Mrs. Fox then wanted to know who the ghost was in life. Maggie and Katy quickly concocted an answer. The spirit, they claimed, was a 31-year-old married man, dead for two years, and the father of five. 'Will you continue to rap if I call in the neighbors,' their mother asked, 'that they may hear it too?'"

Not only did the neighbors come, but the Fox sisters drew crowds from all over, as if they were magnets that could contact the dead. Pretty soon the spiritualist movement was in full swing and mediums, while in a deep trance state, started levitating tables and regurgitating ectoplasm from their mouths, ears and noses. Indeed, spirits were starting to form all over the place and matters were soon out of control as supernatural manifestations became as American as apple pie.

But knocking and thumping soon took a backseat when the Bangs sisters, Lizzie and May, burst on the scene with pretty much just a bucket of paint and a few sheets of canvas. Psychic art has been around, I'm told, for centuries. Mediums in a trance use pencil, pen and paint brush to create paintings from the other side. I can't say this is the way it works in all cases, but the Bangs sisters never touched the paint from the bucket that rested on the floor near where they sat. They would be in a moderately lit room and, over a period of maybe an hour TOPS, an image would start to appear on the canvas which they each held onto with their hands, making it impossible for them to use any sort of brush or hidden device. In spiritualist jargon this is called Precipitated Spirit Paintings.

With the vast and marvelous records of American physical mediumship, one of the most outstanding chapters belongs to the turn-of-the-century mediums Misses Elizabeth S. and May E. Bangs of Chicago, Illinois. Their gifts included aboveboard, independent writing in broad daylight (mostly slates) and independent drawings and paintings, which were all forms of fully-developed clairvoyance, materializations, and direct voices. But their most wondrous and spectacular phenomenon was that of Precipitated Spirit Portraits in full color.

We found this titillating bit of additional information on the Harragate Spiritual Healing Church web site:

"It was August, in the year 1911. A large audience has filled to capacity the auditorium at the world famous Chesterfield Spiritualist Camp in the State of Indiana, America. They have come to witness a demonstration of psychic power, one of the most unique and marvelous in the entire world.

"A select committee has arranged beforehand that upon entering the building, all have been given a numbered ticket, the stub of which was torn off and put into a large vat to be thoroughly mixed up; later on, one stub will be randomly drawn from the collection. Now, after a close examination by the committee to see that there were no markings or paint of any kind, or signs of chemical treatment, a large plain canvas is placed on an easel in the center of the stage. The spirit mediums who will demonstrate the phenomena now enter the auditorium. They are sisters and appear to be about 35 to 40 years of age. Both take their seats on the rostrum, one situated on each side of the easel and clearly four to five feet from it; they will never touch the canvas throughout the entire demonstration.

"A member of the committee now reaches in and selects from the vat and reads the number aloud to the audience; it belongs to Mrs. Alice Alford. Mrs. Alford and her husband are now invited to come up and take a seat on the stage; they will be sitting for a portrait, but, in this particular instance, the painting will not be of Mr. and Mrs. Alford. The artist and the subject of the session are from a different dimension: the world of Spirits.

"When all is ready, the mediums slowly bow their heads and close their eyes as if in prayer and deep concentration; the silence in the auditorium for five straight minutes is so absolute that the air itself seems to stand still. Suddenly, many in the audience lean forward in their chairs, sitting rigidly, their eyes tense and fixed on the canvas, from which a thin, vapor-like cloud, or shadow it seems, sweeps across it, pulsates, and then flickers out.

"More tense moments, shades of definite color begin to appear, as if successive layers of fine dust have been thrown, or precipitated, on to the canvas to form a cloudy background, and this also seems to pulsate and flicker and then quickly disappear. On and on it goes for several minutes; the other-worldly artist, it seems, is making preliminary sketches and trying out different color schemes.

"Suddenly, all at once, the background slowly and steadily now precipitates into view; clearer and clearer it comes, only this time with it an astounding addition: three pairs of eyes have suddenly appeared on different parts of the canvas; two pairs of which are open and the last, situated directly in the center of the canvas, are closed. The two open pairs immediately disappear and the closed eyes remain, only to instantaneously disappear as the audience gasps in astonishment.

"With each successive phase of the unfolding phenomena, the background becomes clearer and clearer and now, a faint outline of a face and bust slowly precipitates itself into view, disappearing and reappearing several times before remaining in focus on the canvas. It is the unmistakable likeness of a young girl, perhaps 14 to 15 years old......many in the audience are now standing, some pointing in wonderment. Gradually, the appearance becomes more clear and more distinguishable; she is transcendentally beautiful and her hair, clearly auburn brown, falls luxuriously to her bare shoulders, revealed by the white dress she is wearing having been pulled down. Her eyes are closed.

"With the portrait now having completely precipitated on to the canvas, to the utter and absolute astonishment of all, the eyes suddenly open, and the audience thunders in applause. To the front of the stage now step the Alfords, clearly shaken by the experience, and Mr. Alford announces to the gathering that the portrait is an exact likeness of their deceased daughter, Audrey. The Alfords, as it turns out, a prominent family of Marion, Indiana, are not Spiritualists in belief, and this was their first visit to Camp Chesterfield. Mrs. Alford wore around her neck, hidden from sight, a locket containing a photograph of her daughter almost duplicate in likeness of the spirit picture obtained, but different in pose and position. The mediums had not seen the locket picture or any photo of the child nor had they ever made the acquaintance of the Alfords. The finished portrait was precipitated on to the canvas in twenty-two minutes. The spirit mediums of this extraordinary event, *THE BANGS SISTERS*."

* * * * *

So our question remains – is this phenomenon a result of some sort of divine intervention? Is it Godly in nature or precipitated by shadowy figures who live in the Summerland? Or might it just be that these individuals – mainly women as we have noted – are tapping into some inner psychic force to produce manifestations that are so bizarre that they are totally out of the realm of the norm? The jury is out, but additional maddening episodes of this nature can be duly noted as we canvas the pages of history.

Mollie was very good at making quilts, though, with all the sleeping she did, one hardly knows where she found the time.

Mollie sleeps forever beneath this grave marker in Brooklyn. Shestill gets an occasional visitor.

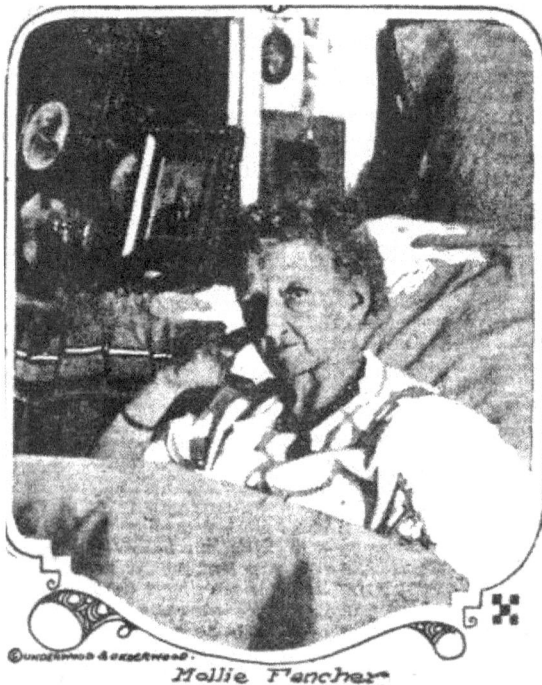

A picture taken shortly before Mad Mollie's passing.

GEORGIANNA W. FANCHER
1850 — 1851
MOLLIE FANCHER
1848 — 1916

MOLLIE
MOLLIE FANCHER KNEW THE SECRET OF LIFE
HALF A CENTURY IN HER BED HER DAUNTLESS SPIRIT
CHEERFUL PATIENCE AND UNFAILING SYMPATHY INSPIRED
MANY WITH COURAGE TO MEET LIFE'S PROBLEMS
FORGETFUL OF HER OWN SUFFERING SHE CARRIED
THE BURDENS OF HOSTS OF FRIENDS
THRU A LIFE OF INDUSTRY GOD GRANTED HER PRAYER
LET ME NOT DIE WITH FOLDED HANDS

FANCHER

Mollie Fancher at age sixteen.

The Fox Sisters were powerful females who jump-
started the Spiritualist movement, which quickly
gathered a huge following.

The Bangs Sisters were loved among the Spiritualist communities for
the phenomenal work they did with spirit paintings.

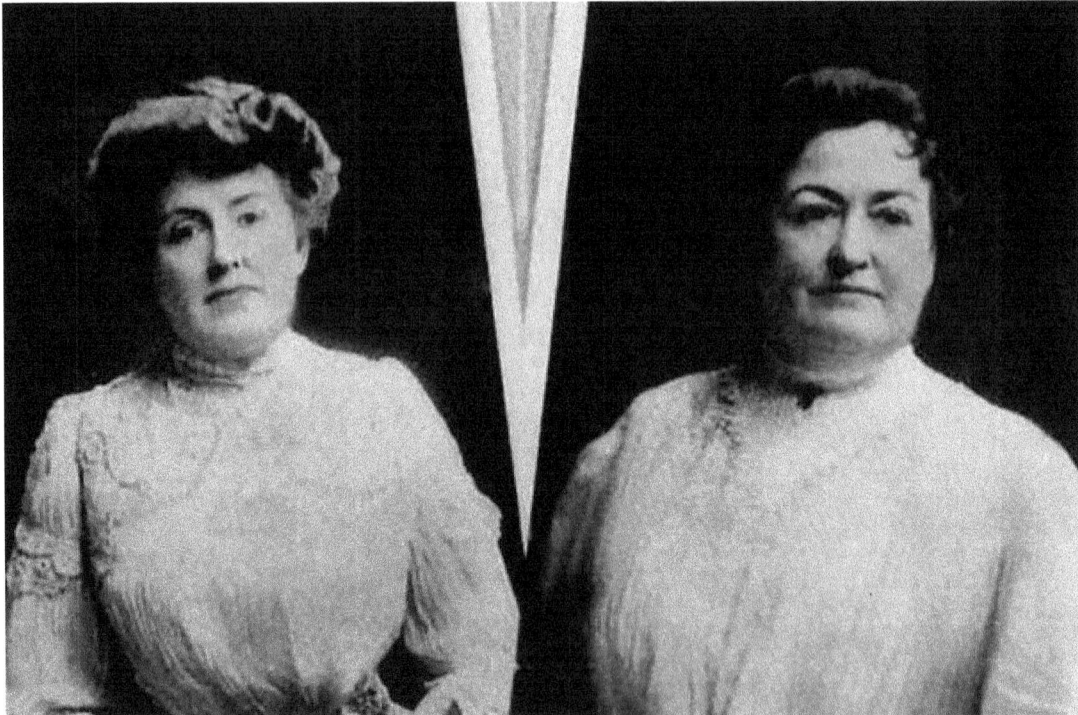

The sisters were very much in demand as they were the only ones who could conjure these types of spirit manifestations.

An Indian spirit guide created without the use of paint or paint brushes. The Bangs sisters merely held onto the canvas while the painting created itself.

A Card from the Bangs Sisters.

CHICAGO, June 9. —[Editor of The Tribune.] —A few months ago when a cowardly raid was made on us at one of our parlor seances at our own home in this city a number of sensational articles appeared in the columns of the press, to the great detriment of our reputation. We then requested the public to withhold judgment until a court of justice had thoroughly investigated the matter. The grand jury of Cook County, after having heard the statement of the witnesses for the State had discharged us, although not a single one of our witnesses was or could be heard by them, thus deciding after hearing the testimony of our persecutors, and without a single word of defense, that the charges were baseless. The object of this card, which we ask a generous press to circulate as freely as it did the articles to our injury, is to inform the public of the final result of this effort to degrade and humiliate us.   BANGS SISTERS.

A card given out by the Bangs Sisters in response to accusations against them.

Spirit paintings done by the Bangs Sisters can be found hanging at Camp Lilly Dale and Camp Chesterfield, enclaves maintained by the Spiritualist community today.

Throngs milled about outside the complex that housed the stove that screamed and cursed.

Many believed that the domestic servant was responsible for the chaos by simply throwing her voice. This was never proven.

Judges and psychiatrists came to evaluate the situation but could find no rational explanation for the phenomenon.

The stove belonging to the Palazon family was said to be haunted. It would talk back to visitors

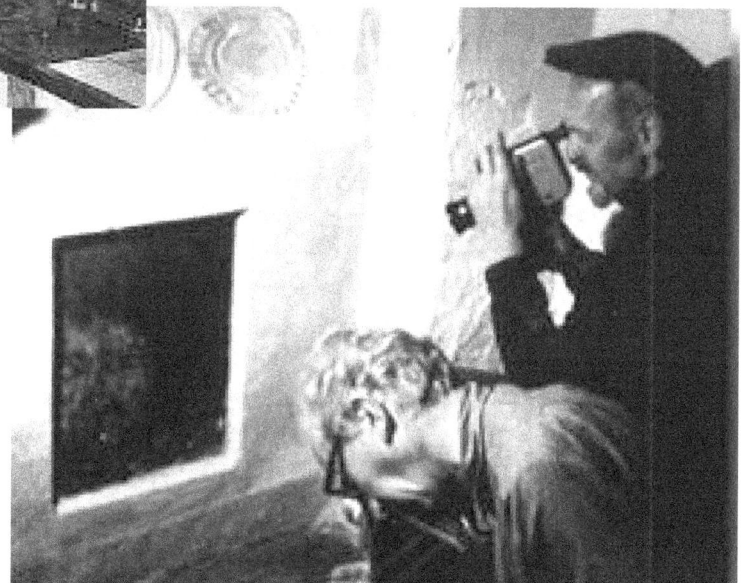

MYSTERY OF SPAIN'S "GOBLIN" STOVE

"You can't be serious," I said to myself when I first heard about the talking "goblin" stove located on Gascon Gotor Street in the town of Zaragoza, Spain. I mean, stoves don't talk, right? Well, this one apparently did and it attracted thousands who wanted to see what the excitement was all about.

And the focus of this phenomena was – well, you might have guessed it by now – a nice lady, a housemaid, who never caused a hint of a domestic problem with any of her previous employers.

It all started one day in 1934 when the Palazon family started to hear insane-sounding utterances and crackling voices coming from inside their modest home. Initially, they thought someone was playing a mean trick on them and that their maid, Pascuala Alcocer, was behind this disturbance. They threatened to let her go if she did not confess.

The maid protested her innocence repeatedly, stating that the wood stove had chosen her in particular to be tormented. Trust me. I know this sounds silly, but, when the maid and the family confronted the stove, it would only get more hostile. But it would also answer inquiries put to it directly, often barking or screaming out its response.

The stove was given the nickname Casa Duende', which roughly translates as "goblin" in Spanish. At first, a few of those on the block were invited in and, while they thought it probably was a hoax, the number of visitors quickly grew until the streets were packed with the curious. Some felt Satan had found a home in the stove, but others thought it was probably the maid throwing her voice.

The frenzied masses were getting to be so much of a problem that the normal flow of traffic was curtailed. We are told that the police were desperate to end the charade and called in several psychiatrists to ascertain whether or not Pascula Alcocer was responsible for these shenanigans. Finding the maid to be of sound mind, they sent her packing, hoping this would put an end to the utterances of the goblin stove.

However, the circus was not to end any time soon.

Ideal Spain, the largest tourist guide to this country, admits that the naysayers were never able to put the case to rest. "It was becoming difficult to prove that this was a hoax. The entity was reported to not only speak, but also to be able to see what was going on around the home. It would guess the number of people that were in a room at a time; it would interact with police officers directly when they asked it what it wanted. In an attempt to solve the mystery, all the people in the block were evacuated, including the maid. It was reported that the voice became angry. The investigators moved in, along with the army and a team of architects. They examined the building from top to bottom. Even the chief architect heard the voice and left the building in a hurry, never to return."

No explanation was ever found and the blame for the voice was pinned securely on Pascuala. She went into seclusion and never did recover fully from the ordeal of being blamed for the goblin voice. In her old age, she refused to speak to the people of the city.

The original building was demolished to try to eradicate the voice and a new building now stands on the plot, Edificio Duende.

An astounding poltergeist disturbance indeed, and, like Mad Mollie, all the clamor and supernatural activity centered around an otherwise normal woman just going about her everyday business.

GEF THE TALKING MONGOOSE

I cannot help but be reminded of the case of Gef the Talking Mongoose who was said to live in a house on the rocky coast of the Isle of Man in the U.K. Like the goblin stove, Gef would rave and rant and loved to curse anyone he disliked.

The mongoose seemed particularly fond of the young female resident of the household who could sometimes get the "animal" to "behave." This unusual haunting, if that's what it can be described as, was validated by the likes of parapsychologist Harry Price, who wrote an entire book about the incident, interviewing those who heard the rummaging of Gef about the out of the way landmark, mostly hiding in the walls but from time to time hitching a ride to town on the undercarriage of the local bus.

Gef is still as popular today was he was more than a hundred years ago. Lectures are given on his demeanor. Price's rare book on the haunting sells for around $500 if you can find a copy, and Facebook even has a page devoted to this little imp who was apparently found dead, at which time the talking stopped.

On the Isle of Man a talking mongoose named Gef was hiding behind the cupboardto snap and curse at anyone who tried to evict him from this coastal home.

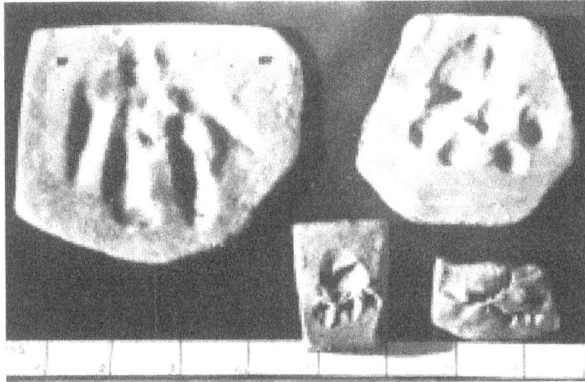

There were those that said no mongoose made their home near the spooked out dwelling, yet traces were found of what appeared to be mongoose tracks.

TALKING MONGOOSE?
✧✧✧ ✧✧✧ ✧✧✧ ✧✧✧
COMMONS MAY HAVE TO DECIDE

LONDON, Dec. 18—(P)—Is there a talking mongoose in the Isle of Man?

Members of the House of Commons soon may be called upon to discuss that question when relations between the government and the British Broadcasting Corporation are debated.

The question already has led to a libel suit in which damages of £7,500 ($37,500) were paid. The debate dates back to a book called "The Talking Mongoose," by Richard Stanton Lambert, editor of the B.B.C.'s review "The Listener," and one Harry Price.

Lieut.-Col. Sir Cecil Levita, former chairman of the London county council, dismissed the Manx ani-

mal's alleged linguistic talents with scorn and ridiculed Lambert's credulity.

Lambert thereupon filed suit for defamation of character and obtained a judgment for £7,500. He also charged persecution by the B. B. C. alleging officials of the company had urged him not to take serious interest in the case. Considerable controversy was aroused over this latter accusation and finally Prime Minister Baldwin named a commission to investigate.

The commission reported yesterday in favor of the B.B.C. but a number of members of parliament were not satisfied and indicated they would move for a debate on the matter. It was understood they would link their questions to those asking whether any of the cabinet had seen an advance copy of the speech broadcast last Sunday to the Archbishop of Canterbury, criticising former King Edward and some of his friends.

Meanwhile the Mongoose is maintaining a dignified silence.

The devilish phenomenon went silent when a mongoose was found dead near the property. Was this a case of a real talking animal, or was the young lady of the household somehow responsible for this odd phenomenon?

THE WEIRD FACES OF BELMEZ

We are told that the Bélmez Faces, or the Faces of Bélmez, Spain, are the result of a true paranormal phenomenon. The faces first started to appear in 1971 in a private house where residents claimed images of faces appeared in the concrete floor, primarily in the kitchen. In the years since, the images have continuously formed and disappeared on the floor of the home.

Located at the Pereira family home at Calle Real 5, Bélmez de la Moraleda, Jaén, Andalusia, Spain, the Bélmez faces have been responsible for bringing large numbers of sightseers to Bélmez. The phenomenon is considered by some parapsychologists to be the best-documented and "without doubt the most important paranormal phenomenon in the Twentieth Century."

Various faces have appeared and disappeared at irregular intervals since the very first day of their materialization and have been frequently photographed by the local newspapers and curious visitors. Many Bélmez residents believe that the faces were not made by human hand. Some investigators believe that it is a thoughtographic phenomenon subconsciously produced by the former owner of the house, María Gómez Cámara – now deceased.

It is said, but never proven, that the faces would follow Maria about even when she visited others or eventually moved. The floors were dug up several times and the tiles cleaned, but the faces always managed to return. The old tiles were eventually destroyed – actually pickaxed – only to have the faces appear on the new flooring.

Though skeptics had a field day with all sorts of "logical" explanations, I don't think anyone ever pointed the finger directly at Maria, the lady of the house.

Other faces and images have appeared over time on floors, walls, ceilings and just about any other place you can think of. Are they imaginary, or is some local "Mad Mollie" out and about causing the phenomenon without even knowing they are responsible for these creations?

This is a mystery that we must still solve!

The face of an unknown woman was among those that could never be erased.

As in most of these cases of paranormal occurrences a woman such as Maria Gomez was normally the center of attention, as in the "House of Faces."

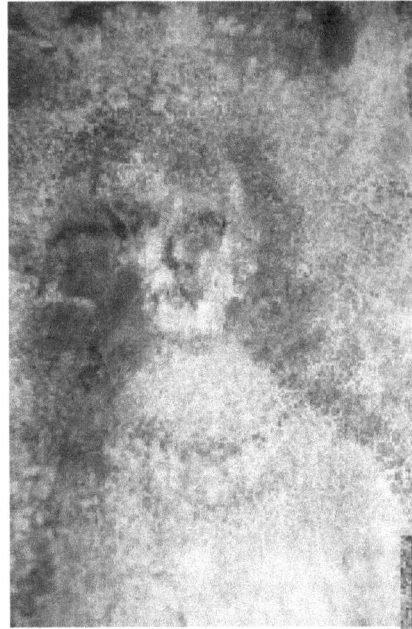

The faces on the floor were as strange and frightening as they could possibly ever be.

Investigators combed the house that Maria Gomez lived in but could find no reasonable explanation for what caused the faces to appear.

The Spiritualist movement was going full steam. Many mediums said that they were able to materialize physical forms out of ectoplasm emitted from their body.

It was rather common for chairs and other objects to levitate and flyaround the room while the mediums, mostly female, went into a deep tranceto contact the spirit world.

Miracle or Madness? The Fasting Girl Phenomenon

By Sean Casteel

There has always been a fine line between genuine religious experience and simple insanity. Philosophers and psychiatrists have long grappled with the complex distinction between the two, and what qualifies as a religious miracle has been a debatable unknown for historians and theologians to argue over down through the many centuries.

The "fasting girl" phenomenon is one such mystery that has yet to be resolved as either fraudulent fiction or supernatural fact. One of the most famous fasting girls in American history was Mollie Fancher, who claimed to have survived – miraculously – without eating a morsel for many years. Little has been written about Mollie except for a lone volume that has circulated among collectors and which documents her sometimes "paranormal" abilities.

Mollie Fancher was called "The Brooklyn Enigma" in her time, roughly the Victorian era, and followed an already established historical tradition. The ability to survive without nourishment was attributed to some saints during the Middle Ages, including Catherine of Siena and Lidwina of Schiedam, and was regarded as a miracle and sign of holiness. Numerous cases of fasting girls were reported in the late 19th century and were regarded as miracles by the credulous. In some cases, the fasting girls would also exhibit the appearance of stigmata. The doctors of the time would blame the entire syndrome on fraud or on hysteria on the part of the girl, while later physicians believed the phenomenon to be an early example of anorexia nervosa.

GROWING UP UNHAPPY

Mollie was born Mary J. Fancher in Attelboro, Massachusetts, on August 16, 1848. She and her two surviving siblings moved with her parents to Brooklyn,

New York, in 1850. Mollie was enrolled in a private school a few years later. Her mother died in 1855, and her father remarried and abandoned his children. Her aunt, Susan Crosby, took over care of the children.

In 1864, Mollie was preparing to graduate from the Brooklyn Heights Seminary, where she had been an excellent student, and looking forward to moving onward and upward. In addition to her academic smarts, she was very attractive – tall, slender, with a good complexion and an overall air of frailty that was the Victorian feminine ideal. Two months before graduation, she began to suffer several health maladies, such as nervous indigestion, weakness of the chest and frequent fainting spells. She stopped eating and her already slender frame began to waste away.

Mollie's doctor prescribed horseback riding to cure her nervous indigestion. Horseback riding had been frequently prescribed for all sorts of nervous complaints among women for centuries. Mollie was thrown from her horse in May 1864; she hit her head on a curbstone, knocking her unconscious, and broke several ribs.

She might have recovered from this trauma and lived a relatively normal life were it not for a second accident that occurred on June 8, 1865. Mollie was engaged to be married and was out shopping for wedding-related items when she stepped off a street car on her way home. Her dress got caught on a hook at the rear of the car and she was dragged a city block before anyone noticed her. She was found unconscious and with several ribs broken. Her suitor broke off their marriage plans, and she was put to bed to heal. She never left her bed, spending the next 51 years of her life there as she suffered varied and strange ailments that baffled observers and physicians alike.

FROM SADNESS TO THE DOWNRIGHT BIZARRE

As she lay in bed with all her miseries to contemplate, Mollie began to experience trances and violent spasms along with lockjaw, vision problems and more fainting spells. She lived on remarkably little food, once allegedly going seven weeks without eating, though there are counterclaims that she was force fed on occasions.

Modern doctors characterize her illness as a kind of hysteria. Hysteria served as a catch-all term for any behavior deemed unladylike in Mollie's day, but today the terms refers to "conversion disorder," where strong, pent up anxieties are converted into physical symptoms. This is similar to how the people in Mattoon, Illinois, believed they were victims of gas attacks and showed symptoms such as fainting, dizziness and vomiting. [For more on the Mad Gasser of Mattoon, see the Global Communications book "America's Strange and Supernatural History."] Mollie's form of hysteria was more likely a form of "motor hysteria," often found in pre-20th century societies where the belief in demonic possession and witchcraft was more common.

Some of the strangest stories about Mollie occurred in the nine-year period from 1866 to 1875. It is claimed that she lay with her arm drawn up over her head, her legs twisted and her eyes closed, yet still managed to write 6,500 letters, sew fine embroidery, keep a diary and make wax flowers – quite a lot for a bedridden woman with one functioning hand. She was also said to read writing from great distances, read minds and have the gift of prophecy. In a country obsessed with spirit communication, ghosts and the supernatural, Mollie became something of a celebrity.

SORTING AMONG THE MANY VERSIONS OF MOLLIE

On top of the many mysterious symptoms Mollie underwent was an even trickier malady: she seems to be a bona fide case of Multiple Personality Disorder. In 1875, she fell unconscious for a month and awakened with no memory of the past nine years. None of the letters or works of art she had created seemed familiar to her, and she resumed conversations where they had left off nine years before. In Mollie's mind, the writing and artwork were the efforts of someone else, someone dead. She began to splinter into several "selves," some cheery and bright, while others were jealous and vindictive. For instance, a personality called "Idol" took great pleasure in undoing the embroidery work of a sweeter personality called "Sunbeam." The transitions between one personality and the next were punctuated by trances and fits, as if the personalities were fighting one another to take over control. The personalities would write letters to one another – in different handwriting.

Multiple Personality Disorder is an extremely rare condition in which a person's self becomes fragmented under extreme emotional strain. Fewer than 100 true cases have been diagnosed, and there is some debate in psychiatric circles as to whether it exists at all. Mollie's case might have been a good candidate for study had the scientists of her day been more alert. Many in the growing field of psychology at the time avoided Mollie's case because of the unscientific supernatural trappings that came with it, so an opportune chance to study the workings of the human brain was lost. Mollie and her various selves succumbed to illness on February 15, 1916, taking her secrets with her.

THE MIRACULOUS WELSH FASTING GIRL

A case similar to Mollie Fancher's took place in Wales and involved a pre-adolescent girl named Sarah Jacob. She is said to have died from a combination of starvation and a hunger for fame.

Sarah was born on May 12, 1857, on a farm in rural Wales to Evan and Hannah Jacob. Her parents held respectable positions in the community; Evan was a deacon in the local church. At the age of nine, Sarah fell ill with convulsions of some type after a bout with scarlet fever. As she recovered, she was allowed to sleep in her parents' bedroom, which was warm and comfortable compared to the loft she normally slept in. She lay in bed all day, writing poetry and reading the Bible and led an easier life relieved of the many farm chores that had been her routine.

Spoiled and pampered, Sarah began to refuse food. She was genuinely religious, but it remains unclear whether her refusal to eat was spiritually motivated or was simply the machinations of a manipulative anorexic. Perhaps her parents encouraged her in her starvation, but in any case, Evan and Hannah later claimed that their daughter had had no food whatsoever from October 10, 1867, until her death two years later in December, 1869.

As the fasting went on, Sarah became something of a local celebrity among her fellow villagers, who were amazed by her ability to survive without food or drink. A local clergyman was so convinced that something miraculous was happening in his parish with Sarah that he wrote the newspapers. The publicity resulted in overnight fame and drew people from throughout England as well as Wales who made the difficult journey by rail and on foot to stand gazing in wonder at this young girl who was reportedly defying the laws of nature.

The visitors brought gifts and money for Sarah, dropping their coins onto the bedspread as Sarah lay, surrounded by flowers, reading and quoting the Bible. People marveled at her appearance; her eyes shown like pearls, in full alertness, and her cheeks were attractively rosy. One person said Sarah looked like "a lily amongst thorns."

Meanwhile, those less inclined to believe in the miracle of abstinence tried to ferret out how Sarah was secretly eating and drinking, but their attempts at observing her were made difficult by her father's constant hovering over the proceedings.

Finally, in December, 1869, Sarah's parents agreed to permit a team of nurses from a Welsh hospital along with other professionals to conduct a watch. Everything was examined for traces of food or liquid, Sarah's bed was moved to a separate area, and visitors were limited to her parents, who could only take her hand. That last condition was required because some suspected that Sarah's sister had been passing her food from her own mouth, similar to when a mother bird feeds her young, under the guise of kissing her "starving" sibling affectionately.

On the first day of the watch, December 9, Sarah was reported to be cheerful, healthy – even plump – with a regular temperature and pulse. She began to decline rapidly. The doctors present urged her father to let them examine her and offer medical care. He refused, saying that he had vowed to Sarah two years before not to give her food. When she died eight days later, on December 17, many felt her death was proof that she was not a miracle child but had been smuggled food by her family, who had wanted to perpetuate the notion of Sarah's supernatural saintliness. Sarah's parents were prosecuted for manslaughter in her death by starvation, and both drew sentences of hard labor in Swansea Prison.

According to author Stephen Wade, there are many factors at play in Sarah's story, including the political tensions between the Welsh and the English, the clash between religious and medical explanations, and the narrow line between pilgrimage and entertainment. Sarah in her bed, surrounded by garlands of flowers and reading pious books, suggested "a deep need for a shrine, for a new 19th century focus for pilgrimage," but may have also been an exercise in mere "show biz" and the cult of celebrity.

THERESE NEUMANN AND THE DAILY HOST

In 1918, 20-year-old Therese Neumann fell into shock after taking a particularly nasty fall off a stool while trying to put out a fire at her uncle's farm. The fall resulted in a spinal injury that led in turn to a whole host of maladies, such as paralysis, gastric problems and blindness. By 1926, a "blood-colored serum" oozed from Therese's eyes and she began suffering stigmata during Lent. The next year, Therese claimed she had been visited by Saint Therese of Lisieux, who told her that food and water were no longer necessary. She could survive on only the sustenance of Holy Communion.

She was closely observed day and night for two weeks in July 1927, with doctors and nurses even measuring the amount of mouthwash she used so they could ascertain that she wasn't swallowing any of it when she spat it back out. By the end of two weeks, the medical team was satisfied that their patient never took or even attempted to take food. Therese lost weight as the observation period began, but she somehow gained five or six pounds by the end of it. The attending physician testified under oath that not a morsel of nourishment, except for one consecrated Host daily, had passed her lips while he and his team were watching.

Therese allegedly followed this devout food regimen until her death in 1962.

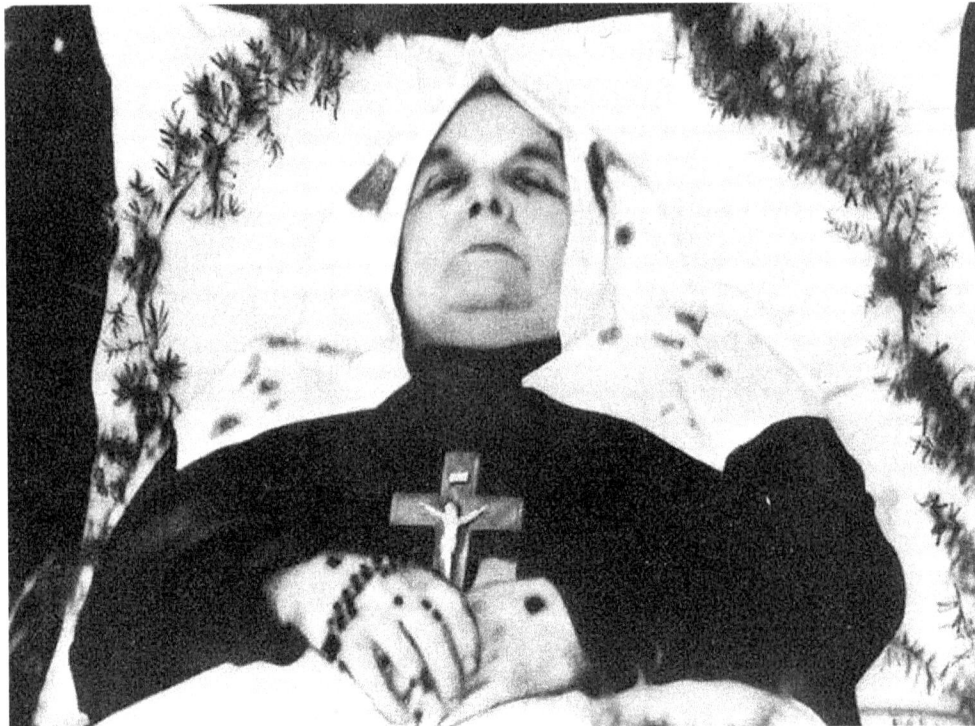

Therese Neumann starved herself and bled with the wounds of Christ. Her faith was never shaken despite the fact that there were those who said she was faking her conditions.

Neumann had the stigmata on certain holy days.

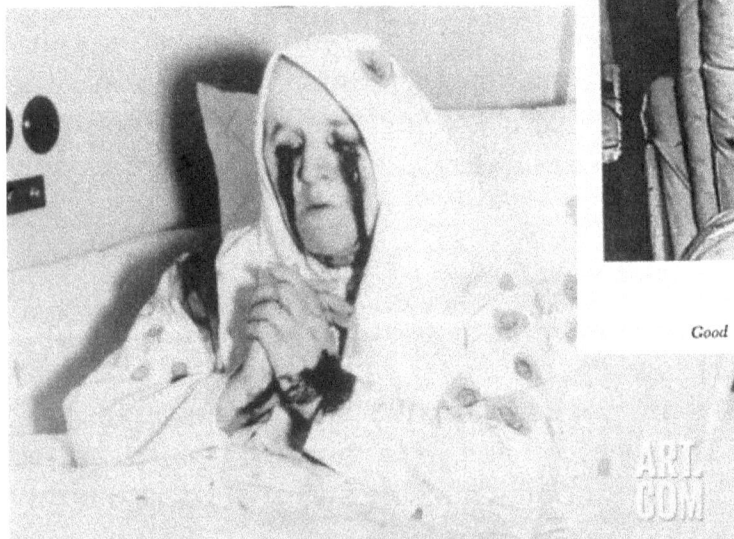

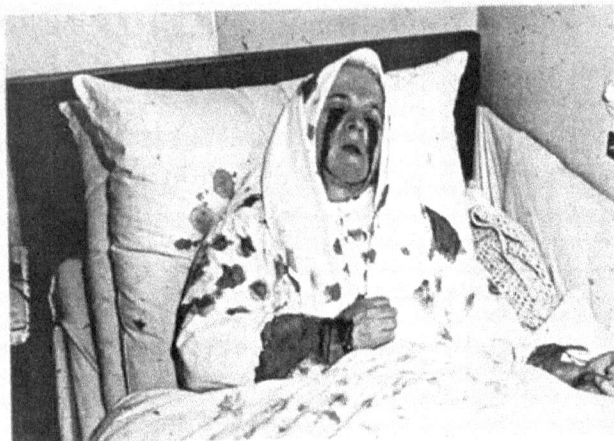

Good Friday, 1953. After the vision of Jesus' death.

On the days of her holy bleeding, Therese was not a pleasant sight to behold.

EXPLOITING THE HUNGER OF THE TINGWICK GIRL

Josephine Marie Bedard, also known as the Tingwick Girl, is an interesting example of how the public was fascinated with these various girls who seemingly did not require nourishment of any kind to survive. When the 19-year-old Josephine claimed she had gone months without eating, two museums in Boston wanted to put her on display so that people could observe her not eating for the low, low price of 50 cents, not unlike a kind of static circus sideshow. The two museums even went to court to argue over the right to "exhibit the girl" publicly.

In 1889, however, Boston physician Mary Walker reported that Josephine was a fraud based on circumstantial evidence.

"At the hotel," Dr. Walker told the Boston Globe, "I searched her clothing and found in one of her pockets a doughnut with a bite taken out of it." At another point, Walker had left a platter with three pieces of fried potato on it in Josephine's presence and then left the room. When Walker returned, one piece was missing and Josephine was holding a handkerchief to her mouth. When Walker accused Josephine of having eaten the potato, Josephine broke down and cried. Though none of this was in fact literal proof, the story was enough to quickly ruin Josephine's credibility.

In spite of all the hoopla and struggle over commercial gain, there was also a certain element of scientific inquiry in regarding Josephine as a medical phenomenon. While a modern institutional review board would not have approved the violation of privacy in the case of Josephine and the other fasting girls for the sake of profit, the practice was allowed in pre-feminist Victorian times.

Anorexia Mirabilis and Saint Catherine of Siena

By Sean Casteel

Mollie Fancher's desire to prove her piety through fasting has many precedents. The term "anorexia mirabilis" was coined centuries ago and means "miraculous lack of appetite." It normally refers to women and girls of the Middle Ages who would starve themselves, sometimes to the point of death, in the name of God. The phenomenon is also called "inedia prodigiosa," meaning "prodigious fasting."

Anorexia mirabilis is both similar to and yet different from the more modern and well-known "anorexia nervosa." In the latter, people usually starve themselves to attain a level of thinness; the disease is associated with a distorted sense of body image.

Anorexia mirabilis, by contrast, was frequently combined with other ascetic forms of self-denial, such as lifelong virginity, self-flagellation, wearing hair shirts, sleeping on beds of thorns and other assorted penitential practices. The self-starvation was mainly practiced by Catholic women who were known as "miraculous maids."

Caroline Walker Bynum, the author of "Holy Feast, Holy Fast," believes that anorexia mirabilis was not simply misdiagnosed anorexia but was instead a legitimate form of self-expression that existed outside the modern disease paradigm. Although the debate regarding whether the two conditions are equivalent to one another continues among historians and the psychiatric community, there remain those who feel that anorexia mirabilis should be understood as a distinct medieval form of female religious piety and placed within its proper historical context.

Many women refused to ingest any food but the Communion host, which was intended to signify not only their devotion to God and Jesus but also to make a point about the separation of body and spirit. The idea that the body could endure for long periods of time without nourishment demonstrated how much stronger and important the spirit was. Popular opinion was unconcerned that the females claimed to go without food for months or even years. The "impossible" length of their fasting only added to the allure of this specifically female achievement.

A SAINT'S REBELLIOUS EARLY LIFE

In the time of Catherine of Siena (1347-1380), celibacy and fasting were held in high regard. Ritualistic fasting was both a means to avoid gluttony, one of the seven deadly sins, and also to atone for past sins. In Catherine's case, as so often happens with anorexic girls in our own time, the fasting had a great deal to do with adolescent rebellion and the need to exert more power over her life.

Catherine was born in Siena, Italy, during the time when the "black death" was ravaging Europe. Her mother was about 40 years old at the time and had previously borne 22 children, but half of them had died. Catherine was an unusually cheerful child, and her family gave her a nickname which is Greek for "joy." She saw a vision of Christ at age five or six, and, by age seven, vowed to give her life to God.

When her older sister, Bonaventura, died while giving birth, Catherine's parents urged the future saint to marry her sister's widower, who was a wealthy but crude and ill-mannered man. Bonaventura had used a strategy of fasting to force her husband to be more considerate, which had shown Catherine that fasting carried with it a certain degree of power.

Catherine also cut off her hair in rebellion against being encouraged to improve her appearance to attract a husband. She resisted the accepted women's options of marriage and motherhood, on the one hand, or a nun's habit on the other, choosing instead to live an active and prayerful life outside a convent's walls in the manner of the Dominicans. Eventually her parents gave up and permitted her to live as she pleased.

The Third Order of the Dominicans agreed to admit Catherine to their order despite the vigorous protests of the other members, who were mainly older women and widows. She was taught how to read by the Order and lived at home with her family in total silence and solitude. Refusing her family's food, she declared that there was a table laid out for in heaven with her "real family."

At age twenty-one, Catherine experienced what she later described as a

"Mystical Marriage" with Jesus in which she received not a ring of gold and jewels but the ring of Christ's foreskin. Later biographers would alter that sexually graphic detail to something more traditional, and Catherine's experience became a popular subject for painters in the Renaissance.

During the visionary experience, Christ instructed her to leave her withdrawn life at home and enter the public life of the world. She would go on to have an active career in papal politics and ministering to the public as she traveled widely throughout Italy and elsewhere in Europe. She died in Rome on April 29, 1380, and was canonized by Pope Pius II in 1461.

Anorexia mirabilis occurred almost exclusively in girls and young adult females and was found most frequently between the 13th and 17th centuries. It was also common, of course, among the individuals described in this book.

A portrait of Saint Catherine of Siena's mystical marriage to Jesus.

Born on 25 March 1347, in Siena, Italy, Catherine was the youngest of 25 children. As a child, Catherine was considered to be very joyful. From a young age Catherine started to receive visions; it is said she had her first vision at the age of five or six while journeying home with her brother from visiting a married sister.

Saint Catherine of Siena's fasting would often make her weak, as shown in this fresco.

WAS THE DECISION TO STARVE DEMONICALLY INSPIRED?

For many years Catherine had accustomed herself to a rigorous abstinence, receiving only the Holy Communion daily. Her extreme fasting appeared unhealthy to the clergy, and her confessor ordered her to eat properly. But Catherine protested that she had an illness that made her unable to eat or even swallow water.

In a paper published by the university in Catherine's native Siena, scholars Mario Reda and Giuseppe Sacco analyzed Catherine's fasting in the light of modern research into anorexia nervosa. Catherine's refusal to marry as her parents wished is for them a clear connection to the onset of anorexia nervosa in modern times, what they call "compensatory anorexia."

"She lost half of her proper weight," the scholars write, "and opposed the demands of [her mother] by fasting, which [in Catherine's mind] confirmed her true dedication to God." Fasting was also a means of renouncing her "corporeality" or the physical demands and appetites of the body, which are "unclean," by definition, for some believers. When the local priest intervened and demanded she ingest food once a day at least, Catherine would vomit each time, saying that God wished her to expiate her sins in this manner.

The priest began to wonder whether to call her a saint or a madwoman. He even considered the possibility that Catherine was being fed through some kind of demonic possession because – in spite of her wasting appearance – she was also hyperactive and possessed great physical and mental strength.

This approach only made Catherine more determined to have her way and starve as she chose. She said Christ, her "Spouse," was rich and powerful enough that she would never be deprived of anything and her every personal need would be provided for.

When her father died, the twenty-one-year-old Catherine prayed until she was exhausted. She suddenly felt an intense pain in her side – the same place Christ had been stabbed by the spear of a Roman centurion. This was a sign to her that her father had been received into glory in heaven. It was also a "sensation" form of stigmata, though no physical wound appeared, and added to the legend of paranormal spirituality that surrounded Catherine.

A SAINTLY SELF-DOUBT

After her father's death, Catherine continued to fast. So as not to cause scandal, she sometimes took a little salad, fresh vegetables and fruit but would then turn around and spit them up. If it was the case that she swallowed even a single morsel, she would vomit until her stomach could not regurgitate any more. "We do justice for our miserable sins," she was fond of saying.

She suffered her share of self-doubt, the Italian authors say, and she pondered over whether she had been deceived by others or had deceived herself about the true will of God. Her inner conflict only accentuated her anorexia nervosa, they believe, and drove her to further self-sacrifice. Their final thesis is that Catherine's "holy anorexia" can be psychoanalyzed as a stereotypical occurrence of the eating disorder, an attempt by an adolescent female to establish autonomy and freedom from parental controls.

"To yield to food was to yield to sin," Reda and Sacco write, "to deceive God, to lose all the power she had laboriously garnered, erasing all the sense of identity gained from the victory over her opposition to family regulation. It is of little matter, then, if she did not feel understood by her opponents. Indeed, incomprehension provided the stimulus to go on. The challenge continued to provide a way for her to confirm her true sense of identity."

Reda and Sacco write that the period of holy anorexia was short-lived, and by the 16th century the church no longer tolerated asceticism. Anorexics were labeled as witches and consigned to the stake. Today, within ten years after onset of anorexia nervosa, seven percent of anorexics die, about twenty-three percent are cured, and seventy percent become chronically ill with "fat-thin syndrome." Confessors of the mind – priests and psychiatrists – are unable to do anything for a large percentage of anorexia nervosa patients while psychiatric biochemists look in vain for pharmacological remedies for the mysterious problem.

The Mystery of Stigmata:
From Saint Francis to a California Housewife
By Sean Casteel

Stigmata is the term given to the mysterious appearance of wounds on the body that correspond to the five wounds suffered by Jesus Christ during his crucifixion. The term was first used by Saint Paul in his Letter to the Galatians. "I bear on my body the marks of Jesus," he wrote, using the Greek word "stigmata," meaning a mark, tattoo or brand like those used for identification of an animal or slave.

A person bearing stigmata is referred to as a "stigmatic" or "stigmatist." The five Holy Wounds or some combination of them are found in the wrists and feet, inflicted on Christ by the nails that bound him to the cross, and in the side, from the lance used by a Roman centurion to confirm that Christ had died. Some stigmatics display wounds to the forehead similar to those caused by Christ's crown of thorns. Other reported forms include tears of blood or sweating blood and wounds to the back, as from scourging.

SAINT FRANCIS, HISTORY'S FIRST STIGMATIC

Francis of Assisi, a noted ascetic, holy man and future saint, was on retreat with some longtime companions in the area of Monte La Verna, overlooking the River Arno in Tuscany. Francis had been contemplating the suffering Christ for weeks, and he may have been weak from fasting and illness. It was September 14, 1224, a Catholic holiday called "The Feast of the Exaltation of the Holy Cross." As Francis knelt to pray, he experienced an ecstatic vision.

According to an early biographer, "He began to contemplate the Passion of Christ and his fervor grew so strong within him that he became wholly transformed into Jesus through love and compassion. While he was thus enflamed, he saw a seraph with six shining, fiery wings descend from heaven. This seraph drew near to Saint Francis in swift flight, so that he could see him clearly and recognize that he had the form of a man crucified. After a long period of secret converse, this mysterious vision faded, leaving in his body a wonderful image and imprint of the Passion of Christ. For in the hands and feet of Saint Francis forthwith began to appear the marks of the nails in the same manner as he had seen in the body of Jesus crucified."

St. Francis of Assisi receives the stigmata wounds of Christ in a vision of the Master, Jesus.

In an article from the website of the Smithsonian magazine, historian Mike Dash explains how and why stigmata had its origins in 13th-century Italy. The church in Francis' time had begun to place much greater stress on the humanity of Christ and would soon introduce a new holiday – "Corpus Christi" – into the calendar to encourage contemplation of his physical sufferings. Religious painters responded by graphically portraying the crucifixion for the first time, depicting a Jesus clearly in agony from wounds that dripped blood. Francis was already a famous name in his era, and his stigmata quickly became known throughout Europe. Other similar cases of the mysterious wounds soon began to appear among the devout.

Francis was not obsessed by the stigmata nor did he allow them to become an object of curiosity. His wounds appeared to some to resemble dark scars; they would open and bleed from time to time, although they remained uninfected and exuded a perfume-like odor. This fragrant smell has also been reported among later stigmatics and is known as the Odor of Sanctity.

The papal document of canonization, written in 1228, two years after Francis' death, makes no mention of Francis' stigmata, though the phenomenon began to exert a significant influence on the later church.

Perhaps the most well known of modern stigmatics, Padre Pio had visions from the age of five and from an early age dedicated his life to the Lord. He became a Franciscan in 1903, and a few years later he became a fully ordained priest. He bled for years in front of humbled crowds of followers.

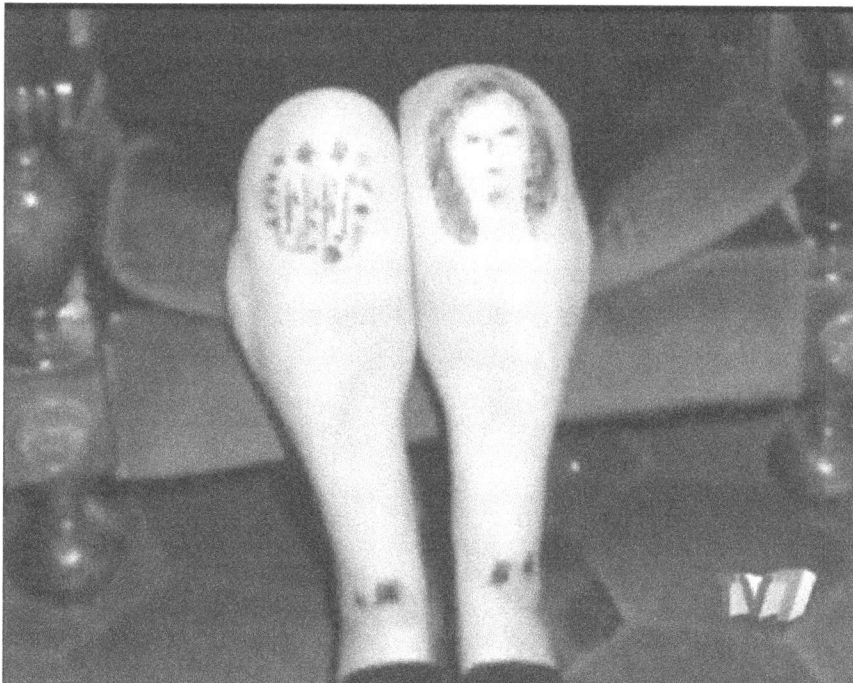

Natuzzo Evolo's stigmata was a bit different than those of other devotees. Her bleeding formed faces that remarkably resembled those found on the film of spirit photographers or "painted" by mediums like the Bangs sisters.

WHAT ARE THE CAUSES OF STIGMATA?

There are various explanations offered by historians and scientists about what causes stigmata. The most frequently offered is that the strange markings are the bodily reaction to intense ecstatic and psychological experiences, such as the vision Saint Francis underwent. Some modern researchers say stigmata are of "hysterical origin," or are linked to "dissociative identity disorders." There is a relationship between stigmata and the same sort of self-starvation practiced by Mollie Fancher and others throughout history who did their fasting in the context of religious belief.

Edward Harrison, the author of "Stigmata: A Medieval Phenomenon in a Modern Age," suggests that there is no single mechanism whereby the marks of stigmata were produced. While he found no evidence that the marks were supernaturally induced, they need not all be hoaxes. Some marked their own body in the attempt to suffer with Christ as form of piety. Others marked themselves accidentally, and their marks were noted as stigmata by witnesses. Often marks of human origin produced profound and genuine religious responses from those who saw them.

Aside from cases of outright fraud, the appearance of stigmata appears to be an essentially psychological condition whose manifestations are determined by the cultural expectations of the stigmatics themselves, according to Dash.

"A large number of sufferers seem to have displayed abundant evidence of low self-esteem, health problems, or a tendency toward self-mutilation," he writes, "a potent mix when combined with exposure to the pervasive iconography of centuries of Christian tradition. It has been shown beyond a reasonable doubt that many have inflicted the five wounds on themselves, sometimes unconsciously, perhaps while in an altered state of consciousness brought on by extensive fasting or intensive prayer."

MORE RECENT CASES OF STIGMATA

However they are caused, cases of stigmata have continued well into our own time.

A young Croatian priest's wounds have been declared by the Vatican to be "not of human origin." Zlatco Sudac's first wound appeared on his forehead in 1999, followed by markings on his hands, feet and side. He says the stigmata fill him with "a tremendous fear of the Lord" but cause him no pain except when he is praying, at which time he feels them pulsing. Sudac also claims to have received the divine gifts of levitation, prophecy and bilocation – the ability to be in two places at once.

Emiliano Aden, a nineteen-year-old Italian man, received the stigmata in 1996 as he walked home from the supermarket with his girlfriend. He felt as though his forehead was being pierced, but there was nothing visible there. Doctors declared he had a migraine headache and sent him home. Once there, he started bleeding from his forehead and collapsed. When his mother sought the help of clergy, they said the wounds were a self-inflicted blasphemy. Aden continues to bleed periodically from his wrist and forehead and spends his days in a combination of prayer, pain and ecstasy.

Briton Ethel Chapman, afflicted by multiple sclerosis and living in a care facility, produced fresh blood from her hands on Good Friday that she could not have inflicted herself, being paralyzed from the waist down and unable to hold things in her hands. She did not suffer from any form of depression, neurosis or psychosis. Ethel told the BBC in 1973 that she had asked God for a sign of his presence and felt the pain of the nails through her hands and feet, all the agony that the Lord himself had gone through. She also claimed to have levitated and smelled sweet perfumes. As her fame grew, she spent the rest of her life devoting prayers to those who asked for help or healing.

The stigmata of an illiterate woman named Natuzzo Evolo ironically took the form of hemography – the process by which blood from the stigmata is miraculously formed into Christian writing, images or symbols on bandages and other types of cloth. In Natuzzo's case, many of the words were in Hebrew or Aramaic. For decades, devout Catholics from all over Italy would come to Natuzzo for advice and prayers, and many spoke of receiving miraculous healings and other graces from her. Thousands came to pay their respects when she died in 2009 and some have since made the case for her beatification.

The best known of the more recent stigmatics is Italy's Padre Pio of Pietrelcina, who suffered from stigmata for over fifty years. In 1918, he had a vision in which he saw himself pierced with a lance; the wound remained with him, and a month later he also began to bleed from his palms and feet. His wounds never closed or became infected and, instead of the smell of blood, they always emitted a sweet odor. He was declared a saint by Pope John Paul II in 2002.

California housewife Cora Evans first received the stigmata in 1947. "I suddenly felt the infinite devotion of God for His creatures with my soul." Simultaneously, she felt the pain and saw the terrible wound in the hand of Jesus. A wound in her own right hand began to appear. Cora claimed to have seen divine visions since the age of three and wrote about her conversations with Christ, whom she often called "The Master," that took place when she fell into a trance-like state. During one such conversation, Christ offered her a choice between coming home with him through all eternity or accepting additional suffering for the good of the world. When Cora chose the latter, the stigmata appeared in both palms along with a crown of thorns on her head. It was reported that the wounds gave off the sweet smell of roses. Over half a century after her death, the church has taken Cora's claims seriously enough to put her on the path to sainthood, declaring her to be a "Servant of God," the first of four steps to her becoming California's first Catholic saint.

Multiple Mollies and Powers From Beyond

By Sean Casteel

The Mollie Fancher story is fraught with complexities and insoluble mysteries. To some who have studied her life, she represents a genuine case of Multiple Personality Disorder, or MPD. That term was changed to Dissociative Identity Disorder, or DID, in 1994.

Whatever term one chooses to use, however, Mollie was clearly not "herself" at all times. In 1875, when she was in her late 20s, she fell unconscious for a month. When she awakened, she had no recollection of the previous nine years. She resumed conversations that had begun nine years previously and claimed that the writing and artwork that had accumulated around her were done by someone else, someone who had died.

MOLLIE SPLINTERS INTO MANY MOLLIES

Sometime after her month in that coma-like state, the other versions of Mollie began to speak. Mollie told her biographer, Abram Dailey, sometime in the 1890s that, "I am told that there are five other Mollie Fanchers who, together, make the whole of the one Mollie Fancher known to the world. Who they are and what they are I cannot tell or explain. I can only conjecture."

Note Mollie's words carefully here. The other personalities, called "alters" by those who study the disorder, are something of which Mollie has no conscious, waking knowledge. She can only make an indirect report of them based on what she has been told by other people around her.

Dailey described the five distinct "other" Mollies, each with a different name, each of whom he met, as did Mollie's Aunt Susan and a family friend named George Sargent. The first additional Mollie appeared some three years after the month-long sleep, around 1878. The dominant Mollie, the one who functioned most of the time and was known to everyone as Mollie Fancher, was designated "Sunbeam" by Sargent, who also named the other personalities as he met them.

The four other personalities came out only at night, after eleven, when Mollie would have her typical spasm and go into a trance. The first to appear was always "Idol," who shared Sunbeam's memories of childhood and adolescence but had no memory of the horse-car accident, the second accident to befall Mollie as a teenager. Idol was very jealous of Sunbeam's accomplishments and would sometimes unravel her embroidery or hide her work. Idol and Sunbeam wrote with different handwriting and often penned letters to one another.

Abram Dailey

The next personality Sargent named was "Rosebud," whom he described as having the "sweetest little child's face" and the voice and accent of a small child as well. Rosebud said she was seven years old and had Mollie's memories of early childhood. She could recall Mollie's first teacher's name, the streets on which she had lived and children's songs. She wrote with a child's handwriting, alternating between upper and lower-case letters. When questioned by Dailey, Rosebud said that her mother was sick, had gone away and the child-persona did not know when her mother would return.

Pearl, the fourth personality, was evidently in her late teens. Sargent described her as "very spiritual, sweet in expression, cultured and agreeable." Pearl remembered Professor West, the principal of the Brooklyn Heights Seminary, along with the school days and friends up to about the sixteenth year of Mollie's life. Sargent added that Pearl pronounced her words with an accent peculiar to young ladies in about 1865.

The last Mollie was given the name "Ruby" and was said to be "vivacious, humorous, bright and witty." Sargent said that Ruby did everything with a "dash," but he was mystified that Ruby, unlike the four other personalities, did not speak much about the history of Mollie herself. "She has the air of knowing a good deal more than she tells," Sargent commented.

IS MPD/DID CAUSED BY DEMONIC POSSESSION?

If we put aside questions as to whether Mollie's MPD/DID was genuine or not, what is the root cause of the disorder? Unsurprisingly, there is a school of thought that believes cases like Mollie's are one result of demonic possession, and there are several Christian ministries, mainly from among fundamentalist Protestants and conservative Catholics, that seek to help victims by performing rites of exorcism.

The more mainstream, psychiatric approach explains the MPD/DID phenomenon this way:

The disorder results from severe trauma, which usually takes place in childhood or adolescence, such as Mollie losing her mother at an early age and the two near-fatal accidents she suffered as a teenager. It can also involve a kind of "role-playing," where the victim, called "a dissociative," plays different roles that he or she has been positively reinforced to play. People with MPD/DID often attempt suicide, hear voices, see things that other people don't, and speak in strange voices. Sometimes the voices speaking through the victim identify themselves as Satan or a demon, further fueling the fire that leads deliverance ministers to try exorcism.

One such deliverance minister is Jerry Mungadze, a native of Zimbabwe. Having grown up in Zimbabwe, he is no stranger to "power encounters." He believes harassment by demons is a rare occurrence, and that someone who exhibits symptoms of MPD/DID, suffered a trauma in childhood, shows no supernatural powers and hasn't made a pact with the Devil has no need for an exorcism. In such a case, working a deliverance session might only "antagonize the created personas" or exacerbate what are clearly only psychological symptoms.

But MPD/DID and demonic possession are not mutually exclusive, according to Mungadze, because detaching a person from his or her personality can open the door to demonic harassment. Even then, the safer approach is to restore the victim's mental health and thus give the afflicted the strength to resist the demons on his or her own.

Nevertheless, victims of demonic possession are believed to exhibit a unique personality – that of the indwelling spirit. The demon will sometimes speak through that individual's vocal cords, often in a language unknown to the person and in a strange inflection. The demons can sometimes cause schizophrenia, depression, mental instabilities, suicidal thoughts or MPD/DID.

Another factor to consider is possession by more than a single demon, as when Christ encountered a demon-possessed man (Mark 5:9) and asked the spirit what its name was. The demon replied, "My name is Legion; for we are many." Many conservative Protestants see multiple possession as the main or only cause of MPD/DID.

Was this the answer in Mollie's case? Were the five personalities she manifested really five demonic entities who commandeered portions of her memories and accurately recalled the traumatized life she had lived?

MOLLIE'S PARANORMAL ABILITIES

Questions about demonic possession are also relevant because it might in some part explain Mollie's paranormal feats, feats that went beyond simply surviving without taking any nourishment.

But a website called "The Rocky Mountain Astrologer" takes what might be called a less fearsome and judgmental view of the situation. An article there, called "Mollie Fancher: Seeing Without Eyes," begins by offering the testimony of the 19th century occultist and theosophist Helene Petrovna Blavatsky, who was a believer in Mollie's powers and wrote about the "Brooklyn Enigma" in her book "Isis Unveiled."

"Miss Mollie Fancher, of Brooklyn," Blavatsky wrote, "a respectable young girl, has lived without any food for over nine years. This extraordinary girl never sleeps – her frequent trances being the only rest she obtains; she reads sealed letters as though they were open; describes distant friends; though completely blind, perfectly discriminates colors; and finally, though her right hand is rigidly drawn up behind her head, by a permanent paralysis, makes embroidery upon canvas, and produces in wax, without having taken a lesson in the art, and with neither knowledge of botany nor even models to copy, flowers of a most marvelously natural appearance."

Madame H. Blavatsky, who was thought to possess special powers.

The physicians treating Mollie unsuccess-

fully tried methods of the time to cure her numerous ailments. Mollie was repeatedly shaved and blistered, electrically shocked, treated with hydrotherapy and submitted to enemas.

In the midst of her injuries, abstinence from food and frightening medical treatments, she began to exhibit some amazing things, like being oblivious to the pain inflicted by the experimenters, reading books without the use of her eyes (a talent that Edgar Cayce also had), predicting future events, gathering information at a distance (clairvoyance), as well as producing large numbers of embroidery pieces and wax flowers despite her blindness and twisted extremities, as in the aforementioned praise from H.P. Blavatsky Mollie also wrote thousands of letters, relating to correspondents through her five separate personalities.

Mollie explained some of the strangeness to her biographer, Abram Dailey, this way: "I received nourishment from a source of which the physicians were ignorant. My spasms and trances were essential to my living; but this my physicians did not know. I have broken the backbone of science and all the 'ologies.'"

THE PARAPSYCHOLOGICAL APPROACH

"The Rocky Mountain Astrologer" examines Mollie's alleged powers from both a parapsychological angle and a more mystical one.

While Mollie's living without food for weeks, months and years seemed to garner the most attention as she became one of the Fasting Girls of the 19th century, what seems of greater significance was her ability to function without the use of her "normal" senses intact for long periods of time. Mollie lost her usual senses of sight, hearing, touch, smell and taste but drew upon other sources to make up for the results of her injuries.

This is in some ways comparable to a blind person developing acute hearing to compensate for loss of sight. But Mollie lost all of her senses for a time and made up for them in very strange ways.

For example, Mollie lost her sight, yet she could "see" to read, among other chores. This is a phenomenon called "paroptic vision," and has been studied scientifically under laboratory conditions. It has also been called "dermo-optical perception," "eyeless sight," "skin reading" and "bio-introscopy," among other names. The simple explanation has been that the blind and others can learn to "see" through their skin.

There is also an extraordinary phenomenon called "transposition of the senses," in which, for example, a person can "see" with the pit of his or her stomach, or a person's senses of taste, smell and hearing wander to the tips of the fingers and toes. Many cases of this transposition have occurred, especially with hysterical subjects.

Paroptic vision and transposition of the senses are scientific or pseudo-scientific explanations for what Mollie was capable of, but they only partially explain what happens to Mollie and others. But what if it all came down to something less scientific but more complete? The astral body.

We all have astral and mental bodies, according to the website, that we use to travel to the inner worlds every night when we sleep. At such times, we don't have the use of our physical eyes or ears to sense anything. Rather, the whole of these bodies is capable of receiving sensory information. The entire astral body sees, hears, feels, smells and tastes. There are no specific sense organs. Consequently, any one astral sense is not, strictly speaking, localized or confined to any particular part of the astral body. It is rather the whole of the particles of the astral body which possess the power of sensation and response.

Therefore, a person who has developed astral sight uses any part of the matter of his astral body in order to see and so can see equally well objects that are in front, behind, above, below or to either side. The same is true with all the other senses. In other words, the astral senses are equally active in all parts of the body.

So, according to *"The Rocky Mountain Astrologer,"* when Mollie became physically blind and her other senses were detached, she merely took advantage of the innate abilities of her astral body – abilities we all use every night. Mollie was forced to use her inner potentials when her physical contacts with the outer world were suddenly cut loose from her.

This is, of course, a more appealing explanation for Mollie's talents than demonic possession or MPD/DID. And while those who are capable of tapping into and even controlling their astral body are a definite minority, they are a minority that any of us has the potential to join.

Sources for Pages xix through xlvi; Sean Casteel

"Mollie Fancher, The Brooklyn Enigma," from the website at: http://www.oddlyhistorical.com/2014/09/22/mollie-fancher-the-brooklyn-enigma/

"Mollie 'The Brooklyn Enigma' Fancher," from the website at: http://www.findagrave.com/cgi-bin/fg.cgi?page=gr&GRid=71987092

"Sarah Jacobs: The Fasting Girl," by Phil Carradice, from the website at: http://www.bbc.co.uk/blogs/wales/posts/sarah_jacobs_the_fasting_girl

"The Girl Who Lived on Air: The Mystery of Sarah Jacob," by Jane Shaw, from the website at: http://www.timeshighereducation.co.uk/books/the-girl-who-lived-on-air-the-mystery-of-sarah-jacobs-the-welsh-fasting-girl-by-stephen-wade/2016836.article

"The True Stories of Four Victorian Fasting Girls," by Stacy Conradt, from the website at: http://mentalfloss.com/article/51477/true-stories-4-victorian-fasting-girls

"Anorexia and the Holiness of St. Catherine of Siena," by Mario Reda and Giuseppe Sacco, from the website at: http://www.albany.edu/scj/jcjpc/vol8is1/reda.html

"The Strange Stigmata," by Dr. Lawrence S. Cunningham, from the website at: http://www.christianitytoday.com/global/printer.html?/ch/1994/issue42/4236.html

"The Mystery of the Five Wounds," by Mike Dash, from the website at: http://www.smithsonianmag.com/history/the-mystery-of-the-five-wounds-361799/?no-ist

"10 People Who Claim to Have the Stigmata," by Michelle Nati, from the website at: http://www.oddee.com/item_98787.aspx

"Quotes About MPD," from the website at: http://www.goodreads.com/quotes/tag/mpd

"Mollie Fancher: Seeing Without Eyes, Parts I and II," from the website at: http://www.rockymountainastrologer.com/MindPower/MollieFancher.html

POST OFFICE BOX 753
NEW BRUNSWICK, NJ 08903

"MAD" MOLLIE
MOLLIE FANCHER, THE BROOKLYN ENIGMA.

An Authentic Statement of Facts In The Life of Mary J. Fancher

The Psychological Marvel of the Nineteenth Century.

UPON the death of Jesus, his apostles and faithful disciples boldly proclaimed the doctrine of Salvation by repentance and good deeds. Regarding truth as divine, and its revelation and promulgation for man's ultimate good, the author takes great pleasure in dedicating this book, its lessons and teachings, to the memory of the noble men and women who in all ages have boldly proclaimed their convictions of the truth, regardless of consequences to themselves.

"MAD" MOLLIE

CONTENTS.

"MAD" MOLLIE

CHAPTER VIII.
The trance condition. What it is. Scriptures cited. Events of nine years lost from memory.

CHAPTER IX.
"Whereas I was blind I now see." Work done during nine years of which Miss Fancher has no recollection. Strange awakening after the long trance. Does not know her acquaintances. Sextuple consciousness. Five different personalities in one self.

CHAPTER X.
Interesting facts from the lips of Miss Fancher. Geo. F. Sargent's experience with Miss Fancher and her several personalities.

CHAPTER XI.
"The forms I see are intangible; I cannot touch them. They are here but I cannot press them to my bosom." Miss Fancher describes what she sees.

CHAPTER XII.
Personal interview with Miss Fancher's different personalities by the Author.

CHAPTER XIII.
Statement of Mr. Geo. F. Sargent. " Light amid darkness."

CHAPTER XIV.
Clairvoyance. Statement of Experiences with Miss Fancher by Mrs. Thos. S. Townsend. Proposal from Mr. P. T. Barnum.

CHAPTER XV.
Miss Fancher's clairvoyant powers. Statements at Hon. H. D. Sisson and Mr. E. T. Blodgett. Mr. J. T. Bishop is seen 40 miles distant. Statements of friends.

CHAPTER XVI.
Testimony of the Press. Brooklyn Daily Eagle makes her case public.

CHAPTER XVII.
Miss Fancher assailed by Drs. Hammond and Beard. Mr. Epes Sargent makes a scathing answer to their assaults in the New York Sun.

"MAD" MOLLIE

CHAPTER I.

The task I have undertaken is self-imposed, and might well have been committed to abler writers. The fear that it might be left undone until too late to be completed in the lifetime of Miss Fancher has impelled me to the work, hoping that her revising hand will make any needed corrections. All of the facts of her life which might instruct, and certainly would be of interest, can not be gathered or collated. They have never been written, and many of those to whom they were known have gone to that realm where Miss Fancher has so long and earnestly desired to follow, that her long continued sufferings which she has so patiently endured, might come to an end. But, happily, some of those who have been witnesses of this lady's sufferings through portions of the long years during which they have continued, and who have observed some of the strange things which are herein related, considered them worthy of note, and from time to time made careful records of what they observed, and it is largely by the aid of these writings that I have been able to put together what is here recorded. These sketches cover a period of over twenty-seven years of her life, some of which were made by her deceased aunt, of whose labors, devotion and self-sacrifice in the interest of her afflicted niece, suitable mention will be made.

I here take occasion to express my obligations to the many friends of Miss Fancher for the services which they have so kindly rendered in this undertaking, without the aid of whom much which will be found of great interest would probably never be preserved, and at least would not be put in suitable form in connection with her life, to make the narrative in any degree complete. The public will certainly be interested in acquiring a reliable history of the case of this remarkable lady, about whom so much has been written and spoken, some truthfully, and some that is cruelly false. It is due to Miss Fancher that the story of her life should be written while she is here to aid in the work, to correct any errors and supply any omissions. Through the story of her life, new lessons will be learned of the strange and mystic relations of mind and soul to the houses we live in—these bodies of ours. What it can yield in the accumulation of knowledge upon subjects imperfectly understood, it is her desire, by this book, to place within the easy reach of all. A thousand times during the long years that she has been confined to her bed, subject to tortures, from the very contemplation of which the mind will naturally recoil, she has said it is impossible to understand why she should be kept here to endure such sufferings, being of no comfort to her friends, but an object of constant care and solicitude. Her prayers for deliverance have not been answered, but to use her own expression, " I have been pushed back when I have struggled for release, and been told that I must wait, to bear it a little longer, a little longer, and this has been going on for over twenty-eight years, and will it ever end? " She has been answered times without number, that her life was prolonged for some wise purpose, and that in the end the reason would be made manifest. It would seem that if the facts of her case, which are so strong and startling, are for the instruction and enlightenment of humanity, and if lessons, in human life are to be learned at such a cost of pain and anguish—such a sacrifice of the choicest privileges vouchsafed to most of us, and if her sufferings are being prolonged to the end that the facts may be recorded, humanity, at least, would dictate that the work be done as speedily as possible.

It is my purpose to state the facts clearly, concisely, and without unnecessary verbiage and whatever comments may be made, will be in such form as to leave the reader free to understand the history of her sickness, and the strange things which she has done and is constantly doing, so that he may form his own conclusions, irrespective of the opinion of others.

I have known Miss Fancher personally for twelve years, and have witnessed some of the strange things here recorded. I have been exceedingly careful to obtain the testimony of the most reliable persons, and in the course of the work copious reference will be made to the same, so that the curious and the doubting, the skeptical and the painstaking may know where to inquire for reliable information, touching the important features of her case.

Unquestionably every age is remarkable to the people of its time; but if the accumulated histories of men and nations faithfully record the past, then we can truthfully say we are living in the most remarkable era of human existence. Wise men will be wiser to no longer dispute that which is vouched for as being true by others possessing reason and judgment, simply because it may be contrary to their own observations and experiences. There is very little as a matter of fact, in the great domain of nature, that we actually understand. To the things that are most common—that we witness every day, we seldom give thought. Why we think, and how we think, involves mysterious operations of our minds imperfectly understood in any respect. Who has been able to tell us what the soul is, where it is, and how it maintains its relations to the body? In asking this, I beg the question as to the existence of the soul, and assume that which many dispute, to wit, that there is a soul, which comprises a part of the being of man. Who has been able to tell us what is the mind, and what is its relation to the soul? Do they exist conjointly, or are they separate forces and powers, but having relations to each other? Is the soul that upon which the mind builds from birth through all life, accumulating knowledge, to be severed and separated from it at the hour of death, or through any untoward occurrence or affliction affecting the brain? Has the soul a particular place where it abides, until released or forced out by some destructive event, or disarrangement of the mechanism so strangely placed and operating within? If so, who has discovered it, and who has answered these questions? The story of the life of Mollie Fancher cannot fail to cause speculations and strange thoughts in the minds of all thinking persons upon these and kindred subjects. Those who have sought to discover the existence of a something answering to the soul, and have found nothing satisfying, will be interested in this work, and if reasonable and fair with themselves and with Miss Fancher, may profit in its perusal. Probably there has never been a case so prominently before the public as that of the subject of this book; and to many of its prominent features the testimony of thousands of reliable persons could be obtained. Sufficient will be here appended to satisfy any reasonable person.

That all will believe in the truthfulness of every statement, is not to be expected. Skeptical people are very apt to erroneously, conclude that it is very essential to the rest of the world, that they should be permitted to examine Miss Fancher for themselves, and that their testimony would be accepted by the rest of mankind as true. The reader will at once see that such a privilege cannot be accorded to all, and if the accumulated testimony herewith presented, is deemed insufficient by some to satisfy them of its truthfulness, it is probable that additional proof would not affect the result.

It is not my purpose to here advance theories of my own. The facts must stand by themselves for the unbiased judgment of the reader. Where comment is made, it will be for the purpose of establishing in the mind of the reader the truthfulness of the narrative, or explaining its character, or for comparing some of its features with similar phenomena occurring in ancient or modern times.

CHAPTER II.

Mary J. Fancher, the subject of this book, was born on the 16th day of August, 1848, at Attleboro, Massachussets, U. S. A. She is the eldest of five children born of the marriage of James E. Fancher and Elizabeth Crosby. Her parents moved to Brooklyn, New York, when Mollie, as she has always been called, was but two years of age. Her mother died several years afterwards. Her father, a highly respectable man, and her brother James E. Fancher, Jr., are still living.* Her sister Elizabeth died ten years ago. She commenced going to a private school kept by a Miss Evans when quite young. Being an apt scholar, when between the ages of eleven and twelve years she was able to enter the Brooklyn Heights Seminary, then under the charge of Professor Charles E. West, where she remained until sixteen, and she was compelled to leave, when within a few weeks of graduating, in consequence of ill health. A few months after the decease of her mother, Miss Fancher was taken in charge by Miss Susan E. Crosby, her mother's sister, who remained with her almost constantly up to the time of her decease.

* Since writing the above he died from a railroad accident.

The mother of Mollie Fancher was a lady of much character and refinement, and during the protracted illness, which resulted in her death, she seemed to look out into the future and discern shadows over the life of her eldest daughter, who was always her favorite child. Her son was a frail infant, with little chance of living more than a few months at best, and, realizing that her life was fast drawing to a close, she called to her side her sister, Miss Crosby, then a young and accomplished lady, and confided to her her forebodings regarding her much beloved Mollie. Speaking of Elizabeth she said, "Elizabeth will be able to take care of herself. But Mollie, I can see, is a child of sorrow, and will need your care, and I want you should make me one promise, and that is, if anything shall happen to her, that you will look after and care for her as your own daughter."

As has been previously said, at this time, Susan E. Crosby was a beautiful, accomplished and refined young lady, and looked out upon life, as do most young ladies, as worth living for its bright hopes of future happiness.

Whether she shared the apprehensions of her sister or not, as to the future of the young child so tenderly committed to her charge, at that time, may never be known. But looking upon the wan face of her sister, and letting the earnestness of her appeal reach her heart, she responded with that nobleness so characteristic of her, and so commendable in its sincerity, and gave the desired assurance, that when she was gone, Mollie should be to her as her own child; a promise which thousands of persons know was faithfully kept, until she was finally forced to leave her charge through her own illness, and eventually to die, longing to clasp once more in her arms the form of her beloved niece, for whom she had sacrificed so much.

A few words touching the life of this noble lady is not only due to her memory, but will be of interest to the reader.

MISS SUSAN E. CROSBY.

At the age of sixteen Miss Crosby made the acquaintance of a young and wealthy planter residing in the city of Mobile, Alabama. They became much attached to each other; their acquaintance ripened into love and they were soon engaged to be married. The day was fixed, the trousseau prepared, her lover set sail to come North, and she looked anxiously forward to the hour when the vessel would arrive, when she would greet him at the landing. The vessel came; she was waiting, but her lover had been stricken with yellow fever on his way, and had died ere the vessel had reached its destination.

This sad affliction was the first great shadow cast over her own life; and after recovering from the shock, her sister having died, she came to Brooklyn, and soon went into the house which Mr. Fancher had then built on the corner of Gates Avenue, and what is known now as Downing Street, where she became the head of the household, and where Miss Fancher has ever since resided.

Mr. Fancher, several years after the decease of his wife, married again, and consequently the entire care of Mollie devolved upon Miss Crosby. The attachment between aunt and niece soon became marked, and grew stronger as years rolled by, freighted with misfortunes and clouded with sorrows. All the care and attention that a mother could bestow upon her own offspring was unreservedly showered by Miss Crosby on her niece. Although a child of strong will and of great determination and firmness, Miss Mollie yielded a willing obedience to the gentle restraint of her aunt, and expressions of endearment and affection were never wanting from one to the other.

Such self-abnegation as Susan Crosby practiced is so rare, as to merit something more than passing mention. Often that which is regarded as a sacrifice, is robbed of its noble-ness by the discovery of a shade of selfishness. If oral promises were sacredly kept, written obligations would be useless. Because they are not, lawyers thrive in drafting, and fatten in enforcing those which are broken. Had Miss Crosby not given her word, what her sense of duty would have impelled her to do, may not be positively asserted; but the reader, I am sure, will agree with me in saying, that few persons would have made so great sacrifices as did she, that she might devote her entire life in ministering to the comfort of her niece. It would have been easy, and, perhaps, pardonable under the circumstances, to have kept to the letter and violated the spirit of her promise, when she found the forebodings of her sister were about to be realized. She observed the gathering clouds and the gloom of darkness, coming into the life of her young niece. Terrible as the affliction then was, its awful nature and long duration could not be suspected, unless by intuition she could sense the extent of the calamity. That she was intuitional, and felt the shadows of impending misfortunes, is clearly evinced by numerous incidents which have been noted in her own life. However we may feel the approach of events, in advance of their coming, we argue that we do not know they will come, and act upon the assumption that they will not; and this in the main is correct, as fortunately the fears of the timid are not usually well grounded, and many persons mistake impressions which are merely worthless imaginings, for intuitions, which are immediate insights to outer conditions, that correctly portend what is to occur.

The day of the first accident to Miss Fancher, Miss Crosby seemed impressed with some misfortune in advance of its coming, and the same was true a year later, when the girl was brought home unconscious from the effects of an injury, which ultimately produced the most appalling results. For some time previous, Miss Crosby had received the attention of a most worthy gentleman, for whom she formed a merited affection, and she had promised him her hand in marriage. Marriage is a relation to which most persons look forward with anticipations of culminating happiness, without which life would be barren of many of its natural pleasures. Woman naturally feels that there will come a time when she will share her fortunes with another, upon whom she will bestow her affections, and in return receive the love and protecting arm of a noble husband. The relation of marriage may not lightly be entered into, because of its sacredness; yet it is natural that it should be formed, and we shall some time learn more of its enduring nature. It was Miss Crosby's misfortune to have made two promises, both of which she felt she could not redeem, with justice to the man she had promised to marry, and at the same time keep the spirit of her promise to her deceased sister, whose child was now a helpless invalid, hopelessly confined to her bed.

The reader is left to conjecture how deep was the disappointment, and how strong the sense of honor of this noble lady, in deciding the question, which she did for herself, without the influence of anything but her own sense of duty. To leave to others the care of her niece to whom she was devotedly attached, who might not be to her always tender and kind, was what she would not do; and to take into her married life such a burden to be shared by her husband she could not, even though he were willing. There was to her but one course, and that was to ask to be released from her promise of marriage, and keep that made with her sister. This being done, her preparations for marriage came to an end; henceforth her thoughts and attention were bestowed upon her niece. What were to be her wedding robes were laid aside; some having never been worn, are yet in the possession of Miss Fancher. The evident affection existing between these ladies was deep and enduring, and unto the end of her life no murmur of complaint escaped the lips of Miss Crosby. Expressions of endearment were ever on their lips from one to the other; and much that forms this narrative is gathered from the writings of Miss Crosby, as from time to time she noted down the strange developments of the most remarkable case in medical history.

CHAPTER III.

Miss Fancher's Adventurous Horseback Rides.

At the time that Miss Fancher was about closing her studies at the Brooklyn Heights Seminary, she was a tall, slender and graceful young lady, a decided blonde, and a universal favorite among her schoolmates, teachers and friends. Her profuse light wavy hair reaching down over her shoulders, her exceedingly fair complexion, regular features, oval face, small and finely chiseled mouth, made her conspicuous wherever she went, and probably no young lady of her time was more widely known in the city than Mollie Fancher. She was ambitious, and possessed a commendable degree of pride to excel in her studies. She stood high in her class, and was soon expecting to graduate, when her teacher observed, as had many other friends, that she was in failing health, and that an immediate change in her course of life was essential to effect her recovery. Her trouble was pronounced nervous indigestion, her stomach rejecting most kinds of food; she had wasted away and become weak, and was the subject of frequent fainting spells, which aroused alarm in the mind of her kind preceptor.

Miss Fancher abandoned the Brooklyn Heights Seminary, with the intention of doing whatever might be deemed wisest, to most speedily effect her restoration to health. Her physician pronounced her trouble indigestion; and horseback riding was advised as just that kind of exercise which would likely produce beneficial results. She first went to a riding-school, then kept back of the Mansion House on Brooklyn Heights, and soon was a graceful and fearless equestrienne. As has been already said, few young ladies in Brooklyn were more widely known than she, and hundreds knew Mollie Fancher by sight, who had not the pleasure of a personal acquaintance. Her skill in managing her horse and retaining her seat, as he trotted or galloped over uneven roads and roughly paved streets, commanded admiration, and she became quite noted as a graceful and fearless rider.

Mr. J. J. Field, a friend of Miss Fancher's, residing near by, had just purchased a handsome pony horse of a Mr. Kerrigan, for his daughter, which he kept at the livery stable of a Mr. Lewis on Aldelphi Street, corner of Fulton Street. He had purchased the animal as a safe horse for his daughter, who was inexperienced as a rider; and, at Mr. Field's request, Miss Fancher took him from the stable and rode him around the city for exercise, without an intimation that he was not safe for a lady to ride; supposing he was used to female horsemanship. She had gone but a few blocks before the animal, which had really never been before mounted by a lady, suddenly started into a run, viciously turning his head and biting at her dress, which was fluttering in the wind, as he plunged through the streets, among vehicles of all sorts, disregarding every effort to hold him in. Weak as Miss Fancher was from her sickness, she realized that any efforts on her part to control him would be unavailing, and she coolly resigned herself to whatever fate there might be in store for her, determined to maintain her seat, however, at all hazards.

Strangers will not know the streets and roads through which she was carried, nor the distance; their names are given for the information of many persons residing in the vicinity, who are familiar with the location. It may be stated that, among others, he ran through Classon Avenue to Flushing Avenue, and through Flushing Avenue, along the Navy Yard, until he came to Clinton Avenue, when he turned again in the direction of Fulton Street. He conturned at a break-neck pace, until he seemed to discover that he was in a familiar location, when he halted in front of a handsome wooden house, and mounting the sidewalk, opened the gate with one of his fore-feet, giving it a backward push with one of his hind feet, to prevent its closing upon him, and deliberately proceeded up the walk to the steps of the piazza, mounted it, and struck the floor heavily with his foot three times, waiting as if he expected to be invited in. All efforts of Miss Fancher to coax or drive him away were fruitless, and she remained seated, awaiting developments, wondering what next was to come. Soon the door opened, and a young gentleman appeared, whom the horse instantly recognized by a whinny of joy, as if he had met an old friend. Miss Fancher proceeded to explain how she came to be an intruder, and besought the gentleman's assistance to lead the animal down into the Street.

The gentleman was Mr. Kerrigan, who was astonished, as might be supposed, at so unexpected a visit from a strange young lady, and at once proceeded to inform Miss Fancher that he had formerly owned the animal, which had been taught tricks and to open gates, and do many unusual things for a horse; and that he had never been ridden by a lady, and was, in his opinion, quite an unsafe animal for her use. He led him down into the Street, and away from the house, and she succeeded in returning him to the stable without further incident or accident.

"MAD" MOLLIE

Many of the readers of these pages will wonder that Miss Fancher should desire—even dare—to venture another experiment with this horse. Those who know her best will wonder least. Few women have greater courage than she; few are more cool and collected in times of peril. The love of venture rises often to the degree of passion, and there are few persons who, when dangers and perils are successfully passed, do not enjoy the recollection of what, at the time, caused feelings of terror or alarm. We are invariably taking chances in life which we should not; frequently blame in others what we are practicing ourselves. Really, what would our lives be without excitement? The savage will venture all his worldly possessions on a horse-race, and people who think they are civilized are doing the same thing. The habit of reading stories of fiction is almost universal, and comes from an innate love, which is soon developed into a passion, for thrilling, exciting accounts of ventures and anomalous occurrences, which the reader knows, but forgets, has no foundation—in fact, are only the productions of the brain of the novelist.

It was not unnatural that, having ridden the horse so far, and at such a speed, she should think that she was mistress, when once seated in her saddle on his back, with bridle in hand, so far as safety was concerned. Her recollections of the exciting ride were pleasing, and she thought she would probably become familiar to him, and he, perhaps, as much attached to her as to his former owner. Unfortunately the brute was not quite gallant enough to appreciate his fair rider, and waited the discovery of an opportune moment, when she would be unguarded, to unseat her. She had continued to ride him without serious danger for some days. Upon one occasion, when he thought the exercise too lengthy, he faced about, plunged through the streets for home, and did not stop until he had carried her down the inclined way, through the low door-way, to his stall. Miss Fancher could not halt him, and seeing she was likely to be swept from her saddle by the lintel of the door-way, she prostrated herself on his back and escaped injury.

But May 10th, 1864, was ominous with fate. If she sensed its misfortunes she did not heed the premonitions, nor those of her aunt, who was impressed with approaching calamity, and besought her niece not to ride that horse that day, as she felt something dreadful was about to happen. Mollie did not share the fears of Miss Crosby, and laughed them away, for the moment, only to return when she had gone. Miss Fancher had safely taken her accustomed ride, and was passing along Gates Avenue toward her home, then only five blocks away, when she accidentally dropped the rein of the bridle on the horse's neck. She reached for it, but her hand being gauntleted, it missed her grasp. She inclined slightly forward to make sure of regaining it. The unguarded moment had come. Suddenly her horse, which until then was quietly walking, plunged forward, kicked his heels high in air, and she was precipitated to the pavement of the Street, the top of her head striking with great force against the curb-stone, and her side the rough stone pavement. Two of her ribs were broken, her heavy hat alone saving the skull from being crushed. She was rendered at once unconscious, and with her foot caught in the stirrup she remained motionless where she had fallen. As if satisfied with what he had succeeded in doing, her horse stood until some one released her foot, when he galloped away to the stable. Unconscious and bleeding, Miss Fancher was taken to a house in St. James' place, while her aunt at home was waiting, anxious to know if her fears and premonitions had been realized. Her physician was at once summoned.

It is probable that Miss Fancher would have recovered from the effects of this fall had not a second misfortune followed a year later. It was nearly two months before she was able to be around; and as soon as sufficiently recovered, she visited friends in Cornwall, on the Hudson, where she remained for two months, Dr. Beattie, since deceased, giving her the required medical attendance. While in Cornwall her physician became alarmed at a huge swelling in her left side, indicating the formation of an abscess. In this respect his fears were not realized; the swelling, being occasioned by the irritation of the flesh from the broken ribs, gradually subsided, and Miss Fancher returned home. All her life she has been subject to severe headaches, which she suffers as an inheritance from her father. Before she left school she was subject to spells of coughing, which, together with weakness and fainting spells, gave warranted apprehensions of consumption. The shock occasioned by her fall, and the injury to her side, were certainly calculated to lessen her chances of recovery, and during the following Autumn occasional hemorrhages from her right lung increased the anxiety of her friends.

Another feature of her case attracted less attention, but is essential to be mentioned to make its history as complete as possible. Her eyesight was becoming defective; her vision was double. She saw two objects where there was but one. When she attempted to thread a needle, she saw two threads, two needles and two eyes. With the return of Spring, in 1865, she was hopeful of regaining her health. For some time she had been receiving the attention of Mr. John H. Taylor, a young gentleman of respectability and of good social standing. At this period they were engaged to be married, and, though no time had been fixed for the nuptials, it was understood that they were shortly to be celebrated. She was expecting to make a visit to Boston—and her preparations were about completed. She desired to make a call upon her physician before leaving, and, having done so, stopped on her way home to do some shopping. This was June 8th, 1865. With her hands full of packages, she took a Fulton Street car, and, when as near to her home as the car would take her, she signaled to the conductor to stop. He rang the bell, the car was halted, and Miss Fancher, with packages in hand, was about to step off the rear platform into the Street, when the conductor rang the bell again for the car to move forward, turned his face and went into the car, evidently supposing she had safely alighted.

Unfortunately, such was not the case, for, as she was in the act of stepping down, she was thrown violently to the ground. Unfortunately, her skirt, which was of strong crinoline, such as was universally worn by ladies at that time, caught in the iron hook at the rear of the car, by which she was rapidly dragged over the rough stone pavements, to within a few feet of an entire block, before the car was stopped, and then it was only by the attention of the driver being attracted to something wrong, by the shouts and cries of people who witnessed the shocking spectacle. She was taken up unconscious; her ribs were broken, her body had been turning round and round, twisting her crinoline into a rope as she was dragged through the Street. This rope she has preserved, but not as a pleasing memento of her misfortune.

She was taken into a neighboring butcher's store, but it was long before she could be removed to her home. She was lifted from the ground and immediately recognized by friends, who gave her such assistance as was in their power. Her aunt was already alarmed at her long absence, and the more so, because of forebodings of other misfortunes about to come, which she had communicated to her niece before she left home that morning.

CHAPTER IV.
Miss Fancher's Indescribable Sufferings.

Up to the accident described in the preceding chapter, Miss Fancher declares that she was unaware of any spinal trouble. She had not experienced any numbness of her limbs, nor peculiar sensitiveness along the spinal column. Three months after the car accident, she suffered from soreness and pain in the spine. "For six weeks," she says, "I was confined to my bed. At the end of that period I was able to go around the room by the aid of a chair, or something to lean upon. During the time I was in bed, the cords of my left limb had so contracted that I was unable to more than get the toes of my foot to the floor. From that time it continued to grow worse until it was useless. My eyesight had continued to fail. I managed to move around the room, anxious to occupy my mind with some employment, and did such work as I was able. Every effort to bring my heel to the floor gave me pain in my back. About September 1st the spinal troubles manifested themselves more severely. Upon one occasion I was assisting my aunt in preserving peaches, when my left arm dropped helplessly by my side, and for the two weeks following I was unable to use it."

In addition to the services of her physician, when the hemorrhages from her lungs became more alarming, a council of specialists was called, comprising the best talent obtainable. In those days the names of the physicians were familiar all over the country. They were Dr. Willard Parker, Dr. Baker, Dr. Ball and Dr. Belden. They all were specialists in lung diseases, and in December of 1865, they met at the residence of Miss Fancher and made a critical examination, and their conclusion was, that she would not survive the month of the coming February, in consequence of the disease in the right lung. Miss Fancher continued to suffer from her right lung until May, 1866, when it ceased to trouble her. To all appearances it is dead. The right side of her chest is fallen; the air- cells are evidently closed, and since then she breathes only with her left lung. We will now use Miss Fancher's own language in describing her case.

"MAD" MOLLIE

"On February 3d, 1866, I was taken with inflammation of the lungs. That night I was attended by my regular physician and his son; the latter remained with me all night. During the night I was supposed to be dying. My friends were summoned to the bedside, and Rev. David Moore came and offered prayer. My physicians said I was dying; I felt and believed that I was, and I bade my friends goodbye. Well, unfortunately, I did not die, as the doctors predicted. The first spasms I had were on the 7th of February, 1866. Again my friends thought I was dying. Rev. Mr. Moore was again summoned. At the intervals between he asked me questions, and my friends sang a favorite hymn with low, sad voices, " Nearer My God to Thee." Again the doctor announced that I was dying, but I put my finger upon my wrist and sensed the beating of my pulse, and as often as the doctor pronounced me dying, I said, l it beats yet.' Again he spent the night by my bedside, sensing my pulse and heart action, evidently very much puzzled. These spasms were followed by my first trance, which lasted three hours. Of course I am ignorant of what transpired about me while I was in a trance, although I am sometimes conscious of what others are not, and I can only relate what I was told transpired. I was told I represented the appearance of being dead, and my physician pronounced me so."

This, it must be remembered, in justice to him, was his first experience in anything of the kind. He had read of trances, but evidently not with such symptoms as mine. My aunt would not have it that I was dead. My jaws were set, but she forced some brandy and water between my teeth, insisting that I was not dead. The spasms had continued during the night of February 7th, and I went into a trance on the morning of the 8th, about six o'clock. My trance lasted about three hours; then I came out, but what had in the meantime transpired was, to me, an utter blank. When I came out of the trance I was conscious for awhile, then the spasms came on and lasted several hours, and from the spasms I passed into a trance again. These trances continued for three consecutive days and nights. The watch at my bedside was necessarily continuous during this time. I was unconscious; my death was momentarily expected. I took no nourishment. At the end of those three days spasms came again. Then I had them day and night, for nine years, alternating with trances. Usually the spasms would last for three hours, and the trances from about five to fourteen hours, and sometimes two or three days at a time. Between these conditions I had spells of consciousness. I am not aware that I have ever been in what is usually understood as insane or delirious conditions since my trances came upon me. I have never heard my physicians say so, with one or two exceptions, which will be explained later on.

"For two months after my trances commenced, fourteen persons were in constant attendance upon me, a relay of seven being required to hold me upon the bed during the spasms. My body and limbs were drawn together until I was almost a ball; then I leaped forward like an arrow, and would have been killed but for the protection of friends and the wadded obstructions placed in the way. These conditions continued until the first week in May of 1866, when I went into a long trance."

Up to this time Miss Fancher had had spells of consciousness, lasting at times a few hours, at others a much less time. It seems quite natural that her physician should direct his efforts to break the coming of these spasms, which were so violent, and seemingly distressing. Anomalous cases are constantly arising, in which the skill and judgment of the physician are powerless to relieve the patient, and I hope to be pardoned by my many medical friends for saying, that at times recovery or death may be the accident of experiment. And it is not always the fault of the physician that this is so. Emergencies often arise in life, where others than doctors are forced to extreme measures to meet a great hazard, where greater danger attends inaction. Theirs is a profession which deals with our bodies for their preservation, as houses for the souls that possess them. We are often astonished at the ease with which the occupant is dispossessed; and then we are amazed, when the house is in ruins, to find the tenant disputing with death possession of the fragments.

I shall let Miss Fancher tell in her own words, as nearly as possible, the treatment she was subjected to for the purpose of breaking these spasms, during the Winter and Spring of 1866. She does not censure her physician, who found her case unparalleled in many respects, and who, under the circumstances, was justified in making all reasonable efforts to save her life and alleviate her sufferings. He was sorely perplexed. How could she live without food, and how recover, or even improve, without medicines? were questions he naturally asked himself, and if either was forced into her stomach, in quantities to accomplish beneficial results, it was at once rejected. There was no medicine in the smallest quantity which did not occasion her the greatest distress. She soon became satisfied that all attempted remedies were hurtful to her, and, in her conscious moments, rebelled against taking any.

"It was," she says, "forced into my mouth, and I kept it there until I got the opportunity, and then I rejected it. My doctor thought I was insane, but, as a matter of fact, I was never more rational in my life. I found every remedy increased my sufferings, and I begged to be let alone. In fact, my spasms and trances were essential to my living; but this my physicians did not know, nor is it astonishing that they should not. It was in these conditions, strange as it may seem, that I got any rest, and it ever since has been so. When they stop I shall surely die. The first remedy externally applied, was brisk rubbing of my body with alcohol, from the moment I went into a trance until I came out of it, to break the trance, my physician believing it was absolutely essential that I should be aroused from these trances to save my life. The spasms preceding these trances greatly exhausted me. As I went into a trance my body and limbs became rigid and immovable, my hands were usually folded across my breast, and my eyes were open and upturned. I am told that my physicians frequently raised me to a standing position by placing their hands back of my head, without the least flexibility of my body or limbs, my body being seemingly as rigid as a piece of statuary. During these times my eyes were not affected by light, nor were they sensitive to the touch, and I was subject to many experiments, to determine if my body was in any degree sensitive to pain; the conclusion of my physicians being that it was not.

"Rubbing with alcohol failing to be of any use, my head was next shaved and blistered, and from this my suffering was very great; but I submitted, hoping that some good would result, but was disappointed. Then I was treated with electricity for awhile; a battery was applied for a few days, with no benefit. Then my physician thought it advisable to change the position of my bed, so that I would lie in line with the earth's magnetic cur- rents; my head was to point directly north, and my body and limbs south; so the bed was wheeled into the required position, and I was divested of all jewelry and metallic substances, and a large horse-shoe magnet was placed at my feet. This occasioned me no suffering, and I was satisfied with it, but it produced no apparent change of condition; so I was next put into a sitz-bath three times in twenty-four hours, and this was kept up for six weeks. The water was made hot, and sometimes it was medicated with herbs. The doctor thought he was doing me good, but he was only adding torture to torture.

" From the sitz-bath he resorted to a steam-bath of dry alcohol. I was placed in the bath-tub, and the tub covered with blankets, and my person up to my chin, and lamps burning alcohol placed in the tub. The heat was not properly regulated, and my body was terribly burned, the skin in places peeling off. My spasms continuing in violence, my physician believing if he could once break them they would not return, and I would get better, and finding hot baths had done no good, he reversed his remedies, and commenced to treat me with cold water. First I was put in a bath of very hot water, and while there pails of ice-cold water were poured upon my head until I fainted from suffering and exhaustion. Then I was taken from the bath-tub and put in bed and my body and limbs vigorously rubbed. I was not permitted to rest even in my trances, which rendered me unconscious, but was constantly disturbed by some method of treatment.

" I was next rolled in wet sheets wrung out from cold water, and made to lie in these until I could and would endure it no longer; then I projected my elbows with all my strength, and burst the sheets, and was at once declared to be in another fit of insanity.

"The next treatment which caused my utter rebellion was the application of ice. First, a jacket was made in the required form, with big open pockets extending from the top of my head down my spine, and around my body. Then five bladders were filled with ice; one was placed upon my stomach, three on my spine and one on the top of my head. Soon my agony was beyond comprehension. I was satisfied that my treatment was but a series of experiments, intensifying my suffering, and preventing any chance of my recovery. I have a temper, and it was then aroused. I seized the bladder of ice on top of my head and hurled it across the room. This was followed by the four others sent in the same direction. Meanwhile the doctor believed I had gone insane, and I was pronounced a raving maniac. Well, I was raving. My vocabulary was insufficient to express my feelings, and I positively refused to submit to any further treatment. I regret to make all of these matters public, and I only do so at the request of my friends, who desire that I shall conceal nothing in giving a history of my case. This physician is dead, and I have no desire now to censure him. My case was anomalous, and he did the best he could for me. His son, a very excellent physician, I esteem as among my friends. He was commissioned at times by his father to apply some of these treatments, and frequently let me off, after exacting a promise that his father should not be informed.

"My aunt believed everything to be right that my physician ordered. She continued to allow him to visit the house, and learn from her my condition. This went on for three weeks, when I desired another physician. Dr. McFail, who then was quite eminent in his profession in Brooklyn, was recommended by a friend. He was called, but, seeing that it was a case which required great attention, he concluded that he could not do me justice, and recommended his nephew, who had just returned from Paris, and was commencing practice here. This gentleman is Dr. S. Fleet Spier, who first saw me April 6th, 1886, and has been one of my faithful and skillful attendants since that time. Some of the physicians who have attended me have been more than doctors; they have been faithful friends, to whom I owe a debt of gratitude I cannot discharge; and I can only pray that they may receive the abundant reward, due from a multitude of good deeds.

"Between the shower baths and ice applications my doctor had, for the time, broken my spasms, and for several days they entirely ceased; but during that time I failed rapidly, being most of the time unconscious. Then my physicians began to recognize the fact, that these spasms and trances served an essential part in maintaining life, and if they were discontinued, I would unquestionably die. Consequently, a new mode of treatment forced itself upon their attention. I took so little nourishment that they concluded I would die from starvation. I was placed in a sitz-bath which was charged with beef tea, that my body might receive nourishment by absorbing it.

"About the middle of March, 1866, when I came out of a spasm, I found my throat paralyzed, and almost every time there was some new complication. For instance, sometimes my sense of hearing was so impaired that I was entirely deaf, and the only way that I could understand or hear, was by having those who spoke to me approach so near to my face, that the sound of the voice could penetrate my nostrils, and in that way communicate with my brain, or organs of hearing. Exactly how it was accomplished I cannot understand; and even to this day my left ear has never recovered its power of hearing; that side of my head is entirely deaf. This loss of hearing occurred about the last of February, t866. On the 22d of February I had a terrific spasm, and my eyesight failed me entirely, and I have never recovered the same. I can see, but not by the use of my eyes. When I first became conscious of my failing sight, I was greatly alarmed, but hoped to recover it again. When I had this terrible spasm that I have just spoken of, and I had come out of my trance, I found it suddenly growing dark, and I supposed it was the approach of night, and asked my aunt to light the gas in my room so that I could see. She replied, 'It is lighted, darling; can't you see it?' I said, 'No, it is all dark.' Then she lighted another burner to satisfy me, and then another, but still all was dark. Then the consciousness dawned upon me that I was blind, and a sense of horror came over me, and I exclaimed:' Oh, my God, I am blind; with all my other afflictions I am blind.'

"Now, bear in mind, that at this time my ordinary sense of hearing was so impaired that I could only distinguish voices in the manner I have described, and with my eyesight gone, I was left to my sense of feeling to recognize those around me. It is somewhat difficult for me now to get the exact dates of the appearance of these different symptoms, but I give them as nearly as I can remember them, trusting to the memorandums made by my aunt, and also those made by my physicians to correct any errors.

"I lost my sight before I lost my hearing. These symptoms and conditions which I am now describing were crowded into the months of February, March, April and May of 1866, and I will give them in their order as I recollect them. I recall that I could recognize Dr. Spier by a peculiarity of one of his thumbs, which had a little roughness of the nail. I recognized my aunt by a pin which she wore. Other friends would place in my hands something which I was familiar with, and then I would know of their presence.

"It was in February that the spasms had closed my throat to such an, extent, that it was almost impossible for any kind of nourishment to be received. The organs of the throat became so rigid, and so hard, that when struck, the sound resembled that of wood or stone, and this rigidity of my throat continued for nine years, with the exception of one instance, when it relaxed for a short time only. After my throat became paralyzed they gave me enemas of beef-tea, brandy and milk-punches. They made bags of Peruvian bark, dipped them in brandy and laid them on my chest. I remonstrated against this, and begged to be let alone, feeling sure that I would get along better without them.

"After Dr. Spier came, he continued to give me medicines for a while, but finding they did me no good, that I could not retain them, they were discontinued. The loss of my power of hearing was followed by the loss of the sense of feeling. I lost the sense of touch, then the sense of smell, then the sense of taste, and then the power of speech.

"During this time my friends were unable to make their presence known to me for quite a time. My power of communicating to them was utterly lost, and, for a time to me, they seemed dead. The doctor was investigating, to find if he could discover any part which was alive to the sense of touch, and finally he found that by putting his finger back of my left ear I knew him. I knew him by the peculiarity of his thumb, which I have already mentioned.

"At times between these trances and spasms, I was in perfect possession of my mental faculties, and I never, to my knowledge, lost them once. Whether I possessed all or not. must be determined from what I saw and did. At any rate, I supposed that I possessed all of my mental faculties and powers.

"Following the loss of these other powers, my fingers became cramped into the palms of my hands, in which condition they remained for a long time, my thumbs being perfectly free. This, if I recollect aright, was in May, 1866.

"About the month of May, 1866, my second sight, a power or sense of seeing without the use of the natural organs of sight—my eyes, and which has occasioned so much comment, began to develop, and it came in this way. First I seemed to have a consciousness of the position of things around me, and the movements of persons, without actually seeing them with my eyes. My watch, a small gold one, was hanging over the mantel-piece on the opposite side of the room, quite a distance from me, and placed in such a way that no persons, with their ordinary sight, could see it, so as to determine the time, from the position where I was lying. Well, I saw, in some way that I cannot explain, the face of that watch, the position of its hands, and I could correctly state the time. My aunt had got into the habit of opening and reading my letters, and communicating their contents to me, and upon one occasion, after I had recovered the use of my hands, and power of speech, and sense of hearing in one of my ears, a letter came, and she proceeded to open it and read it, when I insisted that she should give it to me. She replied, ' Why, darling, you know you can't read it,' but I persisted and she gave it to me. I at once took it in my hands and read it to her. She was astonished; because she saw at once that I did it without the use of my eyes. Then my friends began to make various tests, asking me all sorts of questions as to what they had in their pockets and in their hands, and it was found that I could tell them correctly. My sense of feeling was not gone probably more than a week or ten days, and when it came back I possessed it more keenly then ever before."

Before proceeding further with statements of Miss Fancher, a chapter from the records kept by her aunt shall be inserted.

CHAPTER V.

Miss Crosby's Records.

In the previous part of this book, I have stated that I had access to quite extensive minutes of Miss Fancher's case, which were kept by her aunt, Miss Susan E. Crosby, during her lifetime. I have those now in my possession, in order to confirm many of the features of Miss Fancher's case; and to enable me to speak in detail of some others, as they are contained in those writings, I shall take them up and go through with them, extracting what I deem to be of interest and importance. A great deal would be uninteresting matter, because it is a daily recital of the symptoms and condition in which Miss Fancher was at the time the records were made up, and in many instances they are so similar, that to repeat them would be a useless task. What follows is substantially verbatim, at the commencement of Miss Crosby's diary.

"Mollie Fancher, when a child, and up to the age of fifteen years, was healthy. For a year afterwards she was troubled with weakness in the chest, and a slight cough; then dyspepsia set in, and she suffered from sickness at the stomach, sinking, fainting feelings, and this continued until March, 1864, when her symptoms became more aggravated. She vomited her food, and could keep scarcely anything on her stomach. She left her school in April, being within two months of graduating, and the disappointment was so keen that she seemed greatly disheartened. She was then advised to commence horse-back riding as a cure for dyspepsia. She was then under medical treatment. May 10th she was thrown from her horse; the shock was very severe; her head and side troubled her very much. Under the Doctor's direction she went to Cornwall, in July, where she received medical treatment, constantly complaining of her head and side, and going out to ride one day she was taken ill; the lower part of her body was paralyzed, and during the night she was for a short time unconscious. She remained in a feeble state for several weeks, suffering in her head and side. The Doctor thought she was having an abscess form under her left lung. On examination, however, he found a rib was fractured, which occasioned the swelling. For nine days and nights she had no rest, and remained feeble until September, when she returned home, and seemed to rally, and was quite smart during the Fall and Winter, and up to June, 1865. On the 8th of that month as she was leaving a car on Fulton Avenue, she was thrown to the ground and dragged nearly the length of a block. For an hour or more after the accident she was in fainting fits, and then rallied. Upon examination the Doctor discovered two more ribs in the left side were fractured, and also that her head was hurt. She remained very weak and feeble during the summer, her nervous system appearing severely shattered; she did not seem to gain strength, and at times she would lose the power of her left arm; then remaining at times in fainting fits, suffering most when lying down. She also had a cough.

"The last of August she had a severe attack of illness, the left side and lower part of her body becoming paralyzed. It was several days before she recovered the full use of her bodily power. She then rallied for awhile, then other symptoms, as of spinal disease, appeared, and her head, side and cough seemed worse as the season advanced. She complained of weakness and pain in her chest; also pain through her right shoulder, and was not able to lie down, and was apparently failing very fast. This continued to February, up to which time for eighteen months she had not had a good night's rest. On the 3d of February she was taken with spasms, which continued for a short time, leaving her very weak, until Thursday, the 8th. Her symptoms were great weakness, severe cough, pain in her head, side, spine and chest, and through the right shoulder. She suffered intensely from difficulty in breathing, and was unable to lie down. At half-past four in the evening of that day she commenced having severe spasms, which lasted until one o'clock. Soon after the spasms she appeared lifeless; then she rallied a little, but was thought to be dying; her cough left her, and she remained very weak, without pain, until Sunday, the nth, when she seemed to be again sinking very fast.

"On Monday, the 12th, she rallied and seemed to show signs of life. She suffered intensely in her head, spine and side, and apparently in her heart. Upon Tuesday, the 13th, she seemed to be unconscious most of the time, still suffering in her spine. On the 14th she continued to have spasms once a day, coming on about one o'clock and continuing an hour or an hour and twenty minutes; also suffering and severe pains in her head and spine. On Thursday, the 15th, spasms set in twice a day, at one and at ten o'clock, followed by a trance of from one to two hours' duration. Friday, the 16th, she still remained in the same state, spasms alternating with trances, as above stated. Suffering from head and heart continued. Saturday, the 17th, the spasms and trances were followed by a loss of eyesight. Sunday, the 18th, very hard spasms, and she continued in the same way, the trances following twice during the day, and requiring five and six persons to hold her. On Monday, the 19th, she lost her hearing, having spasms and trance, and suffering intensely from head and spine. Tuesday, the 20th, she was unconscious, having spasms and trance. Wednesday, the 21st, she seemed at times more conscious, but the spasms and trances continued.

"Thursday, the 22d, she had spasms very hard from one to two hours, on coming out of which her body appeared to be paralyzed, and she had her senses, but no power to move. After having been rubbed for an hour with alcohol she rallied and saw, heard and spoke for half an hour. On Friday, the 23d, she lost the sense of smell. On Saturday, the 24th, her hands closed. On Sunday the 25th, her jaws were locked. On Monday, the 26th, her limbs contracted, she still continuing to have spasms twice a day, followed by a trance. During the intervals she suffered much in her head and spine. Tuesday, the 27th, she seemed in a very feeble state, suffering severely with spasms apparently round the heart. She remained very feeble for two days up to March 2d. She had spasms and trances in the same way. From March 3d to March 7th she endured great suffering. On the 7th she had very severe spasms, after which she was paralyzed until the 9th, when her muscles relaxed, and she saw, heard and spoke; her hands also opened, and she remained so for several hours, possessing all her natural powers. Then they again left her. From the 9th to the 13th of March she was very weak, constantly fainting, part of the time unconscious, but had no spasms or trances. On Tuesday the 13th, her spasms returned once a day, continuing for about twenty minutes, followed by a trance of from three to five hours. She was unconscious most of the time, and suffered intensely with her head. Wednesday, the 14th, she had spasms in the head; was very feeble and not expected to live throughout the day. At eight o'clock in the evening she rallied a little, still remaining in a feeble state up to Thursday evening, the 15th, and then rallied and spoke and sung, and appeared to be very happy. Then her speech left her, and her jaws closed. Her sense of feeling left her; she had no power to express herself, but still appeared to be conscious, and remained in that condition up to Thursday morning, the 16th, when the power to perceive and communicate by the sense of touch returned and continued until two o'clock. Then again she had severe spasms and trance, followed by paralysis, until Sunday, when she rallied, and was conscious, but was very feeble up to the 19th. During the day she seemed quite smart, with much unnatural strength; was able to write and work, but in the evening she was delirious.

"Tuesday, the 21st, she again seemed quite smart; her hands opened for a short time. Most of the -week she was absent-minded and had much unnatural strength. Wednesday, the 28th, she again had spasms around the heart, and remained very feeble for three days. After spasms or trances, having fainting spells most of the time, and being oppressed with the loss of breath, and apparently in a sinking condition. Tuesday, the 27th, she appeared to have more life, and the

27

spasms and trances returned. Thursday, the 30th, she was more cheerful, and was able to write during the day, but in the evening was absent-minded, and had much unnatural strength; had spasms and trances up to April 1st, when she was again quite improved most of the day. She had light spasms and a trance lasting from two to three hours. April 2d she seemed most of the time absent-minded and very weak, which continued up to the 4th, then after having very severe spasms and a trance her throat closed; she remained very weak and feeble until the 6th, and was unconscious most of the time. Friday morning, April the 6th, she was very weak, absent-minded at times; spasms alternating with trances. Saturday, the 7th, she was in a weak and fainting condition most of the time, spasms with very light trances in the usual way. Sunday, the 8th, she continued in the same condition. On Monday, the 9th, she was absent-minded at times, and had spasms alternating with trances lasting for three or four hours. Tuesday, the 10th, she seemed quite improved; she had spasms and trances, and at six o'clock in the evening her throat and jaws relaxed, and she spoke quite plainly, and then became absent-minded, and remained in that condition for three days, suffering greatly from nausea; was unable to take any nourishment; spasms and trances continued. On Saturday, the 14th, she was quite improved up to three o'clock, having severe spasms followed by trance lasting from three to four hours, and remaining in an unconscious state all night. On Sunday, the 15th, she was very feeble, her throat closed again, and she had the spasms and trance as usual. On Monday, the 16th, she remained about the same, very feeble, spasms followed by trances; fainting spells, leaving her in an absent-minded condition; her throat remained closed until Monday, the 23d, then it opened for one day. Tuesday, the 24th, her throat closed again, and her spasms and trances continued. She appeared a little stronger and more cheerful, and remained in about the same condition, spasms and trances continuing, until the 28th. On that day her throat opened for a little time. She then became absent-minded during the spasms; then her eye-lids closed; she lost the use of her hands and arms, and at times her speech, and remained in that condition until May 4th.

"During this time she had spasms and trances; her throat was closed, and yet at times, she appeared quite smart and full of life until May 10th, when her throat opened, but was soon closed again during the spasms, which were followed as usual by a trance. She remained unconscious until Sunday evening, suffering intensely with her head and heart. May nth she was more comfortable during the day, was absent-minded in the evening; spasms and trances continued. She was very restless at night. May 13th she was very weak and lost her speech; she had her usual spasms followed by a trance, in which condition she remained a long time, when she rallied, but was unconscious during the night. May 14th her throat was still closed; her feeble condition continued. She was speechless, and the trance followed her spasms up to May 16th; she was unconscious most of that day, during which she had her spasms and trance. May 17th she seemed more comfortable, and was able to write two letters. She had a spasm and trance, and was quite restless, during the night. Friday she seemed much improved; the spasm and trance condition continued, and in the evening she spoke.

"On Saturday, the 19th, she seemed very smart up to two o'clock, when her jaw relaxed, and we forced some nourishment into her stomach. This was immediately followed by severe spasms, lasting from three to four hours, when she went into a trance, in which condition she remained for one hour, and then rallied, but was unconscious, apparently suffering intensely with her head and heart until Sunday evening at five o'clock. That evening she spoke and asked for food; she seemed to be almost famished. She took a small piece of cracker, and one teaspoonful of punch, which was the first food in seven weeks, that she was able to keep on her stomach. Monday, the 21st, she was very feeble, her spasms were light, and she had her usual trance. This condition continued during the 22d, but she suffered severely with her head, and her throat closed again during the day, and the only nourishment she was able to take was two teaspoonfuls of milk punch a day. Wednesday, the 23d, she had spasms and a trance, which condition continued during Friday and Saturday following. On Saturday, the 27th, she appeared quite cheerful in the morning. In the afternoon she suffered severely in her head and heart, and in the evening she was severely shocked by a peal of thunder and lost her speech. On Monday, the 28th, she suffered severely in her head, had very severe spasms, and at two o'clock she went into a rigid trance, in which condition she remained until half-past eleven o'clock the next day, when she fell off into a relax trance, in which condition she remained until Friday evening at eight o'clock, June 1st, when she rallied with a great effort. She breathed with great difficulty, and it seemed as if her natural powers were nearly exhausted. She remained in this condition until the following Monday. June 2d her jaws relaxed, when the opportunity was improved to force some nourishment into her stomach, which was immediately rejected.

"She soon went into spasms, lasting about an hour, and remained unconscious for a short time. She began to be very sick at her stomach, and suffered intensely until Saturday evening, June 3d, when her throat closed, and she was not able to take any nourishment or to utter a sound. On Monday, June 4th, she was very much exhausted and remained weak and feeble until the 6th, when she went into a trance for a short time, the first she had had for six days, suffering intensely with her head and difficult breathing. Thursday, June 7th, she was very feeble during the day, not being able to speak, going into and out of trances all night, suffering greatly with her head and heart. On Friday, the 8th, in the morning she was unconscious, but very restless during the day. She went into a trance during the night, suffering intensely with head and heart; her throat was still closed; she was unable to speak. On Saturday, the 9th, she remained weak during the day, and in the evening at ten o'clock she was taken with spasms for the first time since June 1st. This was followed by a trance and severe suffering in the head and chest. Sunday, June 10th, her suffering continued, and she had spasms and trances until Wednesday, the 13th.

"On the 13th, during the day and night, she had spasms alternating with trances, going in and out of trances all night, and was apparently suffering greatly with pains in her head and chest, and very difficult breathing. On Saturday, the 16th, in the morning she was very weak; at one o'clock she became absent-minded and remained so during the remainder of the day and night, having spasms followed by a trance, which continued up to Sunday, the 17th. The suffering with her head being very intense she was not able to speak, her throat being still closed.

"From May 24th to June 28th she has not been able to take any nourishment. One pint of sweet oil has been used in bathing her chest and bowels, and that has been all the sustenance she has received. She still remains feeble, having spasms and trances during the night, but remains conscious. Her limbs are contracted, her eye- lids are closed, she has lost the use of her right arm, also her hands are closed. Friday, June 28th, she was unconscious during the day, was very feeble, and suffering with spasms, followed by a trance during the night, and coming out of the trance on Friday evening, she lost all power of communicating; her stomach and neck were contracted, her right arm was drawn over her head; both arms were paralyzed. Her lower limbs were contracted, her eyes and throat were closed, her jaws were locked, and she remained in this state, unconscious, until nine o'clock in the evening. She suffered very severe pain in the head up to Sunday morning, July 1st. She remained unconscious until Monday at two o'clock, then went into a spasm, which was followed by a short trance during the night.

"On Thursday, the 12th, she received a severe shock from a fire alarm; she suffered severely from her head, heart, stomach and teeth up to twelve o'clock, when she went in- to an unconscious state, in which she remained until Sun- day morning at nine o'clock, when she rallied and became conscious. From Thursday to Sunday' she had neither spasms nor trance. On Sunday, the 15th, she was very feeble during the day, and in the evening seemed to be in a sinking condition. At nine o'clock she seemed to be in very great distress about the heart. She lay in a fainting condition until nine o'clock the next morning, when she rallied, but was still in a feeble condition. She had very restless nights, suffering still from her head, teeth, heart and chest, and remained about the same up to Wednesday, the 18th. On that day she had a severe shock from a heavy clap of thunder; she suffered intensely in her head and heart. She also had very hard spasms, her body being contracted into the form of a hoop, sometimes bent backward and then forward. These conditions lasted for an hour and a half, when she went into a trance for an hour, then she rallied, but was very feeble. She remained in this state until Friday, the 20th, when she became more comfortable."

CHAPTER VI.
Miss Crosby's Records Continued.

"On Saturday, the 21st, her throat opened and she took a teaspoonful of wine, but could not keep the same on her stomach. On Sunday, the 22th, she was more comfortable. On Monday she remained about the same, and again took a teaspoonful of wine, but her stomach was not able to retain it. At nine o'clock in the evening she began to suffer intensely with her head and went into an absent-minded condition, which continued until twelve o'clock, when for an hour and a half she had very severe spasms, being bent into various forms, and then went into a trance for an hour. Coming out of the trance her lips were contracted and remained so for two days, so that she was not able to take even a drop of water. On Wednesday, the 25th, she was again able to open her lips, swallowed half a teaspooful of wine, which remained on her stomach. On Thursday, the 26th, her throat closed, and she had spasms and trances during the night, which condition continued until Saturday, the 28th. She was very restless at night, had spasms and short trances; was unable to swallow anything; her throat was still contracted; had no power to move her limbs except her feet; her eyes were closed, and she was unable to speak. On Sunday, the 29th, she appeared to be more comfortable during the day. She had spasms and trances during the night.

"On Monday, the 31st, she was quite comfortable during the day, and at eight o'clock began to have very severe spasms, which continued for an hour; she suffered during the night severely in her head and stomach. August 1st she had very hard spasms, which continued for an hour and a half. She then went into an absent-minded condition, and so remained until nine o'clock in the morning of August 2nd. She appeared more comfortable during that day, but had very severe spasms, followed by a trance during the night, and remained in about the same condition up to about August 4th. At nine o'clock in the evening she fell into a fainting condition, and remained so for three hours; she was unconscious during a portion of the night. On August 5th chloroform was administered to relax the jaws, so that some troublesome teeth might be extracted. She went immediately into a spasm, and continued so for two hours and a half. She was unconscious up to seven o'clock. This was followed by a short trance of twenty minutes. She came out of the trance unconscious, and remained so until Thursday, the 9th; then she rallied for a short time. She then fell into an absent-minded state, and remained so until Friday morning at ten o'clock, when she rallied, but was very weak. She was conscious up to Saturday evening, when she went into spasms, which continued most of the night without a trance.

"Sunday morning, August 12th, she was quite cheerful, continuing so during the day; having spasms and a trance during the night. On Tuesday, August 14th, she was about the same as the day previous, until eight o'clock, when she went into ah absent-minded condition, remaining so all night, and was very feeble. On Wednesday, 15th, she appeared in much the same condition as the day previous, with the usual spells of spasms and trances during the night. On Thursday, 16th, she was much more comfortable and had the use of her left arm, and was able to converse considerably by writing, but at eight o'clock she went into an absent-minded condition, in which state she continued until midnight; then she went into spasms and short trances, which continued until morning. On Friday, the 18th, she was very weak; spasms and trances continued during the night, and she remained in substantially the same condition up to and during Monday, the 20th. On Tuesday, 21st, she remained in about the same condition, having the use of her left arm and was able to communicate by writing,but was not able to take any nourishment. She had spasms and trances during the night. On Thursday, 23rd, she complained of intense suffering in her head and had very severe spasms and trances during the night.

"On Friday, 24th, she had become more comfortable, and remained so during the day, with spasms and short trances at night. She remained in about the same condition up to Sunday, 27th, and on that day she swallowed half a teaspoonful of wine and was quite cheerful, but she had severe spasms and short trances during the night. On November 28th she appeared in much the same condition during the day, having spasms and trances during the night, in which condition she remained up to Wednesday, the 30th, when she suffered severely with her head, having severe spasms and short trances at night. On Friday, 31st, she was very feeble during the day; at night she appeared to be in a sinking condition, having neither spasms nor trances. She was in great distress from pains around her head. She continued in this condition, suffering greatly during Saturday. On September 1st she was exceedingly feeble, and she had neither spasms nor trances during the night. She appeared exceedingly weak until Sunday morning, then she rallied. She remained quite comfortable during Sunday, but was very weak in the evening; spasms and trances returned, and she had fainting spells and great trouble with her heart action. On November 3rd she was still very feeble during the day, lying in a fainting condition until night. On Tuesday, 4th, she rallied again, and remained quite feeble during the day; then she had severe spasms which lasted from thirty to forty minutes, and were followed by a trance.

"On Wednesday, 5th, she was quite cheerful during the day, having spasms and trances during the night, remaining in about the same condition until Saturday, the 8th, when she appeared very feeble again, and complained of terrible pains around her head, remaining in about the same condition until Sunday morning, having spasms and short trances during the night. Monday, September 10th, she was quite comfortable again, and continued so during the day; at night she had very hard spasms which lasted about an hour, and were followed by a short trance. Tuesday, 11th, she was suffering greatly with her head and teeth, and was very absent-minded in the evening; she had spasms lasting an hour, and was very restless during the night. On Wednesday, 12th, she was apparently more comfortable, yet went into an absent-minded state, which lasted until four o'clock in the afternoon; then she complained of severe suffering in her head, and she had spasms and trances at night. On Thursday she was very feeble, complained of her head and teeth, and had severe spasms, followed by trances at night. On Friday evening, September 14th, she had severe spasms, her body being contracted into various forms, presenting a horrible sight. Her lower limbs were twisted (in a three-twist), and her feet crossed; she remained in this condition until Sunday, 16th; on that day she suffered intensely with her teeth and head, having hard spasms and trances during the night; her throat being closed.

"On Monday, 17th, she was more comfortable during the day, but had severe spasms followed by trances at night, and she remained in about the same condition until Wednesday, 19th, on which day she had severe spasms and short trances, suffering severely with her head and teeth. On Thursday, 20th, she took chloroform to relax her jaws so that some of her teeth could be extracted. She then went into hard spasms, her body being horribly contracted, taking various forms, which continued from two to three hours. She then fell into a relaxed state, apparently having the power of feeling, and being able to recognize by the sense of touch; she remained in that state until the evening of the 23d; her power of speech returning on that day, and continued from Thursday evening at seven-thirty, until four o'clock P. M. Sunday, when her speech failed again. At times she seemed conscious, but could neither see, hear nor recognize in any way. On Monday, 24th, she was in comparatively the same condition during the day, but in the evening her breathing being very difficult. On Tuesday, 25th, she was still unconscious, in which condition she continued until Wednesday, 26th; in the evening of that day, she appeared to be in a fainting condition, which lasted from nine o'clock in the evening until the following morning, when she rallied and was in a semi-conscious condition, but still unable to recognize any one.

"On Thursday, 27th, she appeared in almost a lifeless condition; her body was cold, she had chills during the day, and her breath was scarcely perceptible. On Friday morning she showed more symptoms of life, but her body was cold; she was suffering from chills and remained so until noon, when her circulation appeared to improve, and the lower part of her body became warm. On Saturday, 29th, she rallied somewhat, but was still unable to recognize any one in any manner whatever. In the evening her breathing became very hard; she was in great distress, and she suffered from spasms in her throat, which lasted about three hours, then she went into a sinking condition, as though her natural powers were exhausted. She remained so until nine o'clock the following morning, then she rallied and showed more signs of life, still remaining very feeble. On Monday morning, October 1st, she rallied, but was still very weak; she was able to recognize; the power of seeing, hearing and feeling returned; she remained very feeble during the night.

(Miss Crosby speaks of her power of seeing having returned, but the reader must not understand that by using the word " seeing," Miss Crosby intends to convey the idea that Miss Fancher was able to see by the use of the natural organs of sight; as Miss Crosby has frequently informed me that from the time Miss Fancher lost her natural sight it never returned to her again, but she saw clairvoyantly, having the power of her spiritual vision.)

"On Tuesday, October 2nd, she was again comfortable, which continued during Wednesday, 3rd. On Thursday, 4th, she suffered severely with her head and heart. She had neither spasms nor trances. On Friday, 5th, she was very feeble and was in an absent-minded state for a long time; she then went into a short trance; during all the night she suffered severely with her head and was very restless. On Saturday, 6th, she continued exceedingly feeble, much of the time in an absent-minded condition; she had three trances at night. On Sunday, 7th, she was more comfortable during the day, but very restless at night; she had no spasms at night. On Monday, 8th, she was quite comfortable until evening; she then suffered severely with her head. On Tuesday, 9th, she suffered with her head and heart; she had short trances during the night; she then went into an absent-minded state and remained in the same condition until Sunday, 14th, when she was more comfortable; she had no spasms, but had short trances day and night, and suffered with her head and heart, which continued from Monday up to Tuesday morning, the 10th; she continued in about the same condition, still living without any nourishment, and remained in this condition from day to day, suffering with pains in her head and heart. For the first time since September 20th her left arm and hand, stomach and neck contracted, becoming distorted, and she remained apparently very feeble until Wednesday, 24th, on which day she had spasms in her throat and in her hand. On Thursday, 25th, she had spasms in her throat in the morning, also in her arm, lasting an hour; she then suffered severely with her head and went into an unconscious condition, in which she remained most of the day. On Friday, 26th, she was more comfortable during the day; in the evening she had spasms in her throat, stomach and chest, and suffered severely with pains in her head. She had spasms and short trances during the night. On Saturday, 27th, she continued about the same up to Monday, 29th, on which day she had spasms as on the 26th, and she still continues to live without nourishment."

This closes the diary kept by Miss Crosby in so far as I have been able to place the same in chronological order. I will state, however, before inserting the additional facts, that she informed me that she kept this record, at the request of Miss Fancher's physician, in order that a correct statement of her condition, as her case developed from day to day, might be preserved. I have refrained from using, in a few instances, her exact language, which was very essential for the information of her physician, but which may very properly be omitted from the recital.

CHAPTER VII.
Continuation from Records.

"On the 4th of April, 1866, her throat closed, and on the 6th commenced nourishing her by means of enema, which was continued for six weeks. After the 31st of May, she was unable to retain them, and they were discontinued. During this time the natural functions of relief were seldom exercised.

"May 28th. Very feeble, suffering intensely with her head and heart; at two o'clock P. M. went into a rigid state, lasting from one to two hours; then into a trance, being quite rigid, and remained so until eleven-thirty A. M. the next day, when she fell off into relax trances, remaining so until Friday evening, June 1st; on that evening at eight o'clock she rallied with effort; breath almost gone; apparently exhausted. She remained in this state until the following morning. During the days she was in this trance, she was nourished with enema four times.

"On June 2d gave her chloroform to relax her jaws in order to give her some nourishment. Shortly after she went into very severe spasms which lasted for two hours; she then went into an unconscious state for a short time, when she became sick, and was unable to retain any nourishment; suffered intensely until Saturday, June 9th, when her throat closed, and she was unable to take any nourishment. From May 31st to June 28th she was unable to take any nourishment in any way. One pint of sweet oil was used to bathe her chest and bowels between June 2d and June 24th. From May 25th to June 28th the natural functions of nature for relief were very seldom exercised. On August 5th gave her chloroform to relax her jaws in order to extract her teeth, when her muscles relaxed and the natural functions of nature were exercised. Since the 6th day of August the natural functions of the body for relief have not been exercised (a period of three months). She now remains in this condition; her eyes, jaws and hands are closed, her right arm drawn up at the back of her head, her lower limbs are twisted in a three-twist, having the use of one part of her left arm and hand, also the fingers of the hand being closed; the only nourishment she has retained on her stomach from April 4th, 1886, to

"MAD" MOLLIE

October 27th, has been four teaspoonfuls of milk punch, two of wine, one small piece of banana and a small piece of cracker."

On a separate sheet of paper, accompanying the foregoing record of Miss Crosby's, is the following:

"Some of the remarkable things which she, Miss Fancher, has done during her sickness are as follows:She could tell the exact time by simply passing her hand over the crystal of the watch; also tell the exact time across the room; she could tell the approach of a thunder storm some hours before it came; she could also tell the fire bells were going to ring sometimes as much as five minutes before they really did ring. She has very often told what parties were doing over in New York, and even further away, and has always been correct in her statements. Persons ringing the door bell at the house, she could recognize before they entered the house. Often in her absent-minded state she would mimic different things and all sorts of characters, sometimes by singing. She once "took off " a wedding party, including the dancing, talking, bowing, shaking of hands, eating and drinking, which were done very naturally indeed.

"She once was hunting and calling her dog, and loading her gun, and taking her swig of whiskey, all of which was done to perfection. She has also done many handsome pieces of embroidery and other work."

It is to be exceedingly regretted that Miss Crosby omitted from her records detailed statements of the wonderful powers that Miss Fancher possesses, and of the remarkable things which she does by their use. She has detailed only in a general way, in her own handwriting, some of the interesting facts connected with the case, showing the powers Miss Fancher possessed, which have occurred from time to time during the long years of her illness. She has stated, however, to a very large number of persons, and among others to me, in more explicit language, some of the remarkable things which Miss Fancher has done, and they, we are told, are only as two in a thousand. We shall perhaps, later on, refer to what may have been the cause, which prevented a detailed statement of the facts connected with these interesting features of her case.

It will be noted that Miss Crosby speaks of Miss Fancher being "in an absent-minded state," quite frequently, during the period covered by her records. She has said that in this absent-minded state, Miss Fancher appeared to be conscious of the presence of those not visible to the eyes of others on this plane of life, and also of brighter scenes, which so impressed the poor pain-stricken girl, that she wept in disappointment when brought back to a realization that she could not remain in the sphere into which she was spiritually permitted to enter, and for a brief period be a partaker with her mother and friends, in the joys and pleasures which were theirs. At times she was talking with them, and seemed fully conscious of their presence; and that they were really visible to her, and held communication with her, cannot be denied, without impairing our faith in the recorded instances of a similar kind in that Book, which is regarded as the most sacred of all throughout the Christian world.

Having said this much with reference to some of the phases of her case, what disposition shall be made of, or inferences drawn from the personating of characters? for this has been of frequent occurrence, as I am informed, by Miss Fancher and her friends, for a long time, some instances of which Miss Crosby has mentioned above. When we consider the terrible physical condition that this poor girl was in; when we call to mind these terrible spasms, by which various portions of her body were moved with incredible force, her neck and throat in a rigid condition, and with this, her right arm drawn over her head, her hands rigidly closed, her lower limbs twisted in a three-twist, which, as any person must know, is impossible without pulling asunder of the very joints; that she has been bent like a hoop for hours, her head and heels meeting, and then her toes drawn up to her head; that she was thrown, plunging, like an arrow from the bed—what person, in view of this state of facts, can for one moment conceive of her resorting to any trick or device, or simulation, to produce these conditions?

Were I to continue the records kept by Miss Crosby of Miss Fancher's condition from month to month, and from year to year, as she has noted the same down, it would be uninteresting to the reader, and of but little benefit to even medical men. There is so much repetition arising from a description of continuing symptoms for a very long period of time, that only matters of special interest will be mentioned.

In several places Miss Crosby notes great suffering to Miss Fancher from the shock of thunder storms, throwing her into severe spasms. She notes one instance in July, when an effort was made to relieve her sufferings by putting her upon a water bed. The change at once" gave her a severe shock, throwing her into spasms, which lasted for a considerable time. This was on the 1st of July. On the 4th of July she received very severe shocks from the firing of a cannon, and from the explosion of firearms near her house. A pistol was fired in the Street, under her window; she was thrown into a rigid condition, and bent in the form of a hoop backwards, her limbs still being twisted, in which condition she remained from five to ten minutes.

"MAD" MOLLIE

On September 20th Miss Crosby make the following note:

"During the day she was quite comfortable, but in the evening had bad spasms in her head, throat, eyelids, and also in her jaw, and her right hand was constantly twitching, which was continued for three days. On September 21st she was able to articulate sounds, and take a little nourishment. She then went into severe spasms affecting every part of her body, which was thrown into various forms. She notes that on the 28th day of February, probably 1868, the year not being given, Miss Fancher was given some chloroform, and instead of going into convulsions, she went into a trance, and was in a perfect state of ecstasy, during which time she was conversing with her mother in heaven; her eyelids relaxed, her power of speech returned, and she claimed that she was having a delightful visit with her mother in heaven, in which condition she remained for two hours."

These records show that Miss Fancher was in, what Miss Crosby styles, an absent-minded condition, for the period of an hour or more very frequently. In one instance she mentions the fact that Miss Fancher seemed very much exercised over the presence of her mother, or that she was in some way holding converse with her mother.

Miss Crosby makes frequent mention of Miss Fancher's possessing unnatural strength. That she received a supply of strength from some source, unknown to her attendants, seems very certain; for how, otherwise, could life have been maintained for so long a period? Occasionally she expectorated blood, apparently from her lungs, which certainly would greatly weaken her. How it was possible to maintain life for several years during the time her sufferings were so great, and the nourishment she received was so very small, is very mysterious. Upon one or two occasions, when they were attempting to force nourishment upon her, which her stomach rejected, and which occasioned her great distress, in reply to Miss Crosby's remark that it was necessary she should receive it to maintain life, she is said to have replied that she received nourishment from a source of which Miss Crosby was ignorant.

Some persons, will undoubtedly discredit the possibility of her having received any nourishment from invisible hands or sources, while others will believe that Miss Fancher stated what was the truth. Those who have studied such cases from a high spiritual standpoint, will readily believe that many persons who are suffering, and are in great distress, are often relieved and succored by help from on high. This leads us to a more complete consideration of some of the remarkable things which Miss Fancher did, and is from time to time now doing, during her long illness, of which brief mention is made by Miss Crosby.

"MAD" MOLLIE

An erroneous impression has been conveyed to the public, through misstatements concerning the exercise of Miss Fancher's powers, many persons supposing that she at any and all times is capable of seeing beyond her room and immediate surroundings, and is able to describe what is transpiring in remote places. This is not the fact. She is in a peculiar state when she is able to see beyond the walls of the room in which she is lying; and yet she is very frequently in that condition. When in that condition she usually is not holding conversation with friends present in the room, but seems to be in a sort of trance condition, in which, if her spirit does not leave her body, it certainly looks out beyond the material surroundings, which shut off the vision of others, and she goes to her friends in different places, and notes what they are doing. She looks around the city and sees what is transpiring, and still comes back to herself and repeats where she has been and what she has seen.

As illustrative, and in proof of this, I will here give an incident within my own knowledge, which is worthy of record.

Some four years ago I called upon her, and during my visit she informed me that on a certain night, which she mentioned, she had been at my house, and had seen me, and noted what I was doing; and described my being present, at about eleven o'clock at night, with a tall gentleman, of thin, spare form, and of dark complexion; and she asked me to go back and locate myself at that time. After considerable trouble I succeeded in doing so, and informed her that I had received a visit from a friend from the country, and at that time was in his chamber, having a few moments' chat with him previous to his retiring. It so happened that Miss Fancher had related what she had seen to Mr. Sargent, who happened to be present at the time I called, and who corroborated her statement. Miss Fancher certainly had no means of knowing, that I can conceive of, where I was at that time, nor of the presence of the friend at my house. Now, a remarkable feature of this case is to follow.

During the winter of 1882 this gentleman, who is the Hon. H. D. Srsson, of New Marlboro, Mass., with his brother-in-law, Mr. Blodgett, called upon me one evening; and I invited them to accompany me to Miss Fancher's home, which they did. Upon entering the room, I asked Miss Fancher if she had ever seen either of the gentlemen before. "Why, no," said she; "they have never been here before; " then she exclaimed: "Oh, yes, this is the man I saw at your house" (pointing to Mr. Sisson) "that night. He has changed some, but he is the man."

Mr. Thomas Townsend, of New York City, who, as well as his wife, is a near and dear friend of Miss Fancher's, and who has witnessed numerous instances of the exercise of her remarkable powers, makes mention to me of the following amusing incident, which will interest the reader.

It is not an uncommon thing for Miss Fancher's friends to joke and laugh with her about her numerous admirers, and inquire about all her beaus, and say many ridiculous things, by way of amusement, and receive rallies in return, for Miss Fancher is an exceedingly witty and keen-spoken lady.

Mrs. T.ownsend, the wife of the gentleman in question, was at the time visiting Miss Fancher, and Mr. Townsend was coming from his office in New York, across the Wall Street Ferry, to meet his wife there. Miss Fancher dropped into a trance, and while in the trance Mrs. Townsend had observed a smile to pass over her face as though she was observing something that amused her. Upon coming out of that condition, she asked Miss Fancher where she had been, and what she had seen? Miss Fancher burst out laughing, but would not tell. In a short time Mr. Town- send put in an appearance, and soon after began to rally Miss Fancher, and asked her numerous questions, when suddenly, to his surprise, she turned upon him and said:

"See here, old fellow, be very careful; that was a very pretty young lady that you was escorting across the ferry, and you seemed to be very much interested in her." It was now Mr. Towsend's turn to blush, and he owned up that he came across the ferry with a young lady of his acquaintance, and was having a very interesting chat with her, when, of course, without his knowledge, Miss Fancher had approached: but how, or in what way, the reader must determine for himself. She saw Mr. Townsend, and was able to describe the young lady, much to his surprise and astonishment. In this way she has visited the homes of friends, and, as will be related by Mr. Sargent, she has been to him when he has been nearly a thousand miles away, and described his surroundings and the persons present so minutely, in advance of any statement from him, that to doubt her powers would be absurd. Many and severe tests have been made to determine the fact of her clairvoyance, and I am not aware that any person who has made the test, has any doubt that she possesses that very interesting and remarkable gift. Miss Fancher's eyes are usually closed, but at the same time it is the belief of some friends, as well as my own, that the optic nerve is not wholly destroyed, but is paralyzed, because she is sensitive to the light; a strong light is exceedingly painful to her. She sees best in a darkened room, and the light from a remote gas jet is always shaded, as well as turned down, so that it will not be thrown upon her face.

"MAD" MOLLIE

Not long since, while discussing the condition of her eyes with Mr. Sargent in the presence of Miss Fancher, he expressed the opinion that she in some way, but just how he did not know, could see by means of her organs of sight. I was very much astonished, and asked him if he had made no test to determine that question, and was still more surprised when he told me he had not. I immediately arose, and securely covered her eyes by placing a double handkerchief over them and covering the lower part of her face, as she lay upon her bed. There was not a movement that any of us could make, or a thing which we could do, which she could not distinctly describe to us, with as much readiness as either of us could have done, had the same been done before our eyes. So many rigid tests have been made of Miss Fancher's powers in this direction, that human testimony fails in its purpose, if it is not believed that Miss Fancher is at times more or less clairvoyant. She is much more clairvoyant at some times than at others. When the day is gloomy and dark, or great storms are about approaching, the atmospheric conditions appear to affect her very sensibly, and then her clairvoyant sight is very much impaired. She sees best, and reads the most readily, when the room is so dark that others can scarcely see the print. The most hardened skeptics in these matters have been compelled to sucumb when in the presence of Miss Fancher.

The question has arisen, and will naturally be suggested, how does Miss Fancher see beyond the walls of her room, by which she is environed? How can she see and describe people who are in the Street, and are ringing the bell at her door? Certainly no human vision, such as is ordinarily exercised, can penetrate through the walls of her dwelling house, and see down through the floors composed of wood and brick and mortar? Is it by spiritual sight? Does her spirit, while still retaining sufficient relation to the body to maintain its seat and hold upon the material forms, pass out through this to other material substances, and, by the use of her spiritual vision, discern what is transpiring? The affirmative would certainly seem the only answer that can be made, unless we resort to the theory, that has come to be with a certain class of people a hobby, that it is done by the means of mind reading. But the question will naturally arise, what mind reading could there be in her seeing and describing persons, who are entire strangers to her, and wHo have not her in mind, and of whom she has never heard?

Mr. Sherk has mentioned an interesting incident which is herewith recorded, to which reference may now properly be made in considering this suggestion.

He sent a man in his employ to Miss Fancher's house, describing it, and telling him to ascend one flight of stairs, to go to the front room, and there hang a certain picture, which he took with him. He proceeded to the place, entered the room, and commenced sounding the wall for a joist into which a nail could be securely driven. While so engaged he heard a voice criticizing the manner in which he was doing the work. He looked around him and saw no one in the room, and supposed himself to be quite alone. He was somewhat nervous, and proceeded with his work, when he was again criticized by an unknown voice, from whence he could not see, telling him that he had not put the picture in the centre, and again; that it was not hung true. He became frightened and hastily finished his work and left the house, and informed Mr. Sherk that he did not like to be sent to places where he could hear voices without seeing the person speaking.

As a matter of fact, Miss Fancher was on her bed in the back room, which was closed by sliding doors from the front room, and by her clairvoyant sight she was able to discern what the gentleman was doing, and to speak loud enough to be heard through the walls, in criticizing the work of the poor fellow, who was frightened out of his wits.

CHAPTER VIII.
Of Miss Fancher's Condition, and of the Trance.

We have now reached a point in the recital of the events in the life of Miss Fancher, when the reader should be informed of some features of her present physical condition, and of some of the peculiar phases of her case, to properly understand what has already been related, and what remains to be written. We have already given her statement of the facts leading up to the long trance, as she terms it, when she lost out of her life all recollection of what transpired for a period of nine years; and how, when she awoke to consciousness, to her, it was as from the sleep of a single night, and in memory she commenced her life again where she had left it nine years before.

Mention has been made of the rigid condition of her right arm during that nine years, it being carried upwards and under the back of her head; and of her rigidly closed hands, excepting the thumbs and a portion of the index fingers. The position and condition of her lower limbs should be more minutely described. They are said to have been twisted around each other, like the strands of a rope, and to have remained so for nine years. This certainly will seem to most persons as absolutely incredible and impossible, unless done by the application of some instrument of torture. .1 cannot vouch for the truth of this statement from personal knowledge, but that it is literally true I firmly believe, and shall give my reasons and authority. Aside from the testimony of others, I can say of my own knowledge that the joints of her limbs are apparently drawn asunder, leaving spaces in the joints into which a finger may be easily pressed, showing the bones to be separated. The ankle joint is drawn apart, and the small bones of the foot seem to be separated; as is plainly seen by examining the instep. The sole of the foot is turned upwards in such a manner as to show a disjointing of the ankle; and I am assured that the heads of the thigh bones are apparently drawn from their sockets, and imbedded in her groins. Her lower limbs are drawn somewhat upwards, and the cords under her knees are hard and seemingly as unyielding as steel. All of these conditions have been produced by spasmodic action. At present when in her spasmodic conditions, a guard around her bed is necessary to prevent her from being thrown to the floor, which, unfortunately, has occurred upon several occasions, despite these and other precautions; and such safeguards have been necessary since she was first taken with spasmodic action, nearly twenty-eight years ago.

The character of these spasmodic actions is beyond simulation or imitation. At times it is most marked in some portion of her body, where natural muscular action is impossible. It is rapid, violent and frequently continues for a considerable time. It agitates her bed, and at times the floor of her room. Her heart spasms are of a character to appall those not familiar with her case. That death does not immediately ensue is astonishing. At present, her body is heavy and flesh soft. About seven years ago she was thrown in her spasms from her bed and struck upon the back of her head, nearly dislocating her neck. This misfortune has greatly increased her sufferings. Following this last accident there is on the back of the neck something of an enlargement like a swelling, which seems permanent in character. She suffers severe pains in and around the heart, and also she has pains in her head. When spasmodic heart actions are most severe, large, dark rings, presenting the appearance of the settling of blood after a severe blow, are around her eyes. These marks disappear when she recovers from one of her severe attacks.

It may, I think, truthfully be said, that Mollie Fancher never sleeps, in the sense that others do. Sleep is a natural requirement. It is asserted by many, and, I think, quite commonly believed, that the mind is never at perfect rest. Every part of our bodies requires rest, unless it be the heart and respiratory organs, which keep up sufficient action to maintain life. Sleep brings many required changes, and it is impossible that Miss Fancher should have lived all these years without it, unless in some other manner the required rest has come to her. In her own recitals of the efforts of her physician to break her trances and spasms, she has stated that he was pardonably ignorant of the part they served in her changed condition of life; that without them she would have died. They afforded her a required rest; and yet they are most unlike a natural sleep. No person would naturally suppose, that any rest could come to either mind or body during the period caused by such spasms as has been described. But ordinarily she is unconscious when in that condition. When that condition is preceded or followed by a trance, and when in the trance state, to most persons she would seem to be in a condition akin to a deep sleep. Most likely this is in a degree a correct conclusion. How it is distinguished from sleep will be now explained.

The Trance.

Considerable mention has already been made, and more will necessarily be required of Miss Fancher's supposed or actual condition of Trance. The reader must form his own conclusions as to what her conditions actually are Before more fully describing her symptoms and experiences while in the trance condition, it may be well to define what a trance is usually supposed to be.

Webster gives among others the following definitions of the word trance:

2. A state in which the soul seems to have passed out of the body into another state of being, or to be wrapped into visions; an ecstasy.

3. (In Medicine.) The total suspension of mental power and voluntary motion, pulsation and breathing continuing, the muscles being flexible, and body yielding to and retaining any given position not incompatible with the laws of gravitation; catalepsy.

The Old and New Testament both contain statements of what different persons are said to have seen and heard while entranced. In the 10th and 11th chapters of Acts are recounted the vision of Peter when he fell into a trance. At the conversion of Paul he saw a great light and fell to the ground and he heard a voice speaking to him. He says that those with him heard the voice but saw no man (Acts, 9th chapter). In II. Corinthians, 11th chapter, Paul recounts, whether of himself or of another he leaves us to infer for ourselves, but evidently his own experiences, and says:

"I knew a man in Christ above fourteen years ago (whether in the body, I cannot tell; or whether out of the body I cannot tell; God knoweth) such a one caught up to the third heaven.

"And I knew such a man (whether in the body or out of the body I cannot tell; God knoweth).

"How he was caught up into Paradise, and heard unspeakable words which it is not lawful for a man to utter."

In the following verse he explains, that his reasons for not saying it was he who saw the vision and was thus entranced, are that others might think he was above what he seemed to be.

Preceding the recital of his wonderful vision on Patmos, John describes himself as being in the spirit on the Lord's day, and he heard behind him a great voice as of a trumpet, and that when he turned his head what he saw caused him to fall as one dead. (Rev., 1st ch.) After he has recited his vision, he closes in chapter 22d,

v. 8-9, by saying:

"I John saw these things and heard them. And when I had heard and seen, I fell down to worship before the feet of the angel that showed me these things.

"Then saith he unto me, see thou do it not; for I am thy fellow servant, and of thy brethren the prophets, and of them which keep the sayings of this book: worship God."

The prophet Joel, 11th chapter, 28th and 29th verses, says:

"And it shall come to pass afterwards that I will pour out my spirit upon all flesh; and your sons and your daughters shall prophesy, your old men shall dream dreams, and your young men shall see visions:

"And also upon the servants and upon the handmaids in those days will I pour out my spirit."

See also Acts, 11th chapter, 14th to 22d verses.

Trance conditions are of rare occurrence and mostly are confined to persons in delicate conditions of health, unless superinduced by effort in the individual. Trance conditions have occurred, if history can be relied upon, in all ages of which we have present knowledge, through historical data. Emanuel Swedenborg claimed to have had visions, and to have heard the voices of angels and spirits who directed him in his writings. The same may be said of Mahomet. That the prophets spoken of in the Scriptures were accustomed to preparing the way for enhancement and visions is certain. Daniel says, "And I set my face unto the Lord God to seek by prayer and supplications, with fastings and sack-cloth and ashes." Daniel, 11th chapter, 3d verse.

"Now as he was speaking with me I was in a deep sleep on my face towards the ground; but he touched me and set me upright." Daniel, 8th chapter, 18th verse.

"In those days, I, Daniel, was mourning three full weeks. I ate no pleasant bread, neither came flesh nor wine into my mouth, neither did I anoint myself at all, till three whole weeks were fulfilled." Daniel, 10th chapter, 2d, 3d and 4th verses. Then follows Daniel's description of the great vision which was presented to him. In the 7th verse he says:

"And I, Daniel, alone saw the vision: for the men that were with me saw not the vision; but a great quaking fell upon them, so they fled and hid themselves." In the 9th verse he says: "Yet heard I the voice of his words: and when I heard the voice of his words, then was I in a deep sleep on my face, and my face towards the ground."

It will likely be possible for some who will read this book, to recall the effect produced upon certain religious persons, with nervous temperaments, by the revivals among the Methodists, many years ago. It was not an uncommon thing to see amid the fervent prayers and shoutings, one or more persons throw up their arms and fall back in apparently unconscious conditions, and so remain for quite a time. They were described as being in a trance. What they claimed to have experienced while in those conditions, I never fully understood. That they were in a state of great ecstasy is quite certain, and their condition would seem to have been produced from excitement, rather than from the conditions which preceded the entrancement of the different persons mentioned in the Scriptures. Some of the readers of these pages may feel that the Scriptural quotations might have been omitted. The feelings of all persons in religious matters are entitled to respect, and the quotations are not made with a view of unduly exalting the condition of Miss Fancher, or her visions in the mind of the reader. They have been made for the purpose of more fully explaining to what the word "Trance," may correctly be applied.

It is quite common now among a certain class of religious persons, to speak of a person being entranced of a spirit, which is understood to represent the person as having his mental and perhaps his physical powers, subordinated to the will and control of a spirit or an angel. The exercise of functions or the enunciation of thoughts the normal power of the individual, is in the New Testament mentioned, as the possession or exercise of spiritual gifts. See the 12th, 13th and 14th chapters of 1st Cor., 1st John (Epistle), chapter IV.

In the olden time, prophets were called seers. In these days a seer is called a person possessing the power or gift of second sight; more commonly now called clairvoyance, or clear sightedness. A person who possesses the gift of hearing what others in their normal condition do not hear, is said to be clairaudient.

Mention is made of the meaning of these terms for the benefit of the few who possibly may not be familiar with them. Keeping these things in mind, the readers will be able to draw their own conclusions as to the nature and character of some of the remarkable powers exercised by Mollie Fancher.

CHAPTER IX.

"One thing I know, that, whereas I was blind, now I see."—
John ix:25.

Who Am I?

Before going further into the details of some of the remarkable features of Miss Fancher's case, it will be necessary to state, and to have it borne in mind, that about a week preceding the first day of June, 1866, Miss Fancher went into a trance, and that of what transpired during that week she has no recollection whatever. That upon coming out of the trance on the first Sunday in June, she found a few persons in her room—Dr. Robert Spier, and other friends and relatives who were interested in her case, and were exercised over her condition. Dr. Robert Spier remarked to her, taking out his watch, "When I come here I always remain longer than I intend. I was to be home to-day at one o'clock to my dinner; we were to have a chicken pot-pie, and you know that is never good when cold." The next day Miss Fancher went into another trance, and from that day for nine years next following, she has no recollection whatever of anything that occurred, or anything that she said or did. During that period her right arm was up in a rigid condition back of her head, the fingers of both her right and left hand were rigidly closed. She had the use of her left arm. During those nine years she had spasms and trances; sometimes her eyes were turned upward and backward in her head, but always remained sightless. During those nine years, as I am informed from unquestionable authority, she wrote upwards of six thousand five hundred letters, worked up one hundred thousand ounces of worsted, did a vast amount of fine embroidery, and a great deal of very beautiful wax work, cutting and coloring the flowers and leaves in the most ingenious and perfect manner. When the use of her two hands was required, the work was done above her head, her left hand being carried up to meet the position of her right hand as described. Her writing was done by inserting a pencil or pen in between the closed fingers of her left hand in the palm, so that the pencil or pen was held in her fist. Her handwriting was very regular and beautiful, her powers of composition very superior. She made numerous acquaintances during that time, as her room was constantly beset by strangers from all parts of the country, anxious to see and converse with her.

The newspapers, in the meantime, had published extensive accounts of the remarkable features of her case, several of the most complete and reliable of which will be incorporated in this volume, and are vouched for as being correct by persons familiar with the facts.

At the end of nine years, she went into a trance lasting one month, at the end of which time her right arm relaxed from its rigid condition, her hands opened, her limbs untwisted, and coming to consciousness, she looked around her room. Observing Dr. S. Fleet Spier, the brother of Dr. Robert Spier, present in her room, she ex- claimed, " Well, Doctor, did your brother get home in time for his chicken pot-pie?" She then looked around her room, and found it in appearance somewhat changed. She looked at her aunt, Miss Crosby, and exclaimed, "Why, Aunt ! What has become of your red cheeks? you look so old and changed." Her brother, who was a lad of thirteen at the time that she lost consciousness nine years before, approached the bedside. He was immediately repelled as being too familiar for a stranger; and when she was told that he was her brother, she could not believe that a boy could so change in what seemed to her but a moment of time—to a man wearing a mustache. Hundreds of people who had made her acquaintance during those nine years, she failed to recognize, and they had to be introduced to her, and make her acquaintance in a formal manner. She burst into tears when realizing that she had been nine years in a sleep, to awake in such changed conditions. When told of what she had done, and shown the work of her own hands, she could not believe what was said, nor recognize the work. She was shown a diary which she had kept during that time, and by this diary she was forced to believe what was in her own writing, although it was very different from her previous hand. She found by taking her pen in her left hand she could write readily and rapidly in the identical style of that contained in her diary, which, to her, was very conclusive that the diary must have been kept by herself.

She says: "Strange thoughts came into my mind, and strange sensations came over me. When I looked upon the wax flowers, the work of my hands, I could not realize that they had been done by me. They were repugnant to me. The sensation that I experienced was that they were the work of one who was dead. I found I could not do some kinds of the work which I had done, without learning again how. I could not realize that so long a period had passed in my life, and that I was part of the same being who had done the work, made the acquaintances, and had the experiences covering those nine years. I was, and still am, an enigma to myself. If anybody can tell who I am, and what I am, when they have heard of the remaining experiences and features of my life, I would be glad to have them do so.

"I am told that there are five other Mollie Fanchers, who together, make the whole of the one Mollie Fancher, known to the world; who they are and what they are I cannot tell or explain, I can only conjecture. I go into trances and spasmodic conditions, sometimes during the day, but most usually about ten or eleven o'clock at night, and come out of them again, and am usually unconscious of what has passed, but sometimes realize and distinctly remember where I have been, who and what I have seen and observed. It seems to me, at times, that I go to various parts of the country or city, and see persons and places, and know what is transpiring; and whenever I do, and I take pains to find out from the persons whom I visit upon these occasions, whether they were at the places at which I saw them, and were doing the things which I saw them doing, if they are able to recall the circumstances at all, they invariably satisfy me that in some manner inexplicable to me, I was either absent from the body and was with them, or was able to make my observations without the obstruction of material objects, unaffected by distance. I have often been hundreds of miles away, in fact as far as Michigan, to observe the whereabouts of Mr. Sargent, my business associate and friend, and have seen and observed what he was doing, and when questioned by me upon his return, regarding the same, he has informed me that I have correctly stated where he was and what he was doing. However incredible these things may seem to others, inasmuch as I have hitherto refrained from making statements for the gratification of the public, I am urged by my friends, and am satisfied that it is my duty to make an impartial statement of my own experiences expressing no opinion whatever as to how they are occasioned, leaving that to be solved by others.

"It has been charged and stated, that this publication is being prepared in the interest of what is commonly known as Spiritualism. Nothing could be further from the fact, in so far as I am concerned; and I believe the same to be true as regards others interested in this publication. The work is being done in the interest of the medical and scientific world and at the earnest request of friends. I have been repeatedly asked to attempt to act the part of a medium for spirit communications, and I have invariably refused to attempt anything of the kind, because I have not, and do not consider myself capable of answering any such requirement; but shall I refuse to make truthful answers to the questions which are put to me by my biographer, as to whether I am conscious at any time of the presence of those of my friends and others who are said to be dead? Would it be just and right for me to refuse to answer those questions? It has already been stated by many of my friends, and it has been published many years ago, broadcast to the world, that when I come out of my trances, I sometimes am grieved because I have been taken away from brighter and better conditions in another world, than what I find in this. It has been said, as the public generally knows, that I frequently speak of having seen my mother and other friends around me who are dead.

"Then, in answer to these questions, I frankly and truthfully say that at times, at least in spirit, away from the scenes of this world, I am with friends in most heavenly places. My consciousness of these things is to me, as real as the experiences of my life upon this earth. I often see my mother and other friends around me, and in my dreary days of sickness, pain and suffering, and when my spirit is depressed, I can hear her tender voice speaking to me words of cheer, bidding me 'bear up, and be brave, and to endure.' Who upon this earth with body and limbs racked and disjointed by disease, and most horribly contracted, and bed-ridden for upwards of twenty-seven years, will not long to be released from pain and suffering, even though that relief is only to be found in utter annihilation? Ten thousand times I would have accepted that alternative, to be relieved from my sufferings. At times I have seen around me, and around my friends who call to see me, the angel forms of those persons who are supposed to be dead. Whether I see what it seems to me I see, and hear what I seem to hear, let others form their own conclusions. I know what I see as well as they know what they see.

"One by one my friends have gone, and what inroads have been made upon their number during those twenty-seven years, others can imagine. Those whom I have loved best, who have been near, kind and tender to me, have been mostly taken away; and when I am told that I ought to be pleased, in being conscious at times, of their spiritual presence, I have repeatedly said, that that is not all I want for in this world; I want to feel the material touch of their hands, to hear their voices, and experience the impression of their kiss upon my lips as of yore. Whatever others may think and feel regarding these experiences, until I am released from the bonds that hold me in the flesh, it will always be a source of grief and sorrow, to lose out of my natural life those who are true and dear to me.

"I have already spoken of other Mollie Fanchers, who are said to be parts of the one Mollie Fancher known to the world. They are said to come one after another, mostly in the night time when I am unconscious. My biography covers my recollection and experiences from early childhood up to the present time, leaving out the nine years of which mention has already been made. I am said in the night time, when passing from the trance and spasmodic conditions, to come to consciousness and to speak and act differently from what I ordinarily do. I am said then to recollect only certain events of my life, and that during those times I see and speak only to those who may happen to be present with whom I am well acquainted. Then I am said to pass into another trance and spasmodic condition, and then to come to consciousness again, and then I appear and act like some other person, but still I am only conscious of certain events of my early life; and so on until four different changes occur, and in each instance, the Mollie Fancher who appears, remembers and is only conscious of the events of the life of the one Mollie Fancher. All these things I am told. I know nothing of them myself. When I come to consciousness, I have no recollection of any of these changes or personations, whatever they may be, of which I have been speaking. I am told that in none of these changes does any one of the so-called Mollie Fanchers, remember any of the events of the nine years of which I have spoken.

"My physician has said, in view of these changes and remarkable experiences, he would not be surprised if I, or a so-called Mollie Fancher, should wake to consciousness of the events of those nine years. At the end of those nine years I could use my left hand quite readily and perhaps more so than my right, and I customarily use my left hand in writing, a sample of which will accompany my biography. Those experiences which refer to the appearance of the other so-called Mollie Fanchers, have not been continuous during all my sickness. They first appeared soon after I came out of what I denominate my long trance, having met with a shock. After awhile they are said to have discontinued their appearances, but having received subsequent injuries by falls from my bed, they are said to have reappeared; and that about every night of my life, at the present time, I am subject to the changes which will be more fully described by my biographer, and by others.

"If anything occurs when I am unconscious, and one of the other, so to speak, Mollie Fanchers is conscious, which gives to her a shock, or creates sorrow, when I recover consciousness I feel the effects of it. I am strangely affected oy my bereavement or cause of grief. It seems to me as if my heart becomes suddenly enlarged, and my chest over the left side is pressed upward so as to present a visible change in appearance. I am sometimes affected by colors. Some are not so agreeable to me as others; I can distinguish them easily by passing my hand over them."

For the purpose of distinguishing these different personalities, or selves of Miss Fancher, they have been severally named "Sunbeam," "Idol," "Rosebud," "Pearl" and "Ruby," and they usually appear in the order named. " Sunbeam" is the one we ordinarily recognize when we visit Miss Fancher.

CHAPTER X.

Interesting Facts from the Statements of Miss Fancher's Friends.

Since the commencement of my task in writing the life of Miss Fancher, I have sought a most thorough knowledge of each peculiar feature of her case, and have found many difficulties, owing to the great lapse of time covered by her strange experiences. I saw the importance of a minute record of her life, a number of years ago, and I then suggested that one should be kept, and understood that the same was being done. I find, however, that some who have quite extensive minutes of what has taken place in her many years of sickness, are unwilling to furnish the same for the publication for Miss Fancher's benefit, and that the most important witness, Miss Crosby, has since died; and I am left to the records of her case made by Miss Crosby, and the recollections of intimate friends for reliable facts.

Among those possessing the most thorough knowledge of the features of her case, during the past seven years, is Mr. George F. Sargent, of the Geo. F. Sargent Company, who is actively engaged in the manufacture of beds, chairs, and all other conceivable articles for the comfort and convenience of invalids, cripples and the deformed. He tells me that he made his first call on the 21st of November, 1866, the expressed object of his visit being to have a conversation about the manufacture of furniture for invalids. I have taken down nearly verbatim his statement, which is substantially as follows:

"I talked very little at my first visit; I was skeptical, and without knowledge of the existence of any such power as Miss Fancher was said to possess; really, my motive was rather selfish, as my actual purpose was to further the interest of the company with which I was connected. I was very much interested in her case, and I was greatly surprised to find her of superior intellect, and of excellent business capacity.

"She was deeply interested in the work of my company, and on the following Christmas I sent her a small present from our factory. We made her a bed, adapting it to her requirements, and it was at this time that she received the last fall, which so severely injured the back of her neck, and gave her such a severe shock. She was in such a terrible condition, that I acceded to the desire of her aunt, and spent considerable time in watching at her bedside. It was at this time that the remarkable features of her case, in regard to separate intelligences or distinct parts of a whole life being manifested as separate individuals, was called to my attention."

Mr. Sargent relates, that since that time down to the present, it is a quite common occurrence, at night, for five distinct changes to occur in the facial expressions, intonations of the voice, language and intellectual quality of Mollie Fancher, and this is corroborated by others. The duration of these changes is often exceedingly brief. Mr. Sargent, for the purpose of distinguishing them, has, at their request, given each a name, which to his mind in some degree indicates or corresponds to the individuality of the one to whom it is applied. Their names are as follows:

"Sunbeam," "Idol," "Rosebud," "Pearl" and "Ruby."

It will be better to use Mr. Sargent's language, as far as possible, in describing these remarkable phases of Miss Fancher's case. He says: "Miss Fancher received the fall from the bed on the 6th day of April, 1887. On the 8th day of April, while I was sitting by her, she came out of a trance, her eyes widely opened. There was a decided change in her facial expression, and she seemed astonished at my presence. It seemed to me that she was another person, and I asked, ' Who are you?' 'Who are you?' was the reply. Then Miss Crosby, who was present, introduced me to Mollie number 2, whom I have since designated as 'Idol.' She remembered her, although she had not seen her for eight years. She then spoke of things and events of eight years before, as though they were but of yesterday, or even of fifteen minutes before. Then we had to get acquainted with each other, precisely as would any other two strangers. I proceeded to question her as to the events of her life; to ascertain to my own satisfaction, if possible, just who and what she was. Since then she has come very frequently when I was present, understanding and claiming that she was Mollie Fancher, and understanding that there was another character or individual claiming also to be Mollie Fancher, asked me to give her a name. After much thought and discussion I bestowed upon her the name of ' Idol.' Our acquaintance ripened into warm friendship, in the same manner as does friendship between any other persons. 'Sunbeam' is the Mollie Fancher usually seen during the day, who manages and gives directions about her affairs, and does the beautiful embroidery, crochet and other fine work, held and highly prized by so many friends of Miss Fancher. She becomes weary and needs rest usually about 11 o'clock at night; her spasms and trances commence, which are now followed by the appearances I have stated. I soon found that when we told 'Idol' of the numerous friends of 'Sunbeam,' of her beautiful work which we showed to her, she seemed to become exceedingly jealous, and was sad that she had no friends, and that she could not do the work that the other Mollie, 'Sunbeam,' could do. She would get hold of ' Sunbeam's ' work and hide it away about the bed, or in other places within her reach, and to prevent this 'Sunbeam' secretes it, or asks others to put the work away. 'Idol' sometimes unravels her crochet work.

"They have written a number of letters to each other. "Idol" writes a straight hand, as Mollie did before she was injured, but, remarkable as it may seem, she has no recollection of being hurt. She does not recall either of the great accidents which befell Miss Fancher, producing her sickness. ,'Pearl' writes the same hand as 'Idol.' 'Rosebud' prints her letters like a little child, makes use of the small "i" instead of the large "I" for the first personal pronoun, and speaks like a little child. Preceding their coming, Miss Fancher first usually goes into a trance, then into spasms, and then these persons, if I may use that expression, come afterwards.

"As we were speaking, Miss Fancher being brain weary, had taken up her crochet work, and was busily knitting, when she suddenly fell into a trance. Her arms were raised, and her hands continued to hold her needles and work in the same position they were in when at work. Her joints were stiffened, and hands immovable. She continued in this state a few moments and then returned to consciousness, apparently refreshed, resumed her w work, and commenced speaking, taking up the thread of the conversation at the precise point reached when she fell into the trance. The first change of condition seemed instantaneous. When asked where she had been, she said she did not know."

Mr. Sargent continues: "I have seen her often go into a trance and her hands remain as we have just seen for a half an hour. She first usually goes into a rigid trance, perfectly dead to all consciousness. The first symptom of her coming back is a relax-trance. To me it seems the dawning of consciousness; and it commences by living over one or more of the important events of the day, and is expressed by her talking to some person who is visible to her, but not to others. She can evidently hear the answers, but we can not. She certainly is at times carrying on a conversation with somebody. She may be asking and answering questions; sometimes she is laughing and sometimes scolding."

[Here Miss Fancher laughingly protested against being thus ' given away.']

"MAD" MOLLIE

She will sometimes be repeating what she had said during the day; living it all over again. When she comes out of this condition, I can easily verify what has transpired in various ways, without being discovered in my purpose. To me she seems like a phonograph, which is repeating what had been spoken into it. In that way I have become familiar with all the family affairs. Miss Crosby was worn out, and solicited my assistance, and I relieved her as much as possible, and often it has been as late as two or o'clock in the morning before I got home.

After going through with the changes I have just described, she would return to consciousness, but would be so weak as to be absolutely powerless. Then we adopted a signal by which she could make known what to do; one gentle touch of the finger indcated that it was 'Sunbeam'; two, that it was 'Idol,' who was conscious; a certain sign signified water, another air, etc. This we designated 'bringing her over the bridge.' Sometimes she will get partly out and then relapse again. We will sometimes shake her, and resort to various methods to bring her back to full consciousness.

Then, again, what transpired in those trances would be very different from what I have now related. I have never been an investigator into any spiritual phenomena, nor had I knowledge of power in any person to either see, hear or speak to beings not visible to the rest of us. But there were evidently times when Miss Fancher was in those trances, when she talked with people not in this world. This was the first and most convincing evidence that I ever had of the presence of spirits around us. Miss Fancher was, and in so far as I know always has been, very reticent in speaking of her own inner consciousness. What she sees and experiences in these trances she is not inclined of her own volition to state. The many cruel things which have been written and said of her, the proneness to ridicule statements of such experiences as hers, upon such a sensitive nature, I believe has had the effect of closing her lips to much that would be valuable testimony, upon subjects now greatly agitating the popular mind in all civilized countries. What I have observed in Miss Fancher's case I shall truthfully and explicitly state irrespective of consequence.

I have seen her at times when she was strangely transfigured; her features were illuminated. She seemed on the very borderland between the seen and the unseen universe. When I have questioned her upon the subject, she has told me that she was conscious of the presence of friends and relations who have died, and particularly of her mother and aunt, whom she sees clairvoyantly. When she came back to consciousness after those instances of her being transfigured, it was through terrible spasms, and all my power was required to hold her on the bed. Sometimes when in these intermediate states which I have described, she sings beautifully and seems very happy.

Sometimes when Miss Fancher is in a very weak condition, she appears unlike anyone I ever knew. She takes to pleating, saying it is for her coffin. When 'Idol' becomes tired she will say to those present, 'I must go now, kiss my eyes down and hold me close,' and the expressive face becomes immediately changed.

One year after 'Idol' came I first saw 'Rosebud.' It was the sweetest little child's face, the voice and accent that of a little child. She was apparently frightened, and was asking for her mother. I asked ' Who is this? ' Without answering she asked me who I was. I asked her whom she knew; she said she knew Spencer, whom I have since learned was a friend and little boy acquaintance in Miss Fancher's childhood days. I learned from Miss Crosby that she came first eight years before, but only at intervals. I began to strike up an acquaintance with her. She asked me if I loved her? I asked how old she was, and she said 'six years old.' I asked her if she went to school, and she said 'yes, sir.' I asked who her teacher was; she answered ' Miss Evans.' [It will be remembered that Miss Evans was Miss Fancher's first teacher.] She told me the names of her playmates. I asked her where she lived when she first came to Brooklyn, and she said Washington Street; that she lived there one year, and then they moved to Hunter Street, now known as Irving Place, and then they ' moved up the Avenue.' I asked her when she went from there; she said, ' I live there now.' She told me her father had a horse, cows and chickens. She is a great mimic and can imitate animals and fowls very nicely. I asked her to sing for me, and she sang ' I want to be an angel,' ' Little drops of water ' and 'There is a happy land.' Then she tried to get up, and was astonished to find that she could not, and wanted to know what was the matter with her, and what made her so 'big.' She asked for her father and mother; was not aware that the latter was dead, and we did not deem it prudent to tell her.

Next after 'Rosebud' comes 'Pearl.' It is impossible to imagine upon this earth a more spiritual being than 'Pearl.' She is like a young lady of seventeen or eighteen years, very sweet in expression. The face of Miss Fancher, when ' Pearl' comes, assumes in features the expression of a young lady of seventeen. Every word and action is smooth, cultured and agreeable. She seems to cover and hold in remembrance what transpired in the life of Mollie Fancher up to about her sixteenth year. What she seems to dwell the most upon are the events which transpired in Miss Fancher's life about the time when she probably took her exit. She remembers Professor West, and her school days and friends up to about the 16th year in the life of Miss Fancher. She pronounces her words with an accent peculiar to young ladies of about 1865. She remembers Miss Evans whom 'Rosebud' also remembers; but she is wholly unlike 'Rosebud.' Her visits are very brief, sometimes five, at others ten or fifteen minutes, and sometimes only a minute, then she makes her presence known by the pressure of her fingers and holds no conversation at all. The longest of her visits is not over half an hour. She seems almost like a spirit. Her life is probably fenced off by one of those accidents; I cannot otherwise account for it.

Next comes 'Ruby,' and she can be contrasted with 'Pearl' as rubies can with pearls. Sometimes she comes with a bound and a shout, full of vivacity and good humor, and departs in about the same way. It is only on very rare occasions that she is sad. She makes light of pain, and nearly everything else. She delights in ridiculing me. She is bright, smart and witty, and it is a great pleasure to converse with her. She is entirely unlike ' Pearl.' She calls me a tyrant because I reason with her, and try to put her to sleep. She does everything with a dash. What mystifies me about 'Ruby,' and distinguishes her from the others, is that she does not, in her conversations with me, go much into the life of Mollie Fancher. She has the air of knowing a good deal more than she tells. They all appear timid of strangers.

CHAPTER XI.

"The forms I see are intangible; I cannot touch them."

At eight o'clock on the 16th day of February, 1893, I called upon Miss Fancher for additional facts within her own knowledge, and to study further the peculiar phases of her case. I hoped to meet Mr. Sargent there, and get from him further information relative to the different characters mentioned in the preceding chapter. I found Miss Fancher alone, excepting, however, the presence of a talking parrot and her canary bird. " Joe," the parrot, bade me " good evening " before I could say as much to Miss Fancher. The heavy, dark, leaden colored rings around her eyes told me too plainly of the dreadful heart spasms she had suffered. She told me she was suffering greatly, and that a heavy storm was coming on, although the evening was bright and cold. Within twenty-four hours, however, a severe snow-storm set in, as she predicted. She informed me that in these conditions her sufferings were very great, and her clairvoyant sight much impaired.

To my inquiries as to the exact date of the first appearance of these other "Mollies" already in some degree described, she replied that all the knowledge she had of them was through her Aunt Susan, and that " Idol " first made her appearance about three years after the long trance, which would be about 1878. She had received a severe nervous shock, and soon thereafter "Idol" put in an appearance, in the presence of Miss Crosby. The fact of these remarkable changes in the intelligence controlling the person of Miss Fancher, she said, was known to but very few persons, for the reason that they usually occur late at night, and whoever they are, and whatever they may be, they are timid of strangers, and will seldom make their presence known to any but those they are acquainted with. And when we reflect that they go back to Miss Fancher's early life, and do not remember anything which has transpired during the last twenty-seven years, excepting that which has come to their knowledge during the brief intervals, when they have been conscious in the night-time, it will be seen that there is very little opportunity for them to meet any but strangers when they come to consciousness.

"MAD" MOLLIE

As Miss Crosby has died, and they made the acquaintance of Mr. Sargent while she was living, they awake to consciousness during the night, and keep silent unless they see some familiar face present.

While waiting for Mr. Sargent to come, I asked Miss Fancher if she had seen her brother since his death? (Except by a marginal note, I have omitted to mention the fact of the death of her brother since the commencement of this writing, by a railroad accident in New Jersey.) She replied that she was conscious of his presence a great deal of the time, and the circumstances attending his terrible death were ever before her eyes, and naturally very much depressed her. I reminded her of one advantage she had over most bereaved persons, that she could see into the spiritual realm, and know they were not wholly lost to her, that they were waiting her coming on the shining shore of the Summer Land. She burst into tears, and wringing her hands said, "Yes, that is what a minister said to me the other day; but do you suppose that is satisfying to me? Here I have lain upon this bed, in this room, all of these years; and I see one after another of those I loved dearest and best, taken away to that heaven I so long for but cannot go to. When I am in my flesh I want my friends in the flesh also, and not be left to the mercy of strangers. I do not despise this gift of spiritual sight, but to me the forms I see are intangible. They are here, but I cannot touch them; I cannot press them to my bosom, as I so much long to do."

I could only respond that she had the sympathy of all who knew the facts of her condition, and that for some wise purpose her life was prolonged, and its lessons were full of instruction to those who learned them. That the remarkable powers she at times possessed were teaching humanity what ought to be better understood.

No person has gone through so much suffering with greater patience and resignation than Miss Fancher. It is not wonderful that at times she is depressed. The period covered by the few months since I commenced these writings has been full of great suffering for her. Not once have the evidences of her pains disappeared from her face. From the shock of the news of her brother's death she has not recovered. It was first announced to her faithful clerk, in her little store under the room where Miss Fancher lies. She did not need to tell Miss Fancher of the accident or of its results; she merely asked her if she had heard from her brother; when Miss Fancher screamed, " My God, he is dead!" and went into spasms. Now, after the lapse of two months, the effect is constantly present. By placing the hand upon the bedding over her limbs, or holding her hand, an incessant tremor is manifest.

"MAD" MOLLIE

At this visit I learned that neither of the Mollie Fanchers, as we shall call them, covers in her memory the events of the nine years following from May 1st, 1869. The one designated as "Sunbeam"—which appellation will continue to be used—at the expiration of the nine years, took up the task of learning to do the same work the otherwise unnamed Mollie Fancher had done during the nine years spoken of. She has since that time learned to do more beautiful work. She attempted to describe to me her feelings, when shown a box containing some wax flowers made by her during those nine years so oblivious to her. She said an involuntary shudder came over her when she first saw them. It seemed to her that it was the unfinished work of a person then dead, and it was many months before she could bring herself to touch them.

There was unfinished embroidery and incomplete crochet work, which had been done with her hands, of which she had no recollection; and whose brain had planned or directed it, was to her a mystery. She related that when she came to consciousness after the nine years had elapsed, and went into trances, upon coming to consciousness, it was no unusual thing to find that she had been crying and pleating lining for her coffin. In this condition she made for herself a white satin waist, as a part of her robe for the grave, which is now turned yellow with age, but which she still keeps. Mr. Sargent informed me that at times, while apparently unconscious of the presence of others, she goes through the form of pleating with her fingers, and will make use of a piece of ribbon or strip of cloth, if within her reach, and form it into pleats.

These occasions, however, are not common, and follow the condition of trance. Her aunt related the conduct of Miss Fancher—that is, "Sunbeam"—soon after she came out of her long trance of one month, at the close of the nine years, in 1875. She manifested the greatest grief that she was "back again in the cold world," and wept and wrung her hands in her sorrow. Miss Fancher herself confesses to a recollection of her grief. She had been for a month as in the sleep of death. That she would wake to consciousness in this world was not expected by her friends. She had taken no food, and there was such an absence of all appearance of life that none but her physician could detect that she still lived. When she came to consciousness all recollection of the events of the nine last preceding years was gone and has never returned.

The leaves of memory containing the record of what she had been conscious of, during that long period in her life, were to her closed and securely sealed. That long trance had relaxed the rigour of her limbs; the right arm which for nine years had closely held its position under her head, came back to flexibility. With it evidently a portion of her brain functions, which had in like manner been held rigidly in abeyance, and yet unimpaired, was released from restraint, and the seat of the operations of her mind was shifted to the other hemisphere of the brain and only took up consciousness where it had been shut off so long before.

This, however, is only a theory of my own, and not being a medical man, it is entitled to little consideration. I have after considerable inquiry found no physician willing to give any statement for publication, as to how the strange workings of Miss Fancher's brain are caused.

CHAPTER XII.

A Personal Interview with the Several Mollie Fanchers.

I had requested and been promised the privilege of spending sufficient of some night at the bedside of Miss Fancher to enable me to see and hold conversation with the different Mollie Fanchers, as they should appear.

It was during the evening of February 16th, 1893, that my desire was unexpectedly gratified. Mr. Sargent was late in coming, and I had considerably exhausted her mental efforts to recall events that I was anxious to locate. Soon after he came Miss Fancher dropped into a trance, and so remained for quite a time, while I pursued him with questions for incidents in his own experience with her. The first evidence of returning consciousness was the relaxing of her arms from their rigid condition; then came violent spasms and twitching of the limbs; then the rapid swaying of her head from side to side set in, followed by moans as of distress; then she violently beat her breast over the region of her heart with one fist, and with the other hand attempted to tear her hair and beat her head. These acts were restrained as much as possible, but the violence of her spasms perceptibly shook the floor. At length a faintly spoken word announced to Mr. Sargent the presence of "Idol." With opened eyes she greeted Mr. Sargent, and extending her hands she asked him where he had been so long. He replied, " Away on business." She asked what business, and to what places he had been. He explained to her how necessary it was for him to attend to his business, and asked if she had missed him. "Yes," she said, "you have been gone five nights. I have been here and there has been no one that I could speak to, and I was all alone."

Just then the parrot, Joe, said " Hello!" She started, turned her head, asking "What is that?" and was very much interested in listening to the bird. During this time I was standing fully in her view, closely beside Mr. Sargent, who was seated on a low chair bending over her. She evidently had not observed me. Had she been able to see clearly, she must have noticed me, but did not. When Mr. Sargent announced that he had a friend present to whom he wished to introduce her, she seemed alarmed, and asked, "Who is he?" Then he pointed to me, and asked her if she knew me. It was not until I had spoken, and she had heard my voice, that she turned her eyes in my direction, and then timidly extended her left hand and greeted me. I then closely interrogated her as to whether she had ever before seen me. At first she said she had not. Then after a moment's reflection she said, " I remember you and of reaching my hand and taking hold of your beard."

She said, "You are the man with the long beard, who came to see the other Mollie and pay her for embroidering a gown for your wife, and I was on the mattress, and it was after Mollie had the fall from the bed. You could not pay for it, because my aunt did not know how much the bill was, and you said you would have to come again."

"Idol" remembered the incidents attending my calling so many years before more clearly than I did, and by repeating them brought them vividly back to mind. She seemed gentle and quiet, and withal somewhat sad. She expressed the opinion that she could learn to work as did Mollie, and after awhile do the work as well as she. When reminded that her visits were short, she replied that she could do a little, and it would amount to a good deal after awhile. She remembered back to early childhood, the incidents of Miss Fancher's life up to about the time of the accident, but was wholly unconscious of anything that had transpired since then, even of the events in the life of "Sunbeam," excepting only those things which have occurred in her presence, in her brief visits or returns to consciousness; those things she recollected quite distinctly. She did not, however, remember the first accident nor anything apparently connected with it. After a few moments' conversation she turned her face away toward Mr. Sargent, and, with a a weary look, the animated expression upon her face disappeared, and Miss Fancher was again in a rigid trance.

During the time of our conversation, she made various efforts to move her limbs in the bed, as if she desired to get up, and seemed annoyed that she was unable to do so. This rigid trance was followed by a relax-trance; then by the violent spasms of her body, and the shaking of the bed and floor; and then came swinging of the arms, the beating of her breast and the top of the head with her fists, and the efforts to restrain her, and finally a reawakening to consciousness. Mr. Sargent was recognized and greeted, and the presence of "Rosebud" was announced. She also was inquisitive to know of Mr. Sargent where he had been so long, what had kept him away, and if he could not have returned sooner.

There is no question in my mind, but that "Rosebud" is limited wholly to the experiences of the life of Miss Fancher up to about her sixth or seventh year. The little songs common among children of forty years ago, she distinctly remembers, and brought to my recollection some which I had entirely forgotten. When asked to repeat all she could remember, she went on to detail a great many events in the life of Miss Fancher, with much greater distinctness than the majority of people could give events in their early lives. After repeating several familiar songs, she began to repeat, working her hands like a little child, the old song, " There was a Frog lived in a well, Kimo, Karo, Kimo;" and she certainly looked, as much as was possible with Miss Fancher's features, and acted, as would a little child of six or seven years, when questioned upon such subjects. I questioned her as to where she first lived when she came to Brooklyn, and she informed me in Washington Street, and from there she went on and detailed the different places as mentioned by Mr. Sargent, until she came to Fulton Avenue, and then stopped.

"Well," said I, "Where did you go from Fulton Avenue?"

Her answer was, "We never moved from there; we live there now." When asked as to where her mother was, she said she had gone away, and was sick, and she did not know when she would come back. Her coming was preceded by a rigid trance lasting a few moments, then by the relax-trance, then by the convulsions already described. It was certainly a strange scene to witness the coming of Miss Fancher to consciousness, as a little child, from these distressing conditions, which indicated considerable physical suffering. Her awaking to consciousness appeared to be attended by a struggle, as if striving to arouse herself from a troubled sleep or dream.

Mr. Sargent's experience in these matters, enabled him by the signals already spoken of, to know who it was that was coming to consciousness. Her action indicated that she recognized him as a friend, whose absence for several preceding nights she had deplored, and asked, as would a little child, what made him stay away so long, and what he had been doing. Like the others, her face was turned, so that had she possessed ordinary vision, she would have detected my presence, but apparently she did not know of the presence of anyone excepting Mr. Sargent, until he called her attention to me, as he did in the other instances. There was a movement of her eyes, which indicated doubt as to what part of the room I was in, and it was not until I approached closely to her, that she apparently recognized me, and then bashfully withdrew herself until reassured by Mr. Sargent that I was a good friend, and had come to see her, when she reached up her hand and greeted me with a kiss. Mr. Sargent is a very good singer, and sang a little piece which seemed to please her very much.

She seemed to have considerable curiosity as to the parrot, which obstinately refused to talk at the precise time desired. I informed her also that I was going to write all about her, and she twisted her hands and said " Nobody wants to know about me." Soon she complained of being tired, and went out of consciousness as in the other instances, passing into a rigid trance.

Probably from ten to fifteen minutes elapsed after Miss Fancher went into this rigid condition, before she came to consciousness again, and her coming was preceded by all the symptoms and actions which she experienced before the coming of the others. At last a faintly spoken name was heard, which was recognized as that of "Pearl." She greeted Mr. Sargent warmly.

She complained of loneliness when she awoke in the night; that no one was there to greet her, and that she went to sleep again without speaking to anyone. When she was told that I was present, she asked where, and when I approached and spoke, she turned her face toward me and seemed to recognize my presence. She was more cheerful than "Idol," and when I was introduced greeted me pleasantly, and I at once engaged her in conversation. She had no recollection of ever having seen me. I was a stranger to her. She forgot entirely having talked with me a few moments before, and it was clear to my mind that she was totally unconscious of any of the facts or events which had transpired in the presence of Miss Fancher, during the evening preceding her coming. She also remembered the incidents of Miss Fancher's early life, and what had transpired down to about the time of the first accident. She could give me the names of her friends and acquaintances during the time she was attending school at Professor West's. She spoke of those experiences as being those in life, and when I called her Mollie Fancher, she said she was not Mollie Fancher; she was Pearl; Mollie Fancher was dead. I asked how that could be, as her father and mother were the father and mother of Mollie Fancher, and that there was but one Mollie Fancher, and that she must be a part of the life and being of Mollie Fancher. She mused for a moment, then smiled and turned her face away and said she did not know how it was. She soon became tired, said she was sleepy, and immediately dropped out, as it were, of our presence, and the person of Mollie Fancher was again in a rigid trance.

One feature I noted, which is common to the exit of each of the characters I am speaking of; and that is, that in the midst of conversation, each one in turn complained of being tired, and instantly seemed to disappear, and Miss Fancher passed into a rigid trance. I took every possible occasion during their brief presence, to question them concerning their individual experiences in the affairs of this life, so that I might be able to state as definitely as possible, what portions of the life of Miss Fancher each covered; what is common to all, and what each individual recollects.

"MAD" MOLLIE

Next came "Ruby," the same symptoms preceding her advent; but the moment she came to consciousness she attempted to move her limbs, putting her arms back, and bracing her body up to a sitting position, and asked Mr. Sargent to support her back; which he did with pillows, and she immediately went into a lively conversation, expressing great pleasure that he was home, and, like the others, wanted to know where he had been, what had detained him, and complained of the exceeding loneliness of her condition when she awoke up in the night and found no one there to whom she could speak. Each one, just preceding consciousness, indicated intense suffering in and about the region of the heart and the top of the head; Miss Fancher beating in both places violently with her fists, which required a great deal of strength on the part of Mr. Sargent to restrain. Sitting upright in the bed, I standing closely beside and somewhat in front of her, she did not at first recognize my presence, but after being introduced she chatted with me quite freely, and accurately described me as a man with a bald head and a long light beard, and when I asked her how she knew, she reached out her hand and took hold of my beard, and said "I can see it and feel it too!"

I was very much interested in "Ruby," for she was quite vivacious, and gesticulated considerably with her arms in giving expression to her words. It is evident that Mr. Sargent had not questioned her so critically with reference to her identity with the life of Miss Fancher as I did, for I succeeded in ascertaining from her that she remembered of being thrown from the horse on Gates Avenue, and injured upon the top of her head, and she also remembered incidents in the life of Mollie Fancher, from Miss Fancher's earliest recollection until after her first serious injury. She remembered going to school to Miss Evans; she remembered Professor West, and also Mr. Taylor, who was her beau, to whom she was engaged to be married, but had ceased to regard with affection. In short, from the brief interview I had with her, I became satisfied that she carried in memory more of the life of Miss Fancher than any of the others, excepting "Sunbeam," and evidently grasps the same events remembered by " Idol," " Pearl" and "Rosebud," and by "Sunbeam" until some time after the first accident. She left without saying "good evening," by complaining of being tired, and dropped out of consciousness. She told me that she knew how to crochet, and that she could learn to do the fine work done by "Sunbeam," had she material at hand and an opportunity to practice.

She appeared quite interested as to what I was going to write about her. She stated that during Mr. Sargent's absence, Mollie had fallen out of bed again, but as the nurse had said nothing about it, Mr. Sargent did not deem it prudent to speak of it. She complained that she had received a shock, and very likely the fall was produced while in this state of semi-consciousness, struggling to awake. Coming, as they usually do, in the middle of the night, or towards morning, the attendant had fallen asleep, and Miss Fancher had received another shock, from which she was suffering considerably.

It must not be forgotten that neither of these characters has any recollection of what transpired during those nine years spoken of, nor of the acquaintance made; and the thought comes, as to whether in the development of this strange case, a sixth Mollie Fancher may not yet put in an appearance, who will recall what transpired during that time. The testimony concerning them might be greatly increased, did each attendant understand these peculiar phases of Miss Fancher's case, and watch their coming and going. Mr. Sargent explained, that sometimes one would seem to be crowded out; and it will be noted that they do not put in an orderly appearance, either commencing with "Ruby" and going backward to "Rosebud," or commencing with " Rosebud" and going in regular succession to "Ruby."

Following the disappearance of "Ruby," "Sunbeam" came back to consciousness, complaining of being very tired, and of suffering greatly, and dreading the long night before her. She seemed surprised when told that all of the Mollies had been there, and that I had conversed with them. They came at a much earlier hour than usual, which most likely was produced by the additional shock Miss Fancher had received by the fall spoken of by "Ruby," but of which "Sunbeam" appeared to have no consciousness, and Mr. Sargent did not then inform her of what "Ruby" had said regarding it.

Mrs. Julia A. Macauley, who attended Miss Fancher for quite a time during the day, and up until about ten o'clock at night, when questioned by me said that she had never seen these other characters to her knowledge, but with one exception; that upon one occasion when Mollie had come out from her trance and spasms, she came with her eyes widely opened, looking, acting and talking very strangely. But this phase of Miss Fancher's case had not then been explained to Mrs. Macauley.

Miss Crosby, and the other nightly attendants upon Miss Fancher, who had opportunities for noticing these apparent changes of the personality of Miss Fancher, as I choose to designate them, had deemed it best to communicate these phases of her case only to a few of their most intimate friends, hoping thereby to avoid the annoyance of additional notoriety, which might be occasioned by stating what they had observed. Hence it seems that whenever these changes in Miss Fancher's condition have occurred, and the characters I have named have appeared in the presence of strangers, the nature of the changes have not been noted as they otherwise might have been.

"MAD" MOLLIE

Feeling that the phenomena of Miss Fancher's many selves should be as fully described as is consistent with the scope of this work, and my statements verified as completely as may be essential, the following chapter devoted to the statement, written by Mr. George F. Sargent, already spoken of, will be read with interest.

CHAPTER XIII.
Statement of Mr. George F. Sargent.

Judge A. H. Dailey,

My Dear Sir:—I am in receipt of your request, that I certify to the correctness of your report of the peculiar features of the case of Miss Mary J. Fancher, usually known as Mollie Fancher, in so far as they relate to the appearance of the several Mollie Fanchers—called "Sunbeam," " Idol," "Rosebud," "Pearl " and "Ruby."

I cheerfully do so; and here state, that I have carefully listened to the same as read by you, and find that your statement of what occurred at the time you were present, is in accordance with my recollections.

You request me also to state any additional features of interest, in regard to those phases of her case, and to furnish such other information as I think may prove interesting for publication, of which I have personal knowledge.

There are, indeed, many interesting matters and incidents connected with them, and my chief regret is, that in endeavoring to comply with your request, I have not the power to depict, through the medium of any language at my command, their full significance, or to make as strikingly apparent to your readers the occurrences as they appeared to me. If you will therefore permit me, I will try and tell in my own fashion, of such scenes and incidents, as seemingly will be of interest, as I can recall them.

My first acquaintance with " Idol " began April 8th, 1886. Three days previous to that date, Miss Fancher had accidentally fallen from the bed, striking her head on the floor, which added injury to injury, causing unusual suffering.

On the evening mentioned, her aunt Susie, (Miss Crosby) and I were sitting

"MAD" MOLLIE

by her bedside, when Miss Fancher went into a trance. While in this condition her aunt left the room. When she came out of the trance I was alone with her, and was startled to see her eyes wide open, as I had never before seen her except with closed eyes. She looked strangely at me and asked: "Who are you?" as though it was an impertinence for a stranger to be sitting by her bedside, and at the same time, asked where is _____, naming a person wholly unfamiliar to me, and then asked about a matter of which I was entirely ignorant, which indicated that she supposed the matter in question was something which was in the immediate present, and that she expected to find the person referred to at her bedside instead of a stranger. I was nonplussed at the situation, and each moment added to my confusion. I tried, however, to explain my identity, and was thus engaged, when her aunt returned to the room. She was almost as much surprised as I, as she said it was three or four years since that Mollie had made an appearance. She was also distressed for the reason, as she afterwards told me, that it meant added suffering for poor Mollie.

She said that the appearance of the second Mollie preluded extraordinary suffering for the first one. The return of her aunt Susie relieved the embarrassment, and I was formally introduced, and during the rest of her brief stay the time was devoted to the cultivating of our better acquaintance, which, owing to the friendly intervention of her aunt, who represented me as a friend of the other Mollie, was entirely successful.

She made all sorts of inquiries concerning the other Mollie; wanted to know if I would think as much of this Mollie as I did of the other Mollie. She said nobody cared anything for her, and quoted one of the other Mollie's friends, as having said to her the last time she was here, when she asked some puzzling questions about herself, that she had better go to sleep, and when she awoke she would understand all about it. She seemed very sensitive about such treatment, saying that they all took some such means as that to get rid of her. Fortunately for our better mutual understanding, I had urged her to stay and tell me all about herself, and I told her that I would always be glad to greet her. After a stay of about three-quarters of an hour she said, " I am very tired," and with the saddest, sweetest expression on her face, and with pleading arms outreached toward her aunt Susie, she said, with a voice of such pathos that I shall never forget it, "Hold me close, kiss my eyes down," and in the twinkling of an eye her features became as rigid as sculptured marble.

After a lapse of some ten or fifteen minutes she returned to consciousness, and the original Mollie again appeared on the scene, and seemed wholly ignorant of what had happened. She seemed to view the occasion when I told her of it

73

as a calamity, and attributed the reappearance of the other Mollie to the extreme suffering she was undergoing, as a result from her recent fall. Whether this was the cause of the reappearance of the second Mollie or not, I leave the problem for others to solve. It is certain, however, that her coming was accompanied by intense suffering, and the weaker Mollie Number 1 became, the more vigorous Mollie Number 2 grew.

From that date, for perhaps a year, the second Mollie came at frequent though irregular intervals, and the length of her visits increased. She seemed to have no note of time; there was no yesterday or to-morrow in her calendar. When she came, it was always through a trance condition, and usually accompanied by severe spasms, and her exit was in a similar manner. If she had been talking at the time of her departure on any subject, on her return, whether it happened to be an hour, a day or a week, she would take up the thread of conversation where she had dropped it, if the same ones were present. If another one was present when she again appeared, she would seem surprised, and ask for the person whom she had left just as though there had been no interval between. She had just as much individuality as Mollie Number 1; so much so, that it became somewhat of a question as to which should retain supremacy.

Each would speak of the others as though they were different personalities, and they would send each to the other messages and letters to be conveyed by Miss Crosby, and on occasions I have been the medium of communication. To illustrate the distinct individuality of the two Mollies, I will state that shortly after the time to which I have alluded as having made the acquaintance of Mollie Number 2, I had occasion to make a trip West, and during my absence I received a letter which reached me May 1st, 1886, directed in the handwriting of Mollie Number 1. On opening the envelope I was surprised to find that it contained two letters, one each from both Mollies. There was no similarity in the chirography; that of Mollie Number 1 being written as she always writes, back-handed, and that of Mollie Number 2 with the letters inclined the other way. I do not think an expert on penmanship would decide that both letters were written by the same hand.

The subject matter of the two letters was also entirely different, each dealing with its own peculiar life. These two letters also tend to demonstrate that the two individualities represent different periods of the same existence. The handwriting of Mollie Number 2, indicates the style acquired while a girl at school, while that of Mollie Number 1, is unquestionably, that which was acquired by force of circumstances during that period of physical infirmity, when it became necessary to hold her pen in a certain way, in order either to write at all, or to write with the greater facility. That period of her life which embraces the first nine years of her sickness, I am unacquainted with except by hearsay, but I have specimens of her writing during that time, which are still different from either.

You will notice that thus far I have spoken of Miss Fancher, or of the circumstances mentioned, only in the past tense, also that I mentioned the two individuals only, as Mollie Numbers 1 and 2.

I have done this, not because they are not individualities of the present as well, but for the reason that covering the time which was contemporaneous with the incidents alluded to, they had no other distinguishing identity than that indicated by numbers; subsequently there have appeared still other Mollies, when it became advisable to identify each by some name by which they would be recognizable by their friends as well as between themselves. I will, therefore, henceforth speak of Mollie Number 1 as "Sunbeam," and Mollie Number 2 as "Idol," and as the others appear, introduce them according to the names given them, beginning with "Rosebud."

The advent of "Idol" had led me to make inquiry concerning the antecedents of Miss Fancher's life, which brought out the information, largely obtained from her Aunt Susie, and corroborated by others, that there had been at intervals covering a period of some four or five years, subsequent to 1875, the appearance of another personality which came as a child. I was not wholly unprepared, therefore, shortly after, for the appearance of a third Mollie, although at the time of my first acquaintance with her, she had not been known to have appeared for eight years by any of her friends.

Her coming was very similar to that of "Idol," through a trance succeeded by a spasm, the only difference being that heretofore, after the exit of "Idol," "Sunbeam" had reappeared, but in this instance this little girl known as "Rosebud," instead, beamed on me with the face, voice and actions of a child. She seemed to regard the event as a matter of course, and with the exception of finding me at her side, it evidently seemed like the waking of a child from a nap. After satisfactory explanations as to who I was, she referred to events which correspond with the date of her last appearance, which was eight years before, as though there had been no lapse of time in the interim. She prattled like a child, and asked for a young friend who was present at her last coming, at which time he was a boy, but in the interim had grown to man's estate. She asked for her mamma, and said she was in New York sick, which indeed was the case some thirty years or more previous. I asked her how old she was, and she said seven years last August (at which time I think her actual age was thirty-seven).

"MAD" MOLLIE

I induced her to tell me all about herself; she told of her school teacher; her girl and boy friends; her Sunday-school teacher and classmates; she sang several songs which she learned in week day and Sunday school, which brought vividly back to me the current songs of my child- hood, some of which would be wholly unfamiliar to children of to-day. She mimicked the cackling of hens; the mewing of kittens; the bleating of sheep; the grunt- ing of pigs and the neighing of horses. She talked of streets in the neighborhood which were not familiar to me, which, on inquiry, I found had been changed in name years before. She asked how it was that she had grown so in size, and after a while she said, " Well, I guess I will get up," and made a futile effort to do so, but the poor body, chained to the bed by years of pain, refused to respond to the bounding activity of the child mind, which could not comprehend its bodily environment. Finally she grew tired, and as a shadow of pain o'erspread the child's face, she bade me a hasty good-bye. And as though clutched by a ruthless unseen hand, she was violently shaken with spasms; struggling there helpless and mute, she seemed like unto an innocent victim, a prey to the vicious sport of an invisible demon, until I could fancy that a guardian angel had suddenly appeared, and had smitten down her enemy, when her body instantly assumed the rigidity of a statue. Every cloud of suffer- ing van- ished, and through a trance which succeeded she came back to (if such it can be called) her normal life.

Since the event I have described, I have had many similar experiences, and though several years have elapsed, according to her own calendar, she is still " seven years old last August." On one occasion, while absent from the city, I received a letter enclosed in the same envelope with a letter from Miss Fancher, signed "Rosebud." The composition was of just such a character as might be ex- pected from a child seven years old. The letters were printed in irregular sizes with capitals and small letters intermingled. The personal pronoun " I " was small and dotted. I had previously seen a letter written by her addressed to her mamma, which her aunt Susie had preserved as a curiosity, written about eight years be- fore. The two productions were as near alike as would seem possible, as regards composition and execution.

Not long after the advent of "Rosebud" there appeared a fourth Mollie, and subsequent to the fourth Mollie, I should say a year later, a fifth Mollie. These are known as "Pearl" and "Ruby," respectively. Their coming was similar to the ap- pearance of "Idol" and "Rosebud," generally preceded by a trance or a spasm, and frequently by both, and their departure is always succeeded by either a trance or a spasm, and frequently by both.

The different Mollies usually follow each other in the following order. After

76

the first trance "Idol," then " Rosebud," then "Pearl" and lastly "Ruby;" then back to normal condition, that of the first Mollie or "Sunbeam."

The two latter Mollies, are more matured than "Rosebud," and less so than "Idol." I have never been able to fully determine which to pronounce the eldest; the chief distinguishing features are that "Pearl" is more subdued, while "Ruby" is vivacious when not absolutely overcome by intensity of suffering. "Ruby" is always ready to joke, and is sparkling with wit, while "Pearl" is quiet and seems to feel the burdens of life more keenly, but she never complains or shows signs of petulance. To make a comparison, I should say they were as near alike as two sisters of nearly the same age and disposition, except that one was of a more buoyant temperament than the other.

The visits of either "Pearl" or "Ruby" are, as a rule, much shorter than those of "Idol" or "Rosebud," and the appearances of "Rosebud" are of shorter duration than those of "Idol." "Idol" at times has manifested jealousy at not being able to do as fine work as " Sunbeam," and Miss Fancher's aunt, Miss Crosby, told me that "Idol" would sometimes get hold of the work done by " Sunbeam" and unravel or otherwise damage it. My belief is, however, that this is not done so much from jealousy as from the desire to make it known to "Sunbeam" that she has been here, or possibly to play a practical joke, for each of the lives invariably speak most kindly of the other.

The disposition and temperament of each Mollie, it seems to me, is quite distinct from all the others, and to me it would be quite difficult to believe that they can be the same being, were it not for the fact that they all seem more or less identified with some parts of the life of Mollie Fancher. Each one seems to be wholly unconscious of the existence of the other, and I believe them to be so.

You ask me to state any facts of interest relative to the clairvoyant powers of Miss Fancher. I am fully satisfied from seeing the experiments tried, that she can see when blindfolded what is transpiring in and around the room. Usually her eyes are closed, and she does fine sewing and embroidering when they are closed. She can distinguish colors by touch, and sometimes works at night without the aid of artificial light. She has often told me of seeing her mother, and has also mentioned the names of other friends as seeing them, who have long since passed away. At such times she is in a condition unconscious as to present surroundings, and there seems to be no obstacle to prevent a direct communion with the unseen. I have watched her facial expression at such times, and though her body would be rigid, the face would portray joy or pain, indicating that an interview was being held with some unseen person, during which the face would be illumined with a joy and a peace that passed human understanding, as though an earthbound soul with loosened fetters was enjoying a brief holiday in the regions of light and rest. Then her face would gradually change to expressions of sadness, deeper and deeper until supplanted by pain, and as the body relaxed it would seem as though a soaring spirit, that had been sporting in the fields of paradise, was saying good-bye to the loved ones, and was retracing her steps downward to the less congenial surroundings of earth, to awake again on her couch of ever present suffering.

She has correctly described where I was, and what I was doing on various occasions; once at a certain hour in the city of Muskegon, Michigan, in the month of October, 1889. She, of course, was in Brooklyn, when to my certain knowledge she could have no means of knowing the same, by any of the known and recognized channels of communication. I had not communicated to her the fact that I was going to sing at an entertainment there. I did not expect to do so until a short time before it occurred. I afterwards sent her an account of it, which was published in the local paper there, but found that in one of her trances she had in some way, inexplicable to me, seen me, or become aware of what I was doing, describing correctly my surroundings, with such particularity as to place the description beyond question as to exactness. Upon coming out of the trance she told Mr. Herbert Blossom, an intimate friend then watching at her bed, what she had seen. I know Mr. Blossom also, intimately, and can fully rely on his word, which was, that upon coming out of the trance, she had described what she had seen me engaged in doing, and my surroundings. He did not credit the statement at the time as being at all correct, and insisted, he said, that she must for once have made a mistake.

Perhaps it may be well to record her own version of this event, which is as follows:

Upon coming out of the trance, Mr. Blossom remarked that she was gone a long time, and he began to be afraid she would never come back again. She answered that she had been far away, and had seen Mr. Sargent. He was standing up surrounded by a lot of people and was singing. Mr. Blossom thereupon smiled incredulously, and said, “I guess that could not be so, as I was a comparative stranger out there.” Miss Fancher replied, “Wait and see; you will find I am right.” The occasion was the opening to the public of Chase Bros’, piano warerooms, which was celebrated by a concert. My appearance there was wholly unexpected a few hour previous. I chanced to be in that city on business, and accepted an impromptu invitation to sing, my name not even appearing on the printed program.

"MAD" MOLLIE

One evening I called at Miss Fancher's and found that Judge Dailey had with two other gentlemen just previously entered. In introducing them Judge Dailey said, " Mollie, have you ever seen either of these gentlemen before? " Pointing to one, she said, " I have never seen that gentleman before," and looking at the other she hesitated a moment and said, " Why, Judge Dailey, this is the gentleman I saw with you that night of which Mr. Sargent made note at eleven o'clock in the evening, a year or so ago."

On one Sunday evening in the month of March, 1887, I called on Miss Fancher about nine o'clock. She was in a trance at the time of my arrival, and her aunt, Miss Crosby, informed me that she had been in that condition for quite a little while. Soon after my entrance she came to consciousness, and after greeting me she said, "I saw you once before this evening." I was, of course, astonished at this declaration, knowing I had not been near her home, and also that it would have been impossible for her to have left her bed. I asked her to tell where she had seen me. She said, "In church; you were standing in a doorway; the door was partially open, and you were shaking hands with a lady." The facts of my where-abouts are as follows: At that time I had charge of the music in the Classon Avenue Presbyterian Church. The services being over I went to the library room to put away some music, and on returning to the auditorium of the church, one of the ladies of the choir was waiting for me to learn about the time appointed for a re-hearsal, which was to be held during the following week. As we talked she stood on the side of the door-sill within the church and I on the side of the library. After a brief conversation we shook hands, said good-night, she going her own way, and I direct to the bedside of Miss Fancher.

The instances I have mentioned all indicate that Miss Fancher was in a trance state at the time of the occurrence. I am convinced, however, that it is not at all times necessary for her to be in that condition to exercise the phenomena of so-called second sight. I have seen it manifested on several occasions, two of which being distinct on my memory. I will relate them. On Easter Sunday night, 1887, 1 had called at her home for a few moments, after evening service at church. There were also present a few others of her friends. We were all engaged in general conversation, when Miss Fancher exclaimed, "There are flowers at the door." A moment after the door-bell rang, and a large basket of flowers was brought to her, having been sent from the Emanuel Baptist Church, of which she is a member. The flowers sent were part of those used in the decoration of the church on that day.

The further incident to which I allude may seem a little ludicrous, but for the sake of exactness I will narrate it just as it occurred.

It was some three or four years ago. It happened that one evening I was in her room when the gas was turned rather low, as is usually the case, a glare of light being painful to her. I held in my hand a little trinket of jewelry, which accidentally dropped on the floor and rolled away. Owing to the semi-darkness I could not have seen it anyway. She laughed at my awkwardness, and said, " I see it." That statement puzzled me, as she was lying with her face in the opposite way from which I had supposed it rolled; and in any event I could not understand how she could have seen it any better than I, owing to the darkness. I therefore questioned her ability to see it. "Well," she said, "do as I tell you and see if I am not right." "All right," I said. "Don't turn up the gas," said she, " but get down on your hands and knees on the floor," and like children, it was agreed that we should adopt the hide-and-seek plan, she to indicate to me after the manner of the old game of hot or cold, i. e., if I was far away I was "cold;" if nearing it I was "growing warmer." So I dropped on all fours, just where I was, and she said I was cold. I moved in another direction and she said I was freezing. I turned again and got warmer, and with every change of direction she indicated my success by the temperature; finally I got "hot" and my eye rested on it, but to further test her power I went away. She was in great glee, and entered into the sport with all the zest of childhood, and said I was getting cold once more. Then I moved toward it, and asked where my hand was then; she said, " Very hot," then I put my hand on it and asked again, when she said, "You have it."

During all this time she had not changed her position nor looked in that direction. Furthermore, had she done so, it would have been useless, so far as ordinary sight was concerned, for the position of the trinket on the floor was about six inches from the foot of the bed, and the top of the foot-board was at least twelve inches above her head, in the position in which she was lying.

GEORGE F. SARGENT.

The following was found in the handwriting of "Pearl" some years ago, in the bed of Miss Fancher, and speaks her feelings as she awakes to consciousness in most touching language. I have entitled it Light Amid the Darkness.

"I am not going to write a book or a story; only the heart's history and experiences of a life that has come truly out of the darkness. My first awakening to this earth life—let me see if I can remember—Oh ! yes. It was a cold, cold night in the winter months—what month I am unable to name, it matters not; only just how I came here and just where I came from, I am to this day in doubt, and a mystery surrounds the opening of my life.

"As I said, one cold winter's night, the gas was burning low, the windows thrown open as if some one was in need of air. The moonlight was beaming in upon me, when I first opened my eyes to what? Was it life? Was I living? It will be impossible for me ever to describe the sensations I had when I first found myself here. Where had I dropped from? Where was I? And where was I going and what was my life? What did it all mean? I questioned in silence. And yet sometimes as I now look back and try to recall or solve the mystery of my new life, I can only think, and could imagine how a lost soul would feel, to fold your hands in slumber and awaken in the arms of Jesus and in Heaven. I was thus bewildered and for the moment thought I was in Heaven. I should have thought so longer, but sharp pains, intense agony and struggling for breath told me I was still on earth. For over there in Heaven there is no pain or sorrow, and I suffered all that. Then it was I realized it was not Heaven with my mamma. Oh, mamma, you know how oft I have implored you to take me with thee and at home.

"This is a long prelude to a small affair. Why am I writing these lines? No other eyes but mine will read them. They are not for critics to look upon and pass their judgment thereon. Oh ! no. I'll tell you why I am writing; it is to relieve a lonely heart—for I am alone. But I must proceed with my story. Take up the thread again, and yet I pause for want of words to explain my feelings. This cold night when my eyes opened after a few moments' silence, a voice said, "And who is this 'Sunbeam,' 'Idol' or 'Rosebud'?"

CHAPTER XIV.

Concerning the Statement of Mrs. Sarah E. Townsend and Clairvoyance.

The following statement, kindly furnished for this publication by Mrs. Thomas S. Townsend, of New York City, is of much importance. It will bear thoughtful reading. The evidence of Miss Fancher's extraordinary clairvoyant powers is so voluminous that no additional testimony could well add to its conclusiveness. In this statement of Mrs. Townsend are two instances where Miss Fancher exercised her clairvoyant powers to a degree almost unparalleled. The instance where she saw and heard correctly, what was transpiring in Cornwall, unmistakably shows that while her friends were fifty miles away from her home, she was holding such relations to them as enabled her to both see what they were doing and hear distinctly what they were saying.

The question she asked while entranced at that moment, clearly shows that her vocal organs were responding to her mental question, "How do you like them?" She says, "I did try so hard to make them see and hear me." The effort caused her lips to utter the question while lying upon her bed. Though she failed to make her friends in Cornwall conscious of her presence, she does not fail to show that she was present with them at that time. One of the lessons we are learning from the life of Miss Fancher is, that a consciousness may at times be had, of transactions in places, distant from the body to which that consciousness is related by the ties of this life, and hence, "being present," may signify far more than that language usually imports.

If, while still related to her body upon its bed in Brooklyn, her spiritual powers instantly carried her to Cornwall, where she both saw and heard her friends as if they were present with her body in her own room, the natural and reasonable conclusion follows, that man has a soul, and can exercise its faculties without the immediate presence of the body, under peculiar conditions, and that distance and material objects are not obstacles to the spirit, as they are to the body. Miss Fancher has lived long in the greatest suffering from pain and physical torture, and thousands of times so nearly has the silvery cord of life been severed that she has been seemingly dead. Thousands of persons have looked upon her wan and rigid features, when her body could have been pierced with needles and burned with fire with no sensations of pain to her, so nearly was the conscious part of her being, the soul, released. These tests have often been applied to her body by her physicians, while she was in her trance conditions, with no response whatever.

We are here taught what has long been claimed and believed by millions of persons of all creeds and faiths, that the soul cannot be tortured by physical sufferings, when it has once severed its relations to the body. It also teaches us that while still holding relations to the body sufficiently strong to awaken again its dormant faculties it may enter realms invisible to us, or places remote from us, and witness what is transpiring there, and hear what others cannot hear, who are with the body.

The incident transpiring at the Street door is important, as showing that Miss Fancher's powers of clairaudience are not confined to her trance conditions. People read their Bibles and believe the seers and prophets possessed the powers they are there recorded as having exercised. There is nowhere in either the Old or New Testament, any authority for the belief so commonly entertained, that the powers exercised by the seers is limited to any class of persons or to any age. On the contrary, the tendency of the Scriptures is the other way. When Peter stood up in defense of the manifestations attending the works of the disciples, he pointed the unbelieving multitude to the prophesies which were then being fulfilled. (Acts, chapter 2.)

Emanuel Swedenborg's wonderful powers of clairvoyance enabled him to witness the burning of Stockholm while he was in England, but the almost continuous possession of that gift by Miss Fancher for so many years, makes her case unique and wonderful.

Mrs. Townsend says:

When I first knew Mollie she had been six years in bed, and Mr. Townsend made her acquaintance about six weeks later. We both became much attached to her. I used to pass one day and night with her every week; Mr. Townsend would come and stay the night with me. At one time, in the seventh or eighth year of her illness, Mollie's brother, now dead, was taken ill, and Miss Crosby went to his home at Cornwall, on the Hudson, so I was a good deal with Mollie, taking care of her.

"MAD" MOLLIE

Opposite to where she lives resided Mr. and Mrs. Parkhurst. That lady and I were seated with her on the day that Miss Crosby had left, when suddenly Mollie went into a perfectly rigid trance. We said, as we always did on such occasions, " Mollie has gone away ! " By-and-by she exclaimed: "How do you like them?" In half an hour she drew a deep sigh and came out of the trance. We asked, "Where have you been?"

"I have been to Aunt Susie (Miss Crosby), and I did try so hard to make them see and hear me."

" What were they doing?"

"Why, they were looking at the presents that we sent them, and I asked her (meaning the wife of Mollie's brother) how she liked them.

Mollie then described how she had seen each person in the house at Cornwall, what they were doing and what they said. When we asked her how she had gone and returned, she said, " Partly by railway and partly by telegraph! " (Surely a joke of Mollie's.) When Miss Crosby returned home we asked her to describe how things had been, and what had been done and said on the evening of her arrival in Cornwall. She gave a full account, and it corresponded to all that Mollie had said, whereupon she exclaimed: "Didn't I tell you so?"

The strangest thing about her is the many changes that she goes through. Of course it is well known that for the first nine years she could keep nothing solid in her stomach. I am positive that she kept nothing in her stomach, and, in fact, could not swallow during the first years that I knew her. She used to call Mr. Townsend and me "Papa and Mamma Tom."

The light distressed her nerves so much that she had her room nearly dark, so that I found it difficult to thread my needle. But she would say, " Oh, do give it to me, Mamma Tom," and in an instant would have it threaded. Whenever I lost anything she told me just where it was, and if anything was missing in Miss Crosby's house, Mollie would go into a momentary cataleptic trance, and would sit upright, which I always loved to see, stretching out her arms and saying, "There it is ! I see it," then fall helpless immediately if we did not sustain her. I have not seen Mollie once for the last few months. I have never seen her sit upright except in the trance; she always has to be propped up. I do not see how she could sit up with her spine as it is.

She made most beautiful wax flowers, and I showed her how to make the leaves. She learned with astonishing rapidity, for she is remarkably clever. She said that some times she saw through her forehead, at others the top of her head seemed to be full of light, and occasionally it was hard for her to see anything at all.

She used to put sealed letters under her pillow and read them; sometimes she read by rubbing her hand over them, and I have seen her read books in the same way.

Very few people have any idea how much Mollie has suffered, and yet she has been such a help to others. I know a prominent minister who frequently went to her, and to me he said very frankly, "I do not come to help Mollie, but to gather strength and consolation from her."

There were times when Mollie could not hear unless we directed our voice up her nostrils, as she instructed us; and when her heart beat with frightful violence she told us to breathe on it, for that relieved her.

It was while I was taking care of Mollie that an agent came from Barnum, who had read newspaper articles about her. He wanted to exhibit Mollie. I talked to the agent at the Street door, and felt very indignant and angry. Mollie could not hear us from where she was, but she afterwards repeated all the conversation to me. When I had shut out the agent and went upstairs again, I found Mollie not angry, but laughing. She said: "Just think of it, Madam Tom; imagine me exhibiting myself for twenty-five cents? I am glad you were so firm with him. Had you not been here he would have certainly got in somehow or other."

I was with Mollie when the change took place in her after those nine years, and it was all very painful. The change took place gradually in about two weeks, during which time Mollie frequently wept and said that something dreadful was going to happen to her. One night the climax came, and then I saw Mollie's eyes for the first time. They suddenly flashed wide open, and never have I seen anything more beautiful, for though sightless, she appeared perfectly angelic. That night was something never to be forgotten. She was wonderful; and she seemed to be on a stage gesticulating with one small hand, and then she sang most beautifully. For several days Mollie was in an unconscious state and we supposed she was dying. When she came out of it everyone and everything was strange to her. She did not even know her aunt. All her surroundings distressed her, and it took her a long time to become reconciled to them. We were entirely unknown to her. When Mr. Townsend approached her with his accustomed friendly solicitude, she drew herself away as if she considered him very impertinent. We had to begin the acquaintance all over again, and she never again addressed us as "Papa and Mama Tom."

But in that second state she used to call me "Lady Townsend."

I have seen so much of Mollie and her strange powers, that nothing extraordinary seems to stand out saliently apart from the rest. I love Mollie very tenderly, and would do anything to serve her. I think that before she dies, Mollie will return to her original self, as I first knew her.

SARAH E. TOWNSEND.
New York, July 16, 1893.

The unsuccessful effort of Miss Fancher to make her presence known to her friends in Cornwall, suggests to the mind of the author, the frequently recorded instances where persons are claimed to have been seen at two places remote from each other at the same moment. These alleged occurrences have given rise to the theory of the " double," which is, that man is a duplex being, and the fact of his being seen at two places at the same moment can be explained upon no other theory. Psychical societies in Europe and in this country, for several years have been collecting and collating all the testimony upon this and similar subjects possible. Students of Psychical Science will do well to obtain from Prof. Richard Hodgson, of No. 5 Boylston Place, Boston, Mass., Secretary of the American branch of the Society for Psychical Research of Great Britain, the proceedings of that society. Psychology is now unmistakably recognized as a scientific study, and, as it bears more directly than any other upon the relations of the mental and spiritual parts of man to the physical parts, it is fast becoming an important and interesting subject for study and investigation.

The recorded instances of the exercise of the remarkable powers of Miss Fancher, which the reader will find in these pages, will afford abundant material for careful consideration. Let no reader hastily reject the testimony here placed before him. It is an adage, that "Whatever man has done, man can do." It has been verified too often to be disputed now. There is nothing which man has done in the past which he may not do now. He is a silly man who believes that nature is not true to herself. Her laws do not change. When we read or hear of anything which seemingly sets the laws of nature at naught, we may safely assume that the seeming mystery can and will be ultimately explained, and that the process by which strange results have been produced will be discovered. Phenomena which have not been explained may eventually be explained, and it is far better to seek out and make known the processes of nature than to attribute them to the direct act of unseen and unstable beings.

In saying this, the author has no desire to be understood as urging the idea that man can comprehend or explain all that is presented to him in the ever-oc-curring phenomena of nature. He is now, and let us hope ever will be, environed by unfathomable mystery. As he will never comprehend himself, how much less will he comprehend the great universe of which he is a part, and in the midst of which he is a burning, glowing fire of intellectual light, peering into and looking upon his surroundings with wonder and amazement. The handiwork of Deity be-comes more grand, and His dealings with His children can be best reconciled with man's conceptions of justice, by looking upon all things as subject alike to unchanging laws. Can He, who is All and in all, do violence to Himself? Can He set Himself at naught? God is in nature, and is to nature all her laws. We learn to know more of Him, and grow to love Him better, as we enter more fully and perfectly into a knowledge of His works. And where shall we be stayed? Who hath set bounds beyond which we may not go? Are there mysteries too sacred to be inquired into? Bigotry and ignorance are akin.

Knowledge is to man as the sun to the world he dwells in. A truly enlight-ened man can be neither a tyrant nor a slave. The soul of man corresponds to his enlightenment. The man who does wrong thereby shows a lack in some part of a well-educated mind, and of a well-rounded nature. Man is rising from grosser conditions to a more perfectly developed being.

Religion should release him from all limitations in the pursuit of knowledge. Arbitrary standards can never be justified except for the security and well-being of society. The spiritual nature of man, and his relations to humanity and the world he lives in, as well to the Deity, should, be studied and understood, if such a thing be possible. However imperfect the beginning may be, anything and everything which can enlighten him, should not be feared but earnestly desired. The lessons we can learn from a knowledge of the experiences, acts and powers manifested in the life of Miss Fancher, are essential and valuable to a better understanding of the nature and powers of man. In the preceding remarks, it has not been the de-sire of the writer, to do more than seek to obtain from the reader a careful consid-eration of the remarkable phases of Miss Fancher's case. He does not flatter him-self that his efforts will be entirely successful. He anticipates the adverse criticism of just such people as was the eminent Dr. Beard, of New York city, who, in his conceit, declared Miss Fancher a fraud, and that the clairvoyant power was pos-sessed by none. But later on, in his greater wisdom, he learned that he had stulti-fied himself, and humbly, to his credit be it said, asked her to forgive him.

CHAPTER XV.

Statement of Mr. Thomas S. Townsend.

Mr. Thomas S. Townsend, of The Newport, Broadway and Fifty-second Street, N. Y., says:

Before the first change took place in Mollie's condition, and while Mrs. Townsend had the care of her, during her aunt's absence at Cornwall, I went to the house every day about half-past three o'clock and remained until next morning. On one occasion a lady, acting as secretary for me, met me at the Wall Street Ferry with some papers which were important for me to have immediately. It being a beautiful afternoon in the month of June, I invited her to take a sail across the river. She did so and walked up Montague Street with me to Fulton Street, where she took a car for the Fulton Ferry, while I took another for the other direction—to Mollie's—arriving there soon after four o'clock. About seven o'clock of that evening Mollie said to me, "Who came across the ferry with you this afternoon?"

Mrs. Townsend then said, that about half-past three o'clock, Mollie had been in a trance, and while in that condition she noticed an expression of amusement in her countenance, and when she again came to herself, Mrs. Townsend inquired what she had seen that was so funny. Mollie would give her no satisfaction. But after having inquired of me, "Who came across the ferry?" she admitted having seen the lady, and gave the name of the person referred to.

THOMAS S. TOWNSEND.

Statement of Mrs. Emily Blossom, Residing at the corner of Atlantic and Clinton Streets, Brooklyn.

Judge A. H. Dailey:

Dear Sir.—In answer to your request for a statement touching my acquaintance with Miss Fancher, and what I have witnessed which may be of public interest regarding her case, I beg to state as follows:

My husband and myself have long been among her most intimate friends. She used to address us by the endearing terms, " Uncle Joe " and "Aunt Em."

Mr. Blossom, who died six years ago, had very interesting experiences with Mollie. Upon one occasion, while he was seated by her bed, a letter was brought to her. She placed it beneath her pillow without opening it, and read it off. Mr. Blossom then said, "Now, Mollie, you let me open that letter and read it to myself so that you cannot see it, while you repeat it to me word for word if you can." Mollie agreed, and read it without making one mistake. Once while we were visiting her, her pet squirrel disappeared and we could find it nowhere, but Mollie said it was in the next room under the bed. That room was quite dark, but we went in and under Mollie's directions chased the squirrel from corner to corner till we captured it. Yes, I have seen Mollie in all her conditions, five, I think, and as she does not know her various selves, I suggested that she should write notes to the other Mollies. This was on one occasion when she woke up from a trance and said to me, " Mollie number one is very much afraid because she is alone." I inquired why she was alone, and said that she should write notes to the other Mollies and ask them. On July ist, 1893, I visited Mollie and she sat up in bed as she has lately done more than once. She took lunch with me, very daintily, but she ate something; while at one time, for nine years* nothing entered her stomach. She could not swallow, the muscles of her throat were completely contracted. She would sometimes take a mouthful of ice cream; something which does not now agree with her, or any other little thing that would easily melt, and the whole of it would be absorbed by the membranes of her mouth.

Yours sincerely,

EMILY BLOSSOM.

Statement by Mr. Herbert Blossom.

I have known Mollie Fancher since 1872, when I was very young, and saw a good deal of her from that time to the year 1881, but after that only once or twice up to 1888, since which time I have seen her occasionally. When I was first acquainted with Mollie she was very loath to show any of her strange powers, but she used to tell me of things that happened in my own room. I remember that when I was a boy, I was in the habit of sitting up reading at night, and she made me promise that I would go to bed at ten o'clock. One night I forgot myself, and when

"MAD" MOLLIE

I closed the book and looked at the clock it was a quarter to eleven. Next time I saw Mollie she asked me what time I had gone to bed that same night. I said about ten o'clock. But she said, " No; I was there, and it was a quarter to eleven."

I used to take newspapers to her, and she would just lay her hand on them and tell me all the news they contained; then I would unfold them, read, and find her quite correct.

Nine years of her life are a blank to her; when she came out of that state she did not know me; I had to make her acquaintance over again. When there was no one else to take care of her I would pass the night watching by her, and as her many conditions generally come on her in the night, she now knows me in all of them except one. When she woke up in that fifth condition one night she said to me:"Well, and who are you?"

During the last year I have seen her in all her different states, from Mollie Number 1 to Mollie Number 5. In fact, during one night, I saw her pass through them all without any convulsion, merely a deep-drawn sigh between each, while generally the convulsions are violent. She displays different characteristics in each, and I always have to wait to hear what she says so that I may know which Mollie is talking to me. In one of her conditions she is very gay and witty. In each, she remembers what has occurred in the same condition, but nothing of the various others. In one she speaks, thinks and acts like a child six years old; for several months she went into that state for a short time in every twenty-four hours. It may not be really the case, but it has seemed to me, that when I have been sitting by her side and talking to her all night, she has not gone into those conditions so much as when she was left alone. When I have been sleeping on the sofa, her spasms have sometimes been so violent that the shaking of the floor has awakened me. Between each spasm she would be a different Mollie, and in the morning her vitality was very low. When she came out of her cataleptic states, I used to ask her what she had seen but she would seldom say a word about it. When I asked how it was that she could see everything, she said she seemed to see through her forehead above her eyes.

Mollie has been a great sufferer. Many years ago, she told me that she never had a moment free from pain. Her heart would often beat so hard that you could see the bedclothes throb. She has always been good and patient. Sometimes when I have been there persons have come to tell her of their own little troubles, and it seemed to me that they were so trifling compared with hers, yet she always endeavored to comfort those who came to her for consolation.

"MAD" MOLLIE

Mollie really is a wonderful person, very clever, and in her patient endurance and kind thoughtfulness of other people, she is certainly a beautiful character. All through her long years of illness she has never been emaciated about her throat and neck; she has been and is very plump. This used to be a source of surprise to me. Again and again I have watched Mollie in spasms, and she continuously rolled her head on the pillow from side to side for a quarter of an hour at a time; she also violently pounded her chest so that in the morning it would be bruised.

I am asked to state what I recall with reference to her having seen Mr. Sargent while in one of her trances. I remember that I was watching with her one night while Mr. Sargent was away in Muskegon, Michigan, where he had gone to organize a company for the manufacture of furniture for invalids, in which Mollie was interested. Mollie went into a deep trance for some time; all evidence of animation being absent, as usual in her trances. When she returned to consciousness and I asked where she had been, she informed me that she had in her trance been to see Mr. Sargent, and said that he was in a large room with a number of persons about him, and on a platform or stage, and was singing. I felt sure that she was mistaken, and told her so; but she said, "We will wait and see." When Mr. Sargent returned, I learned from him that upon the night she was in the trance he was engaged in singing, and that her description of what she had seen was entirely correct.

HERBERT BLOSSOM.

Judge Abram H. Dailey:

Dear Sir.—I was introduced to Miss Fancher a few years ago by the eminent scholar, Dr. C. E. West, in whose seminary Mollie was about to graduate, just before the terrible accident which prostrated her. I have frequently visited her with my husband, Dr. LePlongeon, who, as a physician, was much interested in her case. He found it a most extraordinary one, and told the patient that it would not surprise him if a time should come when she would again stand on her feet.

We are convinced that Mollie sees quite clearly, though her eyes are sightless. On one occasion we took photos to show her. With closed eyelids, and the room nearly dark, she passed comments on the pictures, even pointing out a portrait of myself in a very small group, where my face was hardly bigger than the head of a common pin; we had not told her that my figure was there.

"MAD" MOLLIE

She had a pet cat named Sarah Bernhardt. When it entered the room, noiseless, as those creatures are, she would exclaim, "Here comes Sarah Bernhardt!"

One Sunday afternoon, while I talked with her, a heavy storm came on. Mollie immediately said, "What a pity! That dress of yours will be spoiled."

"Why, Mollie," said I, "you do not know what my dress is like."

"Yes, I do; it is a silver-gray satin."

Her description was correct, and I was much surprised.

We never grew tired of admiring the marvelous wax flowers made by Miss Fancher, and one afternoon her devoted aunt, Miss Crosby, showed us some exquisite portieres worked by Mollie. They were garnet plush, embroidered with silk, old gold, emerald green, pearl gray, pure white, and a rich brown. The design was elaborate, executed with wondrous skill and taste, the work being perfect and the blending of colors most artistic. The garnet velvet was faced with old gold silk. These portieres can be seen at No. 30 St. James' Place, Brooklyn, L. I., the home of Mr. L . There also is a most beautiful lambrequin, made by the same deft and really lovely little hands. The Passion-flower is the design on the lambrequin, that flower having been greatly admired and cultivated by the gentleman mentioned. He interested himself in finding purchasers for some of Mollie's fine work, and it was he who told us of a lady who saw Mollie sketch with great rapidity a beautiful spray of roses, then select needles and silks, thread them without any hesitation and quickly complete the work in the most perfect manner, her eyes being fast shut. The lady said, "Oh, Mollie, your eyes are in the ends of your fingers." Mollie only laughed, and when the piece of work was completed, gave it to the lady to insert in a crazy quilt which the lady herself was making and yet has in her possession.

When Mr. L. kindly allowed us to examine the portieres now in his house he said: "I have known Mollie fourteen years, and have seen many puzzling things for which I cannot find any logical explanation. She certainly sees with precision, though her physicians say that her optic nerves are destroyed. But she has always hesitated to show her powers."

It surprises me that Mollie could, while lying on her back, have worked on such a large piece of goods as the portieres, and have produced such a fine general effect, without having the whole thing spread out before her. She must have had the work, in its completed form, before her mental vision.

"MAD" MOLLIE

(portiere: a curtain decorating or replacing a door. French portière, from Old French, feminine of portier, porter porter, doorkeeper. First Known Use: 1843)

Having been frequently absent from Brooklyn, we have not visited Mollie as much as we might otherwise have done, but we are convinced of her genuineness, her great sufferings, and have often admired her ready sympathy for others less afflicted than herself. Being thoroughly unselfish, she prefers to speak of anybody or of anything rather than of herself. Apart from the interest attached to her phenomenal condition, she is a gifted and lovable woman, worthy of the esteem and affection of her fellow-beings, and is tenderly regarded by those who know her intimately.

Very truly yours,

ALICE D. LePLONGEON.

Statement of Joseph S. Harley relative to his experiences with Miss Mollie Fancher:

I have known Miss Mollie Fancher 15 or 16 years. I am an engraver. I have visited her on an average about once a week all these years. Our conversation is often very general, and she seems to know what is going on as well as do persons who have the use of their senses and are walking or traveling around the city. For instance, upon one occasion she asked me, " What is that large building down there on Bedford, near Lafayette Avenue—are they stores?" I said, " Synagogue. What do you know about it?" She laughed and said "Why do you ask me such a question? Don't I know as much about it as you do?" I have seen Mollie Fancher's several selves, or the ones who come and are said to be a part of her life. Her aunt told me to come and stay late enough to see the other Mollies. I came and saw one come. The Mollie whom I had first seen went into a trance and then appeared to wake up, and her eyes were opened. I had to be introduced to her. She had been told of my coming and was expecting me. She asked me if I knew the old Mollie. I said yes. She appeared quite jealous of the old Mollie. She asked me how long I had known her, and said she wanted to stay and see her some time. At one time the one who appears to be a little child came. She talked and acted as a little child. She asked her aunt, " A stranger?" and her aunt told her I was the one she had spoken of coming, and she said, "Oh, yes." She asked was I married and about my children, if I had any. She said, "I wish mamma would come; she stays so late to-night." Then she said, "I will have to go," and she went into a trance.

I know she distinguishes colors by placing her hands on them. The Mollie I usually see, complained that the other Mollies got, opened and read her letters, and said she was going to wait and see them some time.

JOSEPH S. HARLEY.

Mr. Howard S. Jones, says:
"I have seen Mollie in her cataleptic trances, quite frequently. While I was talking with her she would suddenly become stiff, in whatever posture she had assumed. I have seen her in four of her conditions, and she presents a distinct personality in each, I have no theory or idea as to how this could be explained, but Mollie is certainly a wonderful being. Yes, I have seen her as little ' Rosebud,' the six year old child. Mollie is becoming much more natural than she used to be. She now moves all the upper part of her body quite freely, and her lower limbs, though not straight, are no longer entwined as they were when Mrs. Jones first knew her. My wife was then only twelve years old. If she were here she would herself tell you, that formerly, she had seen Mollie's lower limbs to- gether in three twists; her arm too was at that time up- lifted, so that her hand was at the back of her neck and her eyelids were closed very firmly. Yet she always saw distinctly, as she proved to me over and over again.

"When I was in the room about ten feet from her and it was quite dark where she lay, she would describe what I was wearing, even finger rings. One afternoon when Mrs. Jones was with her, there was a tadpole in a glass case containing fishes. The room was nearly dark and the creatures very small, but Mollie, with closed eyes, followed its movements exclaiming:" There it goes ! Now it is swimming up to the top!' ,etc. I think very highly of Mollie's character and she is very clever."

HOWARD S. JONES.

Rev. Dr. Edward Braislin, says:
I have known Miss Mollie Fancher a long time, and have always been much interested in her, but have not made any close or scientific study of her case. I have seen her in one of her night states, or what she calls other Mollies. Her eyes were then wide open, and she claimed to know nothing of what had happened in

the day. She did not recognize me and I had to be newly introduced to her; apparently she had no knowledge whatever of our former acquaintance. On that occasion, her eyes being wide open, she told me that she had no power of vision, but was absolutely blind. I tested her eyes then, and it is the only time I have done so, holding a lighted lamp close to them. As far as my knowledge goes, I should say they were perfectly well formed, but the pupil instead of contracting only contracted and dilated alternately to its utmost capacity, the eyelids remaining fixedly open, while the full light was pouring steadily on the orbs, so that if the glare acted on them at all, it acted in a very erratic way; but I got the impression that Mollie was quite blind, as otherwise the light which I held to them must have caused her acute pain. I know Mollie well in her normal state, if the term normal can at any time be applied to her, and I consider her sincerity unquestionable. If she is mistaken in any matter regarding herself, she does not knowingly deceive anyone. I esteem her very highly.

EDWARD BRAISLIN.

Mill River, Berkshire Co., Mass., July 8th, 1893.

Having been requested by Judge A. H. Dailey, to certify over my own signature to certain incidents on the occasion of my visit to Miss Mollie Fancher, I willingly do so by stating as follows:

Some three years ago I visited Judge Dailey at his home, 451 Washington Avenue, City of Brooklyn. We were old acquaintances. I came from Massachusetts and spent the night with him. About 11 o'clock at night I retired to my room, Judge Dailey accompanying me, where we spent quite a while in conversation.

I had never seen Mollie Fancher, but had heard of her.

I was subsequently informed by Judge Dailey, that Miss Fancher claimed to have seen us together in that room that night, and to have correctly described my personal appearance. During the last winter, with my brother-in-law, Mr. Edward T. Blodgett, I called again upon Judge Dailey for a social visit. During the evening I expressed a desire to some time see Miss Fancher; whereupon Judge Dailey volunteered to take us to her home that evening, as it was but a few blocks away. When we entered Miss Fancher's room, the Judge asked her if she recognized either of us, Blodgett or myself. She said that we had never been there before. After a few seconds thought she said, that she had never seen Mr. Blodgett before, but I was the man she saw in her trance some years before at Judge Dailey's house; that I had a full beard and other things descriptive that were quite correct.

I will further add, that Judge Dailey was not aware of our intention to call upon him, until we came to his door, and I am quite positive that Miss Fancher could not have known of our coming until we entered her house. The visit was suggested and made on the impulse of the moment, and as unexpectedly to all of us as anything possibly could be.

H. D. SISSON.

I have read the above statement of a visit to Miss Mollie Fancher and know it to be correct.
E. T. BLODGETT.
State of Massachusetts, | .
County of Berkshire,)
Subscribed and sworn to this 8th day of July, 1893, before me
EDWIN ADAMS,
Justice of the Peace.

In connection with the foregoing statements of Mr. Sisson and Mr. Blodgett, it is proper for me to add that sometime in the early part of the year 1890, or latter part of 1889, I called one evening upon Miss Mollie Fancher, and found Mr. George F. Sargent and some other friends with her. Soon after I entered, Miss Fancher asked me to locate myself upon a certain night at 11 o'clock. After considerable reflection I told her I had done so. "Now," said she, "I will tell you where you were; you were in a back room in your house, with a tall dark complexioned man with a full beard. He was rather slender, and there was a bed in the room." She was correct; upon that night a friend of mine from New Marlboro, Mass., spent the night with me, and at the hour of 11 o'clock I was with him in his room, as he was about retiring. Miss Fancher then related to me, that upon that night she went into a trance at 11 o'clock, and went to my house and saw me with the gentleman she had described in the chamber where he was to sleep. Upon coming out of her trance she had related to Mr. Sargent, that she had seen me as stated. The gentleman Miss Fancher saw with me was Hon. H. D. Sisson. During the last winter Mr. Sisson and his brother-in-law, Mr. Blodgett, both strangers to Miss Fancher, called upon me and I accompanied them to her house. Upon entering I asked her if she had ever seen them before. She replied, "They have never been here before," and pointing to Mr. Blodgett, she said, "I have never seen him before, but," pointing to Mr. Sisson, she said, " that's the man I saw at your house that night." Mr. Sisson and Mr. Blodgett have more fully stated what transpired.

The following instance of Miss Fancher's remarkable powers will be found of exceeding interest, inasmuch as it is of very recent occurrence, and I have in my possession the original correspondence touching the same. Neither Miss Fancher nor Mr. Bishop, her correspondent, would likely be willing that I should publish in full the letters as they were written, because of many jolly expressions contained in each letter written by one to the other.

Miss Fancher's letter reads as follows, in so far as I shall insert the same:

" May 17th, 1893. Wednesday, A. M.

"My Dear Friend:

I do not doubt you sent out a ' search,' and now I am sending out one also. What became of you? You last wrote you would put in an appearance, and I looked and expected you. Then, of course, I did not write, for I thought you were coming. I have been very sick, before I received your letter and since, and that is the reason I have not answered. Is the apology accepted?

You seem to be in bad luck when you come to Brooklyn. You hurt your finger when you were in New York, and then you smashed your wrist.

We have had a backward Spring, very cold, and now once more it is pleasant weather. I expect it looks lovely on the Island. The apples and cherries must be in blossom; the trees are budding fast since so much rain fell, and last week was so warm.

How are you and all the family, and the nephew that called with you, and his family?"

She closes her letter by saying:

"I trust you are well, happy and jolly as ever. I can see you standing or posing, wasn't that it, for a picture. With kind regard from

MOLLIE FANCHER."

The envelope to this letter I have in my possession, addressed to Mr. J. S. Bishop, Riverhead, L. I., Postoffice box 561, and it is post marked May 17, 2 P. M., 1893.

The answer to that letter is dated Riverhead, May 18th, 1893, and commences:

" Miss Mollie Fancher,

"Dear Friend:

"Your letter of the 17th inst. was appreciatively read. After referring to some personal matters, the writer uses this language:" You mention in your letter that you can see me standing for a picture; well, I will tell you about it: On Monday, at 6 P. M., a photographer seated the hotel for a picture. He requested me to be included; I complied with his request, and stood in front of, and leaned on one of the pillars that held and supported the veranda, and so I had my picture taken. If not too incompatible with your best wishes and desires, and if you will not think I am too ' inquircus,' I shall be highly pleased to have you inform me how you knew I was having my resemblance copied.

"While dining today I told an intimate friend that I had received a letter from you. A young gentleman then sitting at my right looked up, and acted as though he was greatly astonished. He asked me if I was acquainted with you. I told him I was pleased to say, yes. He said he had the honor of knowing you also. He said his wife was your cousin. He handed me his card. The name of the photographer who took the photograph referred to is Dana Dawens."

Mr. George F. Sargent wrote Mr. Bishop for the return of Miss Fancher's letter that it might be used in this connection.

In inclosing it, Mr. Bishop writes as follows:

"I have mentioned the incident to a large number of reputable people, and they all have said just as I did on the receipt of your letter—it is something wonderful and far beyond human comprehension. The photographer was at the Griffin House a few minutes past 6 P. M., on Monday, May 15, and I received your letter in the evening mail of May 17th. I know to a dead certainty that no one at this end of the line, apprised you that I was standing for a picture at the time you wrote to me about it. Now, Miss Mollie, I want you—'or any other man,' to understand that I want the (your) letters returned to me. With kind regards, I remain
    Yours hurriedly,
    J. S. BISHOP."

"MAD" MOLLIE

Statement of William Kingman, Esq., of Brooklyn, N. Y.:

"I am requested by Judge A. H. Dailey, to state an incident which occurred to my own knowledge with Miss Mollie Fancher. Some three or more years ago, I was residing in the family of Judge Dailey, and one evening he had an appointment to visit Miss Fancher at her house. It so happened that from business engagements, he was unable to keep his appointment, and wrote a note to Miss Fancher explaining the cause of his breach of engagement, and commissioned me to deliver it in person to her, which I was willing to do. I had never seen Miss Fancher, and Judge Dailey remarked to me, ' Mr. Kingman, many people would esteem it quite a privilege to get the opportunity to see Miss Fancher, which you now have.

"I took the letter to her house, holding it sealed in my hand, and as I entered her room and was proceeding to a seat, Miss Fancher exclaimed, ' Oh, Mr. Sargent, Judge Dailey cannot come to-night, he is so very busy now, but will be around in a few days.' I then delivered her the letter and she read it in nearly the identical language she had made use of, as I have already stated.

WILLIAM KINGMAN,
No. 131 Gates Avenue,
Brooklyn, N. Y.
Brooklyn, July 26th, 1893."

Statement of Mr. Jeffrey Simmons.

"Having enjoyed the personal acquaintance of Miss Mollie Fancher during the last five years, it may not be out of place for me to narrate some of the incidents to which my attention has been attracted from time to time while in her presence. Friendly feelings were established or found to exist between this lady and myself during my first brief call at her house, so, on taking my leave she kindly invited me to come again.

"Being intensely interested, I soon became a weekly visitor, and sometimes oftener, having been assured that I was at liberty to come whenever it suited my convenience.

"With that understanding I was treated more as a friend than as a visitor, that is, her work was not put aside to entertain me, nor did she hesitate to utilize my services when favorable opportunities were presented. It finally came about that she had a quantity of worsted to wind, so it fell to me to hold the skeins while she did the winding. It was by no means my first experience in that direction, though I soon realized that Mollie was an expert at disentangling snarls, that seemed to knot themselves up, without the slightest difficulty.

"With surprising deftness her nimble fingers would seize the right strand, and so manipulate it that the ball would soon be whirling again. The absence of any hesitancy on her part, taken with existing conditions, was conclusive evidence to me that normal eyesight was not employed in the operation. Nor could normal eyesight have aided her in threading a fine needle, under circumstances and conditions in which I have frequently seen her do it, without any apparent effort. I can also corroborate what has been said by others, concerning her ability to see and recognize persons at a distance or beyond the range of normal vision.

"This has been demonstrated on repeated occasions, when on going to her house, the moment I entered the hall, she would greet me from where she was lying in her room on the second floor, to reach which I must climb the stairs, pass through one room, and then turn in order to enter her apartment.

"At one time after being thus greeted, on coming into her presence, I said, ' Mollie, did you see me when I was down at the hall floor?' She said, 'Yes, had I not known it was you I would not have said what I did.' A person knowing her, can readily understand that she would not indulge in such familiarity without knowing to whom she was speaking. At the time I made the acquaintance of this interesting person, her store on the floor beneath her apartments, was occupied by a woman whose death occurred a year or two later on. Some relatives on being informed of the decease came on from Connecticut, I think, to attend the burial and to take charge of her effects.

"I knew nothing of this until after it had transpired, when one day following, on entering Mollie's room I met three persons leaving it. She informed me that they were relatives or heirs of her former tenant, and that they were desirous of closing up the business at once. To accomplish their purpose, they had brought the books and papers belonging to the store and placed them on the bed within reach of Mollie, who had undertaken to perform that laborious and unpleasant task, and was proceeding with as much deliberation as though she was familiar with the entire detail, and knew the significance of every item.

"At another time on coming into her presence, a light table having legs of a suitable length, so that when placed on the bed its top was raised so as not to rest on her person, was in that position. Spread upon its surface was a large sheet of drawing paper on which was displayed numerous tines and curves made with different colored pencils, which together with other implements used in drawing, were lying near. Acting on my first impulse, I said what are you doing? To which she replied, that Mr. Sargent was anxious to have this drawing completed as soon as possible, and had worked upon it till very late last night, when he gave it up, and asked her to finish it for him to-day. This was said as though it was some ordinary work that any one might do if he felt so disposed. That surprising genius, manifested in so many ways, is in keeping with a high order of mentality, which aided by keen perception, enables her to grasp ideas and principles, and also to unfold and present them in a clear and logical style of reasoning.

"Add to this an amiable disposition that inspires her to bear intense pain, with the heroic fortitude of a martyr, who can smile when suffering the pangs of death, and you have a faint picture of Mollie Fancher entertaining her friends, forgetful of herself, while endeavoring to make their visits pleasing to them."
JEFFREY SIMMONS.
825 Lafayette Avenue,
Brooklyn, N. Y., November 17, 1893.

Statement of Louis Sherk.

Judge A. H. Dailey,
"Dear Sir:—My first acquaintance with Miss Mollie Fancher dates from 1878, when I unexpectedly visited her upon an invitation extended to me by her aunt, Miss Crosby, who had never seen me, but knew of me through my brother, who had treated Miss Fancher magnetically by request of Dr. Speir. My brother is now dead.

"When I called, it was upon a dark and stormy day. I was wrapped in a cloak, wearing a slouch hat. As I entered the hall, on the floor below, I heard my name called to come up stairs. I did so, and this was the first time that I had seen either Miss Crosby or Miss Fancher. I asked Miss Crosby how she knew who I was, and she said that Mollie had told her while I was down at the door.

"The room in which Miss Mollie was lying was very dark. At that time she could bear scarcely any light in the room, as the light pained her, notwithstanding she was blind. There was no fire in the room and it was cold and chilly. She at once remarked that I wore an imperial, which my brother did not. On account of the darkness I could not distinguish Miss Fancher's features at the time. She took hold of my hand and passed into a trance state, and when she came out of it she was covered with cold perspiration. On another occasion she made a little button-hole bouquet of wax flowers, selecting the colors from a box of wax sheets which I handed her. It was so dark in her room that I could not find the box at first, but she pointed it out to me.

"Upon another occasion I asked her the definition of a certain word. She handed me a little dictionary. It was after sunset, and the print was very small. My eyes are poor, and to discern the print I would require a magnifying glass, but she took the book, turned over a few leaves and pointed to the word and the definition. I afterwards took the book and examined the word with a glass under the gas light, and saw that she had directed me properly.

"At another time I found her when she did not appear to be the same personality, so far as actions and conversation are concerned, as upon other occasions. She called herself, however, Mollie Fancher, and was quite anxious that I should take as much interest in her as I did in the " other Mollie," to use her expression.

"Upon another time I sent a man to her house to hang her picture in the front room, but did not inform him who occupied the house. I gave him instructions where to hang it if no one should be in the room. It so happened that no one was in the front room, and as he reported to me, the folding doors between the front and back room were closed. In the midst of his work he heard somebody severely criticizing him as to the manner in which he was hanging the picture. He looked around, saw nobody, and proceeded with his work, when he was again interrupted. He became alarmed, looked under the piano and back of the chairs, saw nobody in the room, went back to his work, when he was further criticized. He hastily finished his work and left the house. He told me that he would not go back to that house for any money, for he did not want to come in contact with the devil. I then informed him that this devil was Miss Fancher, and that many wealthy people would gladly pay a large sum to have had the experience which he had. The explanation to the whole thing being, that Miss Fancher from her bed in the back room, saw what he was doing, and had something to say as to the manner in which the work was done; but to see him she had to see through the partition intervening. I have had numerous other experiences with Miss Fancher, but I have mentioned sufficient to indicate what I know concerning her."
LOUIS SHERK.

CHAPTER XVI.

Testimony of the Press.

The history of the case of Miss Fancher will never be comparatively complete unless authenticated by contemporaneous reliable newspaper publications.

On the 7th of June, 1866, the Brooklyn Eagle published the first article which ever reached the public concerning her. My attention was first called to her by her physician, Doctor S. Fleet Speir; and by searching the files of the Brooklyn Eagle, in the Brooklyn Library, this article has been found; and having ascertained that it is in the main, quite correct, it is here inserted. It will be found very interesting reading, as showing Miss Fancher's condition at that time, and of the beginning of public interest in her case. The facts were obtained chiefly from her own physician. The article is from the pen of Col. William Hempstreet, an able writer, and the author of a recent publication, entitled, " The Substance of the Soul."

A REMARKABLE CASE

Terrible Condition of a Patient—The Nerves in Rebellion—A Continuous Trance—Persistent Muscular Rigidity—The Gift of Second Sight—Physic Raffled—The Sufferer Lives Seven Weeks without Food.

It has been held by many medical men, that the remarkable vigor which characterizes the present century, is a result of the preponderance of nervous energy in the races that people the earth. This would seem to hold good from the slowest to the most active race. Where nervous energy is clogged and embedded in flesh and bone it is less conspicuous in results; an African of Africa, can hardly be said to possess the talent for fretting himself to death; an anxious mother of the Saxon-Yankee race, can do it upon the slightest provocation. Where the driving, go-ahead-ativeness of Yankee energy and thrift is found, there is found an atomic element known as nerves. Upon these all high pressure people build and work, and in this country they are " run" at various rapidity, until "Nervines," "Soothing Syrup," "Laudanum Troches," etc., become indispensable to about half the population.

It has longed seemed the especial province of Americans to abuse their nerves from the cradle to the grave. The first trouble to be encountered is the paregoric epoch, from which a child just escapes in time to begin the imbibition of tea and coffee. These are finally reinforced by cigars or tobacco, and finally malt and fermented liquors are brought into requisition. These, not to mention other equally inimical agents, are sure to weaken the wonderous net work of sensation, and thus impaired, the nervous system is transmitted from father to child.

Over-worked and over-stimulated, the nerves are full of short-lived vigor, just the thing for a short raid as flying artillery, but utterly failing when the heavy work of bombardment is demanded. As an illustration of the condition of the nervous prostration to which a young person, previously healthy, may be brought, the following Very Extraordinary Case finds place in these columns. It will be read with melancholy interest by all, and should be well heeded by those to whom are confided the education of our youth of both sexes, as well as parents, who allow the intellectual faculties in their children to be stimulated to an unhealthy action, and thus render them liable to all the suffering now experienced by a young lady, whose case is here partially described.

In the Twelfth Ward in this city, not very far from what may be termed the Clinton Avenue section of town, there resides a family, consisting of a father, mother and several children, among them a daughter of nineteen years. The parents are moderately circumstanced, respectable and intelligent, and well connected. This daughter, whose name must remain unmentioned here, in deference to the manifest wishes of her relatives, is a fine looking, capable young lady, and of good apparent promises. She is what would be termed spirituelle, with light hair and complexion, a fragile figure, pale countenance, large sparkling eye, with a forehead and features indicative of thought rather than execution. Up to the time that her nervous system gave way she was deemed a bright student, and stood deservedly high in one of the Montague Street schools. Her books were her delight; like many another she neglected all for them, and would arise late in the morning in consequence of weakness, hasten away to school without a breakfast, fearful of being tardy, and then at evening, in her anxiety to learn her lessons, again neglect a meal for which she felt little inclination. In this manner Her Vitality Gradually Ebbed until she seemed too frail to carry the assortment of text books, with which city pupils load themselves in going to and from school. In this way, neglecting her physical weakness, and allowed by her parents to do so, she continued an assiduous student until about three months since, when she met with an accident. In riding upon a horse which was rather spirited, she was thrown with considerable violence to the ground, and the shock rendered it necessary that

"MAD" MOLLIE

she should undergo medical treatment.

After a time she recovered slowly, and impelled by a mistaken enthusiasm growing out of the spirit of class emulation, she recommenced her studies, looking more like parchment than flesh and blood.

Disaster followed disaster in her case. One day in leaving a car in Fulton Avenue her crinoline caught, and the weakened young lady was dragged some thirty or forty feet before she could be relieved from her dangerous position. Occurring just at this critical time was most unfortunate, and almost immediately she was reduced to her present deplorable condition. She is engaged to be married to a wealthy young man, and the ceremony was to have been solemnized this fall; this fact in connection with her gradual decline had its effect upon her mind, as she felt that she could not conscientiously assume the duties of a wife. A day or two after the second accident she was Suddenly Seized with Spasms of which she has daily been a victim to the present time.

For the last nine weeks she has alternated from a spasm to a trance, and extreme rigidity of the muscles has succeeded their complete relaxation. At first the spasms were not general, but after a day or two the entire body appeared affected. While in these spasms the contortions of the unhappy patient become vital; it appears at times almost impossible to hold her. Each one is succeeded by a trance of about three hours duration. When some half a dozen of these attacks had passed off, it was discovered that the sight, hearing and power of deglutition had de- parted. This latter deprivation—or ability to swallow—was most serious, as it prevented the administering of medicine or food in the ordinary manner. Although the two Avenues of sense—seeing and hearing, were cut off, it was discovered that the interesting patient could see and hear by second sight, or clairvoyant appreciation. A dim realization of sights and sounds, is borne to the brain along the weakened nerves, by which she is enabled to appreciate the unwearied kindness of her friends. She is, whenever able to communicate, in a perfectly conscious state, and all the mental operations appear to progress as usual.

Occasionally the muscles controlling the throat relax, when for a time she is able to articulate indifferently through her clenched teeth. For the most part she is compelled to communicate by writing, an operation rendered additionally difficult by the fact of the tentanic action of the muscles of the hands, which are closed forcibly and in which a pen can be held only by forcing it between the closed fore-finger and the rigid thumb. In this way she writes beautifully, and in a letter to her physician—than whom no member of the profession in this city stands higher—she explains in beautiful, regular chirography, her exact condition. One time the right hand was paralyzed, and she then wrote with her left. This paralysis appears never to leave the body, it appears successively in the arms and lower limbs.

Her Clairvoyant Condition.

When in the quiet condition of rigidity, the patient is in a trance. Her eyes closed, the ears are dead to sound, the muscles cease to act, respiration is hardly perceptible, and once or twice a state of ecstacy indicative of mental unsteadiness has resulted. These seasons last for four days, or two hours each. When in this condition, she is powerfully clairvoyant in her faculties. She can tell the time by several watches variously set to deceive her, read unopened letters, decipher the contents of a slate, and repeat what "Mrs. Grundy says," by serving up the gossip of the neighborhood. She appears to possess the faculty of second sight to a remarkable degree. In this condition she lays herself out straight, folds her arms, if able, and stares in a look of unmeaningness with calm, fixed eye at the ceiling. Thus, in all the appearance of death, she remains until she is mysteriously relieved to be plunged into the Spasmodic State, which includes trismus and tetanus as well. The spasms cause paroxysms of the muscles of voluntary motion, and produce an incurvation of the spine to an alarming degree; in one case she rolled up like a hoop, her head and feet touching. She then became curved the other way for some hours. In the spasms as in the trances, the action of the organ of excretion is natural and normal, while the respiration differs materially; in the latter condition the patient is quiet, motionless, rigid and breathes almost imperceptibly, while in the former she is continually in motion, her contortions absolutely fearful to witness and almost entirely beyond control. And yet, amid all this idiosyncratic action, her mind is as clear as ever, enabling her to smile at a good joke and compliment the maker thereof.

Of course the unfortunate has been treated for her malady, without any particular encouragement; the treatment is as peculiar as the disease. The practice of medicine, in all cases experimental to a degree, is entirely so in this one. During last week the patient fell into a deep trance while sitting in a chair, her head fell back, the limbs straightened out, the hands were clenched in a grip which no power could break, and a cold condition of the body prevailed. Thus she remained—a living corpse—the incarnation of vitalized death, until Saturday morning last, when the muscular rigidity ceased, except in her right arm and lower limbs. During all this time she could neither hear, see, feel, taste nor smell, all the Avenues of life and communication were cut off. To test this, the flesh was perforated with pins, knives were used and the most powerful blisters applied to the cuticle, but without the least visible effect. The nerves were thoroughly paralyzed,

"MAD" MOLLIE

no sensation could be communicated through them, and the prostrated girl, living in the rigidity of death, remains unconscious of the usual painful operations performed upon her. The strongest mustard plaster will have no more effect upon the appearance of her skin even, than would an application of water. Every function appears as if held in abeyance, every Avenue of communication obstructed.

What was Tried.

At first a homoeopathic physician was engaged for the sufferer; but little pills and teaspoonfuls of A and B were useless, as deglutition was important in consequence of the almost hermetical closing of the throat. Homoeopathy was then succeeded by hydropathy and the unnerved young girl was showered with cold water to produce a shock and thus restore the action of her nerves. Her spine was frozen by ice, and finally by this " treatment," long since abandoned even in insane asylums, she was very nearly washed into her grave. Her abnormal condition became aggravated instead of yielding, and a change of physicians was effected. An allopathy representative came next and found his patient in a trance.

He began by administering food and nourishment by enemas, and on Saturday, for the first time in seven weeks, the tracheal muscles of the patient relaxed slightly, and her physician, by forcing the pliable extension of a throat syringe past the obstructed point, was enabled to inject a little soup and milk punch into the stomach. Last Sunday she had a spasm but no trance followed. This is found as a good sign by the physician, who now dares to hope that the unfortunate young girl may ultimately be restored to a moderate degree of health.

Persons who believe in Spiritualism, as expounded by Andrew Jackson Davis, table-tipping, Rochester rapping, etc., claim that this is simply a case of spirit mediumship in which a bevy of bad spirits capture a human body vi et armis, and hold it as the Board of Health proposes to hold the westerly point of Coney Island. The physicians hold that it is simply an utter prostration of nervous power, susceptible of cure under careful treatment. Non-professionals will, of course, side with those whose hypotheses appears the most rational.

"MAD" MOLLIE

CHAPTER XVII.

Mr. Epes Sargent's Defense of Miss Fancher and Correspondence.

As might have been expected, the publication in the Brooklyn Eagle, aroused public curiosity, and a hunt was at once commenced to ascertain the whereabouts and name of the remarkable invalid. Her identity could not long be concealed. Then her home was at once invaded by reporters, and hundreds of other people, anxious to learn more of the phenomenal parts of her case, or to satisfy their curiosity and be able to say that they had seen Mollie Fancher. From that time to the present, at short intervals, the press has flamed out with statements concerning her. Some have been founded upon previously published accounts, with imaginative interviews added by the enterprising reporter. The determined efforts of Miss Fancher not to be constantly before the public, and her refusal to permit physicians, other than her own, to visit her bedside, tended to create adverse criticism, from which she was destined to suffer in any event. She denied the right of the public to be informed of her condition, and even forbade her physicians and intimate friends to give out for publication anything concerning her. But even these precautions were insufficient to secure the privacy she desired. Some of the publications concerning her were cruel in the extreme.

By some persons she was pronounced a fraud and an impostor, and the fact that she was living so long without food was denied. She was publicly accused of deception, and such physicians as Doctors William A. Hammond and Geo. M. Beard, of the City of New York, spoke and wrote of her very disparagingly, without ever having seen her!

On November 25th, 1878, the report of an interview by a reporter of the New York Sun, was published in that paper, with Dr. William A. Hammond, in which the reporter informed Dr. Hammond, that Miss Fancher had the testimony of such men as Rev. Dr. Duryea, the Rev. Dr. Van Dyck, Prof. West, Henry Parkhurst, the astronomer, and such physicians as Drs. Speir and Ormiston, as to the genuineness of her case.

108

Dr. Hammond in reply is reported to have said, "I know that they are all deceived—lied to by this hysterical girl."

"But," said the reporter, " see what tests she was subjected to. How can there be any deception? " To which the doctor replied, " Well there is deception in all. It's all a humbug. Why, my dear fellow, she is not the first girl that has deceived learned and good men. There are plenty of cases of simulative hysteria, and Miss Fancher's is one. I haven't seen her, never heard of her before; but I have heard of so many other similiar cases that I do not hesitate to speak strongly about it."

"But," said the reporter, "how do you account for her second sight; her reading a paper that she doesn't see; her telling the contents of a sealed envelope?"

"She can't do it," said the doctor, vehemently. "She can do nothing of the kind. I'll bet $3,000 she can't do it before me. I will write a check for over $1,000, and if she will tell me the exact amount, the bank on which it is drawn, and describe the check generally, I'll give it to her. Why, I can read you case after case where these hysterical girls have deceived thousands. Take the matter of visions. This girl in Brooklyn is a Protestant so she confines her visions to seeing heaven and her dead friends. Were she a Catholic she'd see the Virgin Mary or the Saviour, like that girl at Lourdes, who sees the Virgin, and who actually has been the means of having a church built on the spot where the vision appears. You have seen accounts of the excitement she has created. Why, she is Simply a Cataleptic.

"I have myself, had under my immediate charge, fifty girls and women who in the condition of ecstacy, have had visions of all sorts, all the way from God himself down to the schoolmistress who had locked them up in dark closets. I tell you that those people in Brooklyn are of two classes—those who lie and those who are deceived. Mind you, I do not say that Miss Fancher is to blame, that she does all this intentionally. Hysteria prompts deception. It is a characteristic of the disease. She has probably not will enough to overcome the desire to deceive. But she should be aided in every way to overcome the desire, not assisted in her deceptions. For all this is simply the deception of a hysterical girl."

"But she has deceived clergymen and physicians."

"Oh, that's nothing. Clergymen are the most gullible men in the world, and physicians who have not made a study of nervous diseases are apt to be imposed upon by these girls."

"MAD" MOLLIE

In an article published in the New York Sun, December 23d, 1878, is an extract from a tract entitled "The Scientific Lessons of the Mollie Fancher Case," by Geo. M. Beard, M. D., New York, in which he says:"Unsought-for evidence has been brought to me from various quarters—from physicians and from clergymen as honorable and able as any whose names have appeared in connection with this case—that Mollie Fancher intentionally deceives; that she lives on the fat of the land; that the fancy articles she professes to make are made for her; that her reading without eyes is done by trickery; but all this, like the evidence on the opposite side, is of a non-expert character, and can, in science, receive no consideration."

To these attacks, numerous answers were made through the press, and among others who took up the cause on behalf of Miss Fancher, was Mr. Epes Sargent, a man of great literary attainments, a careful student of psychology, a well-known writer. He wrote an exceedingly able article which was published in the Sun of December, 1878, in answer to these unworthy criticisms and assaults upon Miss Fancher. The publication of his letter called forth from Miss Fancher a note to him, expressing her thanks for his kindness in defending her.

The following is Mr. Sargent's reply to the assaults upon Miss Fancher, and also a personal letter to her, in reply to a letter of thanks to him.

CHAPTER XVIII.

Mr. Epes Sargent to the New York Sun.

To the Editor of the Sun:

Sir.—In a tract entitled " The Scientific Lessons of the Mollie Fancher Case," by George M. Beard, M. D., New York, the writer says: "Unsought for evidence has been brought to me from various quarters, from physicians and from clergymen as honorable and as able as any whose names have appeared in connection with this case, that Mollie Fancher intentionally deceives; that she lives on the fat of the land; that the fancy articles she professes to make are made for her; that her reading without eyes is done by trickery; but all this, like the evidence on the opposite side, is of a non-expert character, and can, in science, receive no consideration."

So it would require an expert, would it, to decide whether Miss Fancher "lives on the fat of the land;" an expert like Dr. Beard? No butcher, cook, maitre d'hotel, or lovers of good eating would be competent to decide the question!

I have no acquaintance whatever with Miss Fancher or any of the persons who have testified in her case, so I will leave it to her friends to answer (if they have not already done so), what seems to me a very gross and uncalled-for attack on a lady prostrated by disease. It is very much as if one were to publish a paragraph like this: "Unsought for evidence has been brought me from various quarters, by most honorable and trustworthy persons, that Dr. Blank is a forger, a thief and a murderer; but as the testimony is of an entirely non-expert character it can, in science, receive no consideration."

Could Mrs. Candor herself have done it better than Dr. Beard in this attempt to slay a reputation? Sheridan's lady limited her scandalous remarks to the drawing room; the doctor sends his broadcast over the land in a published tract.

It is not surprising that Dr. Beard should be very much disturbed by the strong and respectable testimony, recently published in The Sun, in regard to certain remarkable phenomena similar to those which he has been denouncing lustily for several years as impostures or delusions. He is committed to a theory which would dismiss all supersensual facts as impossibilities. Having claimed that only an "expert" is qualified to observe a fact in clairvoyance, to comprehend whether Miss Fancher, or any one else, really ever did read through the folds of a sealed letter, or utter certain words, indicating prevision, or execute a piece of fancy work in the dark; and having further claimed that in the whole world at this time there are only seven or eight experts of the kind needed, he gives us very clearly to infer that Dr. Beard is one of those seven or eight highly gifted persons, nay, the very Corypheus of the band.

But when we come to inquire into his claims to be recognized as an expert, we find that they are mainly of a negative kind; based, not on his acquaintance with inductive facts, but on his estimate of his own remarkable cleverness at "deductive reasoning" Great as a physician, it seems he is greater as a metaphysician; and it is in this latter capacity that he appears in assuming to decide what things are subjects for scientific inquiry, and what are not, and whether or not Miss Fancher is an impostor.

Why is clairvoyance untrue, according to Dr. Beard? And he gives us to understand that it is untrue, because "absolutely disproved by deductive reasoning," and because the "special sciences," to which its claims must be referred, know them "to be false, without any examination!"

So it appears that his "expertness" is derived mainly from not knowing certain facts which certain weak-minded persons, like Sir Wm. Hamilton, Dr. Wm. Gregory, Professor of Chemistry in the University of Edinburgh; the nine members of the five-year Special Commission on Mesmerism of the French Royal Academy of Medicine, together with Archbishop Whately, Dr. Elliotson, Dr. Ashburner, Dr. Esdale and others, after long and patient investigation, have claimed to know.

If this be not a somewhat arbitrary extension into the domain of positive science, of the etymological process by which lucus was said to be derived a non lucendo, what is it? Truly, it saves a deal of trouble, but how is it made available in the education of an expert? There I confess myself nonplussed.

Deductive reasoning may err, as well as intuitive judgment. It was deductive reasoning that led Bacon, Melanchthon, Luther and other learned men to reject the Copernican system. Deductive reasoning opposed the introduction of gas, the system of cheap postage and ocean steamship navigation. It refused to look through Galileo's telescope. It was very incredulous also as to the possibility of Edison's talking machine, and it has stood in the way of many great inventions and wise reforms.

Dr. Beard divides the universe into the known, the unkown and the supernatural; and he tells us that "in the realm of the supernatural all things are possible and all things are undemonstrable."

Now, would it not be a little less unscientific to say that we really do not know whether there is anything supernatural; that what seems to us such may be merely the natural unrecognized or misunderstood? What possible reason has a man claiming to be a man of science, for saying that "in the realm of the supernatural all things are possible," when he does not even know of the existence of the supernatural?

Ruling out the supernatural as merely the imaginary, what right, then, has Dr. Beard to say that certain well-attested facts are legitimate subjects of scientific inquiry, and others are not? How, except under his arbitrary metaphysical assumptions is he going to make even a show of a defense? He would subject the proof of a fact to the same a priori limitations as the proof of a hypothetical proposition. The rotundity of the earth would not have been proved to this day if men of science had been " experts " of the type of Dr. Beard, and maintained that facts cannot be demonstrated as well as propositions, or that they can be annihilated by his deductive reasoning.

The trouble with him is, that he confounds deductive evidence with intuitive, and vice versa. Now, it is demonstrative evidence only that is in the true sense scientific; and how, out of his purely negative notions, is he going to give us any demonstrable proof of his negations? In his claim to judge of scientific possibilities by his "deductive reasoning," he is simply an idealist or an intuitionalist; and in his presumption that he can truly test the delicate psychical phenomena in Miss Fancher's case by his rude, material, dictatorial process, irrespective of the subtle influence which his very presence, in his aggressive, positive, unsympathetic state of mind, would introduce, he is a coarse realist and no more qualified as an "expert" to discover the real facts of such a case than a blacksmith or a pavior (a paver).

To show how far Dr. Beard is merely a despotic idealist in attempting to invalidate by his "deductive reasoning," certain perfectly well established facts, let me call the reader's attention to the following:

"MAD" MOLLIE

In the year 1826 the Royal Academy of Medicine in Paris appointed a commission of eleven members, who inquired into the whole subject of mesmerism for five years, and, in 1831, reported in full, and in favor of the reality of almost all the alleged phenomena, including clairvoyance. Of the eleven members, nine attended the meeting and experiments, and all nine signed the report, which was therefore unanimous. They say:"We have seen two somnambulists distinguish, with their eyes shut, objects placed before them; name cards, read books, writing, &cetra. This phenomenon took place even when the opening of the eyelids was accurately closed by means of the fingers."

Here was a body of nine trained and skeptical physicians, undoubted experts (though, perhaps, not after Dr. Beard's definition), who examined the subject experimentally for five years, and then unanimously reported that clairvoyance is a fact. Does Dr. Beard flatter himself that he can annihilate such testimony by his "deductive reasoning?" Or that his claim to be an expert on this one subject can be admitted by those who have studied it practically not only for five, but for forty-five years?

Dr. Georget, of Paris, in his day an expert in nervous and cerebral pathology, was the author (182 1) of a much esteemed work on the "Physiology of the Nervous System," in which he boldly professed materialism. But in his last will and testament he writes: "Hardly had my 'Physiology' appeared, when renewed meditations on a very extraordinary phenomenon, somnambulism, no longer permitted me to entertain doubts of the existence within us, and external to us, of an intelligent principle, altogether different from material existences; in a word, of the soul and God. With respect to this I have a profound conviction, founded upon facts which I believe to be incontestable. This declaration will not see the light till a period when its sincerity will not be doubted, nor my intentions suspected."

It was not published till after his death.

And this expert in nervous disease, Dr. Georget, was converted from materialism by facts quite similar to those attested by Dr. Duryea and others in Miss Fancher's case. But Georget was not the only eminent expert converted from materialism. Dr. Beard has of course heard of Cabanis, author of " Rapports du Physique et du Moral de l 'homme." His writings have been a vast storehouse of facts for materialists. Yet in a posthumous letter, published by Dr. Beard, Cabanis emphatically abandons his materialistic conclusions, and formally recognizes the necessity of an immaterial or spiritual principle. Few of the writers, who are now using the arguments of Cabanis against the existence of psychical power in man, ever mention the interesting fact that he lived to retract his error.

A clairvoyant boy at Plymouth, England, whose case will be found reported in the " Zoist " (vol. IV, pp. 84-88), was subjected to the examination of a skeptical committee whose names are given, and who seem to have done their work very thoroughly. First his eyes were examined, and it was found that the balls were so turned up that, even were the eyelids a little apart, ordinary vision was impossible. Then he was closely watched, and while the eyelids were seen to be perfectly closed he read easily. Then adhesive plaster was applied, carefully warmed, in three layers, and it was watched to see that the adhesion was perfect all round the edges. Again the boy read what was presented to him—sometimes easily, sometimes with difficulty. At the end of the experiments the plaster was taken off strip by strip by the committee, and it was found to be perfectly secure and the eyelids so completely glued together that it was a work of some difficulty to get them open again.

Is a case like this one in which " deductive reasoning " must be permitted to make us insensible to the force of facts, perfectly well attested, continually repeated, and more common now than they have been for the last fifty years? If facts are to be thus left to the mercy of an individual's deductive reasoning, why not dispense with a jury in our courts of law, and employ some expert of a judge to render verdicts?

Dr. Schmitz, Rector of the High School at Edinburgh, whose school books, published by the Messrs. Harper, are used in many American schools, had a clairvoyant at his house, who accurately described Prof. Gregory's house, and the persons at that time in the dining-room (afterward ascertained to be correct.) As a further test, Dr. Schmitz was asked to go into another room with his son and do anything he liked. The boy then described their motions, by jumping about, the son going out and coming in again, and the doctor beating his son with a roll of paper. When Dr. Schmitz returned, Prof. Gregory repeated all the boy had said, which the doctor, much astonished, declared to be correct in every particular.

A party of experts, of whom Sergeant Cox, a well-known lawyer of London, and President of the Psychological Society, was one, was planned to test Alexis, the famous French clairvoyant. A word was written by a friend in a distant town and enclosed in an envelope without any of the party knowing what the word was. This envelope was enclosed in six others of thick brown paper, each sealed. The packet was handed to Alexis, who placed it on his forehead, and in three minutes and a half wrote the contents correctly, imitating the very handwriting. (See "What am I?" by Sergeant Cox; vol. 2, page 167. It may be found in the Boston Public

Library.)

Robert Houdin, of Paris, the greatest of modern conjurers, whose exploits were well known, took his own cards and dealt them himself, but Alexis named them as they lay upon the table and even named the trump before it was turned up. This was repeated several times, and Houdin declared that neither chance nor skill could produce such wonderful results. He then took a book from his pocket and asked Alexis to read something eight pages beyond where it was opened, at a specified level. Alexis pricked the place with a pin, and read four words, which were found at the place pricked, nine pages on. He then told Houdin numerous details as to his son, in some of which Houdin tried to deceive him, but in vain; and when it was over, Houdin declared that the facts reported were correct, adding: "The more I reflect upon them the more impossible do I find it to class them among the tricks which are the objects of my art." His two letters were published at the time in La Siecle, May, 1847.

Will Dr. Beard contend that Houdin, the most expert of conjurers, and whose business it was to find out every trick that he could utilize to strike one with astonishment, was not, after all, so much of an expert as himself; that he did not know how to investigate by "deductive reasoning" and that what he thought he saw did not happen? If the doctor can find any persons simple enough to believe such a claim, he is quite welcome to such converts.

Capt. R. F. Burton, the famous English traveler and explorer, in a letter to the London Times (Nov., 1876), writes: "The experience of twenty years has convinced me that perception is possible without the ordinary channels of the senses;" and he remarks on the subject of clairvoyance, that it is to be proved or disproved, not by hard words, nor by mere logic, but by experiment and facts."

A very different opinion, it would seem, from that of Dr. Beard, who wishes us to take it for granted that his " deductive reasoning " must settle the matter, and if facts contradict that, why then so much the worse for the facts !

Dr. F. Lefebre, Professor of Pathology in the University of Louvain, a very learned physician, would not have discredited Dr. Speir's testimony even to an instance of prevision on the part of Miss Fancher, for he writes: "It is possible that the power of foresight by somnambulists may be raised to a degree far above the ordinary level, and that they can sometimes penetrate into the future so far as to excite our utmost astonishment."

Unnumbered incidents, similar to those I have related, might be quoted. I have witnessed many myself during the last forty years, and I have seen what the cleverest conjurers can do in imitation of clairvoyance and mind-reading; but I will take the word of the best of them that the process by which the genuine clairvoyant gets his knowledge is incommunicable. Mr. Bidder, the highly esteemed English arithmetician, who excited wonder when a boy by his instantaneous answers to complex questions in arithmetic, on being asked, how he did it, replied, "I don't do it—I see it." And the clairvoyant can give no better explanation than this.

The only true experts in such a phenomenon as clairvoyance are those who have studied it experimentally for a long series of years, coordinated the facts, ruled out all that was doubtful, and by repeated tests satisfied themselves, under a great variety of conditions, and through many clairvoyant subjects, young and old, the sound in body and the unsound, the ignorant and the educated, that the existence of such a faculty is proved beyond a question. The very element of positive, aggressive distrust, which Dr. Beard would bring to the investigation of so subtle a phenomenon, would be fatal to any satisfactory result.

A name or a fact which we try to force ourselves to remember may evade our most anxious endeavor. But if we give it up, and think of something else, it may soon start up, automatically, as it were, and summon consciousness to seize it. Every experienced investigator knows that the most wonderful proofs of clairvoyance are those that are unexpected and spontaneous. Try to extort them by your imperious manner, or manifest distrust, (and you cannot well feel it without manifesting it to clairvoyant sympathies) and you spoil the conditions, and perhaps go away ignorantly pronouncing it all a delusion.

" Fear of experts," says Dr. Beard, referring to Miss Fancher's case, " s one of the symptoms, almost pathagnomic." Not a fear of genuine experts, but a sense of the folly of dallying with those persons who are strongly committed against the fact, and who bring the predetermination not to be convinced, is the real motive that makes the sensitive subject shy of such experimenters.

Dr. Beard tells us that " human testimony is the product of the human brain." It was but just now that Dr. Hammond, who also denounces the Fancher narrative as "all humbug," and who asserts that " there never was a case of clairvoyance," told us that " the spinal cord and sympathetic ganglia are not devoid of mental power." How, then, do we know that human testimony does not come from the ganglia? Once it used to be thought that mental manifestations came from what the simple still call the mind; and that the brain was merely an instrument for thought, even as the eyes are for seeing, and the ears for hearing. But "nous avons change tout cela."

Thought is now merely a product of the movement of certain kaleidoscopic molecules in the brain; and if I think differently from Dr. Beard he must not blame me, since it is merely because the molecules in my brain get disposed, or shaken up, differently from those of his own.Thus thought lacks the character of logical necessity, and universal truths are impossible, all except those that come from his own individual " deductive reasoning." Here are his words: "Human testimony is the product of the human brain, and its scientific study belongs to those who, like physicians, devote themselves to the study of the brain in health and disease."

So, then, it now appears that all these books that have been written on mental philosophy, the human understanding, logic, and the laws of evidence by the Aristotles, Lockes, Berkeleys, Humes, Kants, Hegels, Hamiltons, Mills, Von Hartmanns, Blackstones, Kents and Storys must be displaced as rubbish to make room for the writings of Drs. Beard and Hammond!

And if Dr. Beard is an expert in judging of human testimony, why not in judging of other "products of the human brain," and for the same reason? Why can he not lay down for us laws of taste in poetry, painting, music, and general literature? Are they not all, equally with human testimony, products of the human brain, and does not their "scientific study" belong to one who devotes himself "to the study of the human brain in health and disease?"

Dr. Beard says: "We have not in our profession a more honorable or able body of men than some of the Brooklyn physicians who have been, directly or indirectly, connected with the case of Miss Fancher; and yet the instincts of the majority, both of general practitioners and specialists of nervous diseases, reject all of their testimony relating to the claims of clairvoyance, mind reading, and prophecy."

This time it is instincts that must be admitted to the witness stand under Dr. Beard's ruling. When it comes to quoting the "instincts" of certain physicians as any authority in a question of clairvoyance, is it not in order for Dr. Beard to explain how it is that the instincts, coupled with the long and multiplied observations of men like the Rev. Dr. Duryea, Prof. Chas. E. West, Henry M. Parkhurst, and Dr. Speir, all in Miss Fancher's favor, should not be as authoritative as the instincts of professional persons experimentally unacquainted with the facts, probably not knowing Miss Fancher, and who now, on purely a priori grounds, mere instincts, would impugn her honesty? "Instincts and deductive reasoning!" Does Dr. Beard really suppose that men seriously in search of facts, are to be staggered by arguments like these?

But Dr. Beard is not without a precedent. There is another eminent authority, one who in a certain department was himself an expert, who thought as highly as he of instinct, and said:"Beware instinct ! The lion will not touch the true prince. Instinct is a great matter. I was a coward on instinct. I shall think better of myself and thee, during my life; I for a valiant lion, and thou for a true prince."

"Studying the subject through the reason," says Dr. Beard, "we know deductively by the law of biology that no member of the human species can have any quality different in kind from those that belong to the race."

If anything were needed to show the shallowness of Dr. Beard's pretensions to be an expert in regard to clairvoyance and cognate phenomena, this one sentence would suffice. What real expert denies that clairvoyance is a faculty probably latent m all human beings, but developed only under certain conditions, abnormal or infrequent? Because an adult man may not be able to tell one tune in music from another, and little Mozart at five years of age shows marvelous powers both in executing and composing music, do we infer that Mozart had "a quality different in kind from those that belong to the race?"

Dr. Beard takes certain facts gleaned from his experience as a medical advisor in nervous diseases, and rejects, simply because they do not harmonize with his foregone theory, a large class of other facts gleaned by competent persons giving special attention to the mental phenomena manifested. How, then, can we place any reliance upon the deductions made by him from laws or rules derived not from all the facts, but from only a few, and those, perhaps, purely physical in their nature? In what possible way has he qualified himself to pronounce against facts which he has not witnessed, but which are amply attested by other persons, including physicians?

" Why, by my deductive reason!" he will reply, while the truth is that there is no reason in his deduction, since he has accepted but a portion of the facts and arbitrarily excluded others which he claims to know, " without examination," are false. It follows, then, that what he calls his deductive reasoning has no more scientific value than the "instincts" which he felicitates himself on, as having led some of his professional brethren to charge Miss Fancher with fraud.

Unless the Fancher case is overturned by something very different from the impotent and unscientific antagonism of Dr. Beard, its well attested facts must be a valuable contribution to that enlarged science of psychology, the materials for which have been fast accumulating during the last hundred years, and never more rapidly than during the last ten.

EPES SARGENT

P. S.—I have just learnt that Dr. Hammond proposed to test Miss Fancher by placing in an envelope a check for a sum of money over $1,000, and having her tell, in the presence of three scientific examiners, two of them being competent neurologists, the amount, number, date, on whom drawn, signature, etc., she to have the money in the event of her success.

Ever since Puysegur's experiments in 1784, offers like this have been repeatedly made, as Dr. Hammond must be aware, and declined generally in cases where some experienced person had charge of the sensitive subject. And why declined? Because you might as well expect the needle to point true while you are agitating the compass as expect to elicit clairvoyance under the stress and excitement of an anxious motive, or under the disturbance produced by the simple presence of an uncongenial person, aggressively disposed.

Suppose some "expert" should go to Dr. Hammond and say, "Here is a certified check for ten thousand dollars, and now you shall have it if you will mention right off, within thirty seconds, the names of six classmates with whom you went to school when a boy." Would not the doctor (if he were in need of the $10,000, which I hope he is not), be likely to feel some little tremor and doubt, which would paralyze the effort of memory? And yet, in familiar conversation, where nothing was exacted and nothing at stake, and he was not limited as to time, how readily might he mention the six names in the thirty seconds!

Clairvoyance is a phenomenon as delicate and uncertain as that manifested in the caprices—the sudden flashes and sudden eclipses of memory. A subject's lucidity is always impaired or spoiled by anything that excites anxiety or irritation, or appeals to cupidity. Nay, the very presence of a person convinced that there is imposture and eagerly bent on detecting it, would, without any external manifestation, be felt by a sensitive as readily as she might feel, in her normal state, a freezing current of air.

Every patient investigator knows all this; and it was the reason why such physicians as Dr. Gregory and Dr. Haddock, having the command of clairvoyants, always refused to subject them to the money test. Such negative proofs of indisposition to act, under conditions that would introduce all these adverse influences, do not reach the real truth, for, as Mr. A. R. Wallace remarks: "How can any number of individual failures affect the question of the comparatively rare successes? As well deny that any rifleman can hit the bull's eye at one thousand yards because none can be sure of hitting it always and at a moment's notice."

Of course, by the skeptical and ignorant, the answer to these reasons will be an incredulous shrug. The reasons are good and true, nevertheless, and all eminent students of the subject of somnambulism, whether spontaneous or induced by mesmerism, have come to this conclusion.

" I think we may now regard it as established," says Dr. Gregory, "that (in clairvoyance) the subject often possesses a new power of perception, the nature of which is unknown, but by means of which he can see objects o r persons, near or distant, without the use of external organs of vision; and my own prolonged experience amply confirms all this."

The over confident attacks of Drs. Hammond and Beard are merely repetitions of what has been going on the past hundred years; and when the money test has been proposed and rejected, the ignorant have cried out, as perhaps they will cry now, " This settles the thing." But, no; the thing has been many times settled in that way, and has not stayed settled. Where there were ten believers in clairvoyance thirty years ago, there are ten thousand now. It is useless for vis to point to the interminable accumulations of ever-recurring testimony in behalf of the great phenomenon; for these soi-distant experts take the ground that the testimony of the whole human race would be of no avail against their own " deductive reasoning." Of what use is it, then, to dispute with such persons, since they substantially tell us that facts of nature, abundantly attested and proved, must give way to their own individual preconceptions of what it is proper for nature to permit? But, as Lord Bacon well remarks:"The voice of nature will consent, whether that of man do or no, instincts and deductive reasoning," prepossessions and metaphysical crotches, to the contrary not withstanding.

Mr. Epes Sargent to Miss Fancher.
Dear Miss Fancher:

Your interesting letter of January 4th gave me much pleasure. You owe me nothing in the way of thanks, for to me you were an impersonality (though now— I hope a friend) and what I wrote was for the impersonal truth. I knew that your two principal assailants, Doctors Beard and Hammond, were as ignorant as they were audacious on the subject of clairvoyance. What can be said of the discretion or good sense of a man who could publish a sentence like this by Dr. Beard: "It is a fact, capable of absolute proof that no phenomena of this kind" (clairvoyance) "has ever appeared in the world in any human creature, in the trance or out of the trance." That is to say, it is a fact "capable of absolute proof," that Christ never told the woman of Samaria—"all things that ever she did." That Henry the Fourth of France did not say, as he was going out on the day of his assassination, "I shall meet with misfortune." That Swedenborg did not describe the great fire at Stockholm, and that Miss Fancher never read a letter clairvoyantly. A physician who affirms that it is "capable of absolute proof," that such occurrences never took place, is quite as much of a blockhead as the Irishman, who, being on trial for stealing a pig, wanted to call in a dozen of his neighbors to testify, that they did not see him steal it.

Gross insinuations from such a quarter must not disturb you. The psychical faculties manifested in your case are undoubtedly the property of all men, though rarely developed to consciousness in this stage of being. Dr. Beard founds the objections of what he calls his " deductive reasoning" on a stupid misconception, this—namely, that your case contradicted the principle that " no human being ever has any faculty different in kind from that conferred on the human race in general." Now, there is no such contradiction. What your case helps to prove is— that there are psychical, supersensual or spiritual faculties in the human being generally. That these faculties, being independent of the appropriate physical organs, and transcending all material limitations, must inhere in an entity, of which the physical body is merely the temporary instrument, must belong, in short, to what St. Paul calls " the spiritual body." And thus your experiences help to corroborate the pneumatology of the Hebrew and Christian Scriptures, and to give us a rational and strictly scientific ground for regarding the term immortality, or not death, as etymologically correct, and as directly applicable to the individual man, since all of him that dies is the external husk—whose atoms have been always in a state of flux and departure, and which death disintegrates, leaving the spiritual organism emancipate and unharmed.

Now this view, scriptural, aboriginal, and common even to uncivilized tribes—a view also in strict harmony with absolute science—is one against which the physicists of our day are arrayed in deadly hostility. They have perfected their opinions, and a phenomenon like clairvoyance would be a disturbing element, would compel them to go to school again, and to learn something from cases like yours. This they cannot afford to do. That anything substantial, though unseen, leaves the body at death—that there are supersensual faculties—they will not believe. Physicists like Tyndall and Youmans, tell us that the psychic realm is ultra-scientific, and does not belong to the realm of nature; that theologians and speculative philosophers may amuse themselves in that fanciful region, but that grave men of science cannot recognize its existence. Now this is all untrue and mischievous; untrue because directly contradicted by such phenomena as your case has developed; and mischievous because such assumptions lead to a Sadduceean philosophy, that rejects immortality as a myth, and religion as a chimera fit only for children and old women. We hold that the phenomena of your case belong strictly to the realm of nature, and that the psychic faculty may be proved equally with the mathematical or the musical.

And so, dear Miss Fancher, I hope it will be a joy and a comfort to you, to realize that your life has not been fruitless. That you have been highly privileged by Providence in helping us to strike a telling blow at the wretched Sadduceeism of our age, towards which the physical sciences seem to be leading those who ignore such facts as your case exhibits, though all positive and genuine science is, as it advances, helping to confirm and illustrate these supersensual facts, and must ever be in full harmony with them. I fear I must have wearied you with my long letter, if so, let the motive exculpate me, and believe me.
Very sincerely your friend,

EPES. SARGENT.

P. O. Box 2985.

Miss Mollie Fancher, Brooklyn, N. Y.

CHAPTER XIX.

The Testimony of Prof. Charles E. West and Henry M. Parkhurst.

No gentleman in Brooklyn has more respect in the community, than Prof. Charles E. West, principal of the Brooklyn Heights Seminary, with whom Miss Fancher studied so many years before her accident.

This gentleman is well and hearty, though upwards of eighty years of age. He retains all his intellectual faculties seemingly unimpaired. He visited Miss Fancher soon after the features of her case began to develop in producing the phenomena which have attracted so much attention. He made careful notes of what he observed upon the occasions of his visits to her house, and for the period of about twenty-six years, it is seldom that two weeks have gone by, without his being at her bed-side, as a friend, to talk with her, and give her cheer in the midst of her sufferings. He has placed in a scrap-book, numerous clippings from the newspapers, of publications concerning her. Those regarding himself I understand from him to be substantially authentic.

His letter published November 10th, 1878, in the Buffalo Courier, will be found of great interest. Although repeating some things which have already been written, it is deemed important to publish it in full. It is as follows:

MOLLIE FANCHER.

Buffalo Courier.

Sunday Morning, November 10, 1878.

Dr. West's Account of a Most Remarkable Case—Twelve Years Without Food —Extraordinary Physical and Mental Conditions—Clairvoyance and Other Preternatural Faculties—"Nothing to Die."

The interest that has been aroused recently in this city in the remarkable case of Miss Mollie Fancher, will insure an eager perusal for the following letter from Dr. West, principal of Brooklyn Heights Seminary, which we are kindly permitted to publish. It was written to a lady of this city in answer to inquiries as to the facts of Miss Fancher's condition:

The Letter.
Brooklyn, October 8, 1878.

Dear Madame:—You request me to write a brief sketch of Miss Mollie Fancher in answer to the many questions which have doubtless been asked by those who have examined the beautiful specimens of her needlework, which have been sent to your loan exhibition, which were wrought during a most extraordinary illness of more than twelve years' duration. To give anything like an adequate account of this remarkable girl would require a treatise. This I cannot attempt.

Miss Mary J. Fancher was born in Attleburough, Mass., August 16, 1848, and was educated at the Brooklyn Heights Seminary under my care. She was a sweet girl of delicate organization and nervous temperament, and was highly esteemed for her pleasing manners and gentle disposition. She was an excellent scholar, excelling in belles lettres studies; but her delicate health led to her removal from school a short time before the graduation of her class in 1864. For three years I lost sight of her, till I learned from a Brooklyn paper of her singular condition, which resulted from a remarkable accident.

Her aunt soon after called and invited me to visit " Mollie," as she is familiarly called. I did so March 4, 1867; and from that time to the present I have been an intimate visitor of the family. I have kept a journal of my visits and noted all that was important which came under my observation. I have used all the sagacity I possess to detect any fraud or collusion; but I have never seen anything to excite my suspicion or mar my confidence in her integrity. She is a lovely Christian girl and shrinks from any public exhibition of herself. Spiritualists and curiosity-seekers have sought access to her, but have failed. The power of discriminating character is so great, that she is rarely ever imposed upon.

The Facts to which attention is called can be fully verified. They are as follows:

May 10, 1864—She was thrown from a horse and severely injured.

June 8, 1865—In attempting to leave a Street car her skirt caught and she was dragged for a block over the pavement.

"MAD" MOLLIE

February 2, 1866—She was taken seriously ill. Her nervous system was completely deranged. Her head and feet coming together, she would roll like a hoop; she would also stand on her toes and spin like a top. Several persons were required to prevent her from doing personal injury to herself.

Feburary 8, 1866—She went into a trance and was to all appearance dead.

February 17—She lost her eyesight.

February 18—She lost her speech.

February 19—She lost her hearing.

February 22—She saw, spoke and heard for half an hour, and then for a time lost these faculties.

February 23—She lost the sense of sound.

February 24—The fingers closed.

February 25—The jaws locked.

February 26—The legs took a triple twist.

March 7—The spasms were violent.

May 20, 1866—She asked for food, ate a small piece of cracker and took a teaspoonful of punch; it being the first food she had taken in seven weeks, and was able to retain on her stomach.

May 27, 1866—She was shocked by thunder and again lost her speech.

May 28, 1866—She went into a rigid trance at 2:30 o'clock, which lasted till 11:30 A. M. the next day. She then passed into a relaxed trance till June 1.

June 2, 1866—Nourishment was forced by a pump into her stomach, which threw her into convulsions. She was unconscious and deadly sick with nausea, and suffered intensely till Sunday evening, June 3d, when her throat closed and she was unable to take any nourishment or utter a sound.

These items are taken from the diary of Mollie's aunt, who made a daily record of her condition. I have copied but a few of them to show the beginning of her remarkable illness.

My first visit, as I have said, was March 4, 1867. I found her lying on her right side with her right arm folded under her head. Her fingers were clenched in the palm of her hand, her thumb lying parallel with them. The thumb and fingers of her left hand were in a similar position. The right hand and arm were paralyzed, as was her body generally, excepting her left arm. She was in a trance, sighed and seemed to be in pain. She remained in this trance till the 8th, a shorter time than usual at this period of her illness. Her trances often lasted from ten to twelve days.

I find my letter is growing so large I must condense my journal observations and neglect any chronological order.

I will speak of her Mental and Physical Condition.

First, her physical. For twelve years or more she has lain in one position on her right side. For nine years she was paralyzed, her muscles only relaxing under the influence of chloroform. For the last three years she has been in a new condition—the limp instead of the rigid. Her muscles are so relaxed that her limbs can be moved without the aid of choloform. While passing into this state her sufferings were intense. For days it did not seem possible that she could live. Her eyes were open and staring. For nine years they had been closed. Now they were open and never closing day or night. They were sightless. She could swallow, but take no food; even the odor of it was offensive. During this twelve years' illness there have been times when she had not the use of any one of her senses. For many days together she has been to all appearance dead. The slightest pulse could not be detected; there was no evidence of respiration. Her limbs were as cold as ice, and had there not been some warmth about her heart she would have been buried.

During all these years she has virtually Lived Without Food. Water, the juices of fruits and other liquids have been introduced into her mouth, but scarcely any of them ever make their way to her stomach. So sensitive has this organ become it will not retain anything within it. In the early part of her illness it collapsed, so that by placing the hand in the cavity her spinal column could be felt. There was no room for food. Her throat was rigid as a stick. Swallowing was out of the question.

Her heart was greatly enlarged, severe pains passed from it through her left side and shoulder. With slight exceptions she has been blind. When I first saw her she had but one sense; that of touch. With that she could read with many times the rapidity of one by eyesight. This she did by running her fingers over the printed pages with equal facility in light or darkness. With the finger, she could discriminate the photographs of persons, the faces of callers, etc. She never sleeps, her rest being taking in trances. The most delicate work is done in the night. She performs none of the ordinary functions of life, except that of breathing. The circulation is sluggish, and as a consequence there is very little animal heat. She longs to die, but says she cannot, as there is nothing to die. Such is a brief statement of her bodily condition.

Second—To me

Her Mental State is more extraordinary. Her power of clairvoyance, or second sight, is marvelously developed. All places in which she takes any interest are open to her mental vision. Distance interposes no barriers. No retirement, however secluded, but yields to her penetrating gaze. She dictates the contents of sealed letters, which have never been in her hands, without the slightest error. She visits the family circles of her relations and acquaintances in remote places and describes their attire and their occupations. She points out any disorder of dress, however slight, as the basting thread in the sleeve of a sack which to ordinary sight was concealed by the arm. Any article which has been mislaid she sees and tells where it may be found. She discriminates in darkness the most delicate shades of color with an accuracy that never errs.

She works in embroidery and wax without patterns. She conceives the most beautiful forms and combinations of forms. She never studied botany or took a lesson in wax-   work, and yet she Never Mistakes the forms of leaf or flower. Leaves with their ribs or veins, their phylotaxis; flowers, with calyx, coralla, stamens with their anthers are given with a most truthful regard to nature. Holding pen or pencil in her left hand, she writes with extraordinary rapidity. Her penmanship is handsome and legible. She once wrote a poem of ten verses in as many minutes—her thoughts flowing with the rapidity of lightning. In cutting velvet leaves for pin-cushions, like the sample sent you, she held the scissors by the knuckles of thumb and forefinger of the left hand, and bringing the velvet with thumb and finger of her right hand, she cut the leaves as sharply and without ravel as though they had been cut with a punch. These leaves do not differ in size or form more than leaves growing on tree or shrub. In the early part of her sickness, she cut more than two thousand such leaves. In April, 1875, she worked up two hundred and fifty ounces of worsted; to December, 1875, she had written six thousand five hundred notes and letters. She has kept an account of all the expenses of the family during her sickness. She keeps a daily journal, except when in trances of longer duration than twenty-four hours. In passing into the new condition, three years ago, of which I have spoken, she forgot everything that had occurred in the previous nine years. When she was able to speak, she inquired about matters that occurred at the beginning of her illness—the nine intervening years were a perfect blank to her.

Study for the Psychologist.

But I must take leave of this subject. The incredulous will not accept it—and it is not surprising. Miss Fancher is not to be judged by ordinary laws. Her state is abnormal—a species of modified catalepsy, which has deranged the ordinary action of mind and body. It is a rich mine for investigation to the physiologist and the psychologist; and with them I leave the case.

Very respectfully,
CHARLES B. WEST.

Prof. Henry M. Parkhurst, an astronomer of note, and a thorough scientist, who resides nearly opposite the residence of Miss Fancher on Gates Avenue, Brooklyn, and, whose family was on intimate terms with the family of Miss Fancher, made a careful investigation of her case, which, as will be seen, caused much comment, and the following publication resulted. Prof. Parkhurst has at my request reaffirmed, in writing, his conclusions made in 1869. His article appeared in the New York Herald, November 30th, 1878, preceded by the following:

(Editorial.)
EXPERIMENTS IN CLAIRVOYANCE.

Professor Parkhurst's interesting letter detailing an attempt to test the clairvoyant powers of Miss Fancher, the Brooklyn lady whose strange case has aroused a form of curiosity which seems latent in every man and woman, is the most important paper yet called forth by the discussion of this case. It seems hardly probable that a man of scientific bent and methodical business habits, as the writer of the letter is known to be, could have been deceived at any stage of the experiment, the details of which he gives so minutely to the public, and it is equally improbable that any of his assistants could have been familiars of the lady and thus unconsciously assisted her to that second sight which, under certain conditions, seems possible through the eyes of another. The supposed clairvoyant reading of Miss rancher was imperfect, which is a peculiarity of all attempts at second sight; but this fact is rather of the nature of proof than disproof, if there is any real connection between exhausted physical force and unusual mental vision, as has sometimes been argued by materialists, who deny that there is anything more in clairvoyance than is explicable upon physical grounds. While the intelligent public will wish the lady good riddance of the swarms of inquirers who beset her without respect for her feeble health, it will also hope that some competent person or persons may be allowed opportunity for investigating a case which, if all that it is said to be, is of exceptional importance in its relations to physical and mental science.

(New York Herald.)
IS IT MIND READING?
Miss Mollie Fancher's Talent—How She Told the Contents of Papers in Sealed Envelopes—

Professor Henry M. Parkhurst's Statements.

To the Editor of the Herald:

In view of the recent publications with regard to the remarkable case of Miss Mollie Fancher, I think it is time for me to make a statement in detail of the test of clairvoyance which I made by means of a sealed envelope in June, 1867. These publications have been thus far made without her consent and against the wishes of Miss Fancher and her friends; and as one of her friends I shall continue to keep silence with reference to the physical aspects of the case. But I have obtained from her permission to lay before your readers an exact statement of this one experiment, because it demonstrates, as it seems to me, so far as it is possible for a single experiment to demonstrate a general principle, that there may be a clairvoyance independent of mind reading. I have before me the contents of the original envelope and two statements, one of which was written at the time, and the other, containing more detail, prepared two years later at the request of her physicians. These have been returned to me for this purpose by Miss Fancher, who had possession of them; and as they will be much better evidence than my present recollection, I will give the two statements in full. They are as follows:

Tests of Mind Reading.

The accompanying envelope and its contents were prepared to test the mode in which Miss Fancher reads unopened letters or sees, to learn whether it is through the mind of some other person or direct vision. The smaller envelope was first prepared, but not being entirely satisfactory was not inserted as a test. The printed slip was so selected that no living person could by any possibility have any conception of its contents. It is probable that no human being had ever read a word of it. I knew that it was taken from the bills of the Maryland Constitutional Convention, and knew what subjects were treated of in that constitution. I have since ascertained that it was cut from the original Judiciary bill, being now section 7 of article 4.

After making several statements with regard to the contents of facts known to me, she stated that the printed slip was about ," court" and "jurisdiction" (the words being there) and contained the figures, "6, 2, 3, 4." Subsequently she was reported to me to have said that it contained the words, " No judges can see it." The letter was returned to me with the seal intact, and was opened in my presence. These I still have.

I regard the proof as complete that she read the printed slip so far as stated above, absolutely independent of all human knowledge of its contents.

HENRY M. PARKHURST.

New York, June 3, 1867.

P. S.—The words, "No judge shall sit," passed through two messengers before reaching me, and were changed on the way. I have good reason to believe they were accurately read at first.

Independent Clairvoyance.

In order to test the mode by which Miss Mollie Fancher could read unopened letters, or see, whether through the mind of some other person or by direct vision, I enclosed in an envelope a printed slip, so selected that no living person could by any possibility have any conception of its contents. It is probable that no human being had ever read a word of it. She first stated correctly several facts concerning writing within the envelope and known to me, the writing being too small to be easily read without a glass, while she seemed reluctant to read the large print which was not known to me. I do not know how she read this writing excepting that it must have been either directly or from my mind. She then stated that the printed slip was about "Court." I was not satisfied; for although I did not know it was there I might have guessed it, and by a not very remarkable coincidence the word might have been there. She next read the word "jurisdiction," stating positively that the word was there.

I was still not completely satisfied, for the same reason as before. She then stated that the slip contained the figures "6, 2, 3, 4." This I regarded as decisive, for I had no idea that there were any figures upon the slip, and should have guessed that there were not. The letter was returned to me with the seal intact, and was opened in my presence. The word " court" occurs four times, "jurisdiction" once, and the figures " 6, 2, 3, 4, 5," and no other figures.

Two points, perhaps, deserve further explanation:First, The selection of the printed slip. As an official reporter of the Maryland Constitutional Convention in 1864 I rceived several copies of every bill, portions of which I had cut out and used. I took a pile of these bills and cut through so as to form a large number of slips of envelope size, of which I saw only that on the top. The outside portion was destroyed. A friend in my presence placed the package behind his back, selected one from the interior and placed it in the envelope and destroyed the remaining slips. We then sealed the envelope, other papers having been placed in it so that no sunlight could penetrate it.

Second—The envelope was first sealed as usual, with mucilage, and then with sealing wax. The seal was intentionally done with some roughness, so as to leave an irregular edge. In order that myself and friends might know that the seal had not been tampered with, we each carefully scrutinized the accidental configuration of the edge of the sealing wax, and selected certain minute peculiarities as the test. Those peculiarities would have been destroyed by the opening of the seal. We were all satisfied each by his own selected tests, that the seal was precisely as we left it, entirely irrespective of any opinions we might have as to the moral probability of any deception. While, therefore, I am rather strengthened in the belief that that clairvoyance which derives its knowledge from other minds is most common and most easy, I know beyond the possibility of doubt that independent clairvoyance is also possible. Nearly two years have elapsed since the experiment, and no one has suggested any point in which it fails to be an experimentum crucis.

HENRY M. PARKHURST.

Is It Mind Reading?

Nearly ten years have elapsed since this second statement was written, and I have not yet been able to conceive any respect in which any test could have been made more satisfactory. My former statements are so definite that I need add but little. At that time she could not speak, so that all that was expected or desired from her was so much of an indication of the contents of the printed slip as should be absolutely beyond guessing or chance. It was for this reason that she gave me the numbers in preference to words, because they could be easily indicated by raps. When she first stated to me that the paper contained those figures in that order, and I am not sure that she was not interrupted and thus prevented from adding the number 5, I could not understand how the figures could be there at all. Then it occurred to me that probably they were some small figures put by the printer at the bottom of the bill. It was not until the envelope was opened, and found to contain section 6, with the lines numbered 2, 3, 4, 5, that the idea occurred to me that the line numbers could possibly have been upon the slip.

The only other point that seems to have been omitted in my former statements is that I entered at the time upon my pocket memorandum book at her house the contents of the envelope as she stated them to me. Then I took the envelope unopened to my office in New York, which the "friend" mentioned in the second statement occupied with me, and the envelope was carefully scrutinized by each of us, and by another gentleman whom we invited to be present. I then communicated to them the contents as stated to me, and immediately afterward opened the envelope in their presence with the result already given. This, therefore, was as much an independent test to my friend as to me, for he knew it was impossible that there could have been any collusion on my part. This friend was Dr. Edwin Leigh, well known to educators as the inventor of pronouncing orthography, which is now used in teaching children to read in all the public schools in St. Louis, Boston, Washington and other cities.

Dr. Leigh's Statement.
From Dr. Leigh I have obtained the following:
I have read the above statements and they exactly accord with my recollection. I think William Henry Burr, now of Washington city (possibly it was William Blair Lord) was present at the time of the sealing up of the envelope, but was out of the city at the time we opened it. John H. Bazin, then the printer of the Christian Leader, f and one of his compositors were present at the time the envelope was opened. We were all satisfied that it could not have been tampered with. I may add that from the manner in which the paper was selected and inserted in the envelope I think it was absolutely impossible for any one to know or to find out by the ordinary use of his senses what paper was in the envelope without opening it. The opaque papers placed on each side of the contents were such as to render it impossible to read them by transmitted light. It seemed to me conclusive proof that if there be such a thing as mind reading this could not be a case of it.

EDWIN LEIGH,
No. 1,035 Fulton Avenue,
Brooklyn.

For myself, with my other knowledge of the case, I should not have regarded the sealing of the envelope important; but I wished the test to be such as not to involve the possibility of deception, and to be so corroborated by independent observers that in the mouth of two or three witnesses every word might be established. I still believe that in this I was successful. I may add that one reason why Miss Fancher and her friends have objected to the publication of any of the facts of her case is, that the result has always been that she has been immediately beset by that class of persons who are so wanting in delicacy and common sense that, although strangers, they will intrude upon the home of a sick woman to gratify their own selfish ends. It is true that many of them profess to believe that they can do her good; but if they were honest in that they would go to her friends or her physicians, and not make that profession the excuse for annoying her. Even her circle of friends has now become so great that, unless they exercise much consideration, she will have no time for rest.

HENRY M. PARKHURST.

I have carefully reviewed the above publication of my correspondence in relation to Miss Mollie Fancher, and may add that I have never had occasion to change my views as therein expressed.

HENRY M. PARKHURST.

"MAD" MOLLIE

CHAPTER XX.

Nov. 24, 1878.
(New York Sun).

DEAD AND YET ALIVE!

The Extraordinary Case of Miss Fancher of Brooklyn.

FACTS VERIFIED BY ABUNDANT TESTIMONY.

A Mental Sight that is not the Clap-Trap of Clairvoyance.

Lying for Thirteen Years Almost Motionless, and at Times Cold with the Chill of Death and Pulseless; Blind, yet Reading with Perfect Ease; Seeing and Describing Acts and Persons Far Removed from her Bedside—Mental Phenonema that might seem incredible except for the Testimony of Physicians, Clergymen, Teachers, and Trustworthy Friends—Without Food for Months at a Time—Seeming Never to Sleep.

In Downing Street, Brooklyn, has lain for thirteen years Miss Mary J. Fancher, much of the time in a trance-like condition, with feeble heart pulsations, sluggish and almost imperceptible respiration, and the chill of death upon her flesh. At times she has been transformed into a cheerful, vivacious, intelligent, entertaining young woman, and then she has relapsed into speechlessness, blindness, deafness, and entire paralysis of the senses. She has developed most astonishing powers, resembling second sight or clairvoyance, reading with ease the contents of sealed letters, describing articles in hidden packages, perusing books while absolutely blind. Sometimes her powers are voluntary, at other times they are unconsciously exercised.

"MAD" MOLLIE

So little nourishment has she taken that it may be said she lives without food. She is surrounded by persons of social standing and refinement, and has always been exceedingly sensitive to any public mention or knowledge of her condition. She has ever repelled any effort to couple her manifestations with those of clairvoyants; has begged to be allowed to live and die in the retirement of her home, unmolested by strangers, and accessible only to her friends. Clergymen, physicians, men of letters and of intelligence have visited her. Among many who have taken a special interest in her are the Rev. Dr. Joseph T. Duryea, Pastor of the Classon Avenue Presbyterian Church; the Rev. Dr. Henry J. Van Dyck, pastor of the Clinton Street Presbyterian Church; Prof. Charles E. West, principal of the Brooklyn Heights Seminary; George W. Benson, Henry M. Parkhurst, the astronomer; James B. Smith, the well-known architect; the Rev. Mr. Moore, former pastor of the Washington Avenue (Brooklyn) Baptist Church, but now of Geneva, N. Y.; the Rev. Dr. Prime, editor of the New York Observer; Dr. S. Fleet Speir of 162 Montague Street, Dr. Robert Ormiston of 74 Hanson Place, Dr. Mitchell of 129 Montague Street, Dr. Kissam of 100 Joralemon Street, and Dr. Crane of 163 Clinton Street.

Of these gentlemen, Messrs. Speir, West, and Parkhurst have made voluminous memoranda of Miss Fancher's physical and mental changes and conditions. Miss Fancher herself has written at great length descriptions of her feelings and sensations.

PHYSICAL PHENOMENA.

The Nervous System Deranged—Sight, Hearing, Speech, and Consciousness Lost and Restored—Life Without Nourishment.

At the age of 12 years Mary J. Fancher was sent to the Brooklyn Heights Seminary, in Montague Street, and there she remained for four years. She had not vigorous health, yet she was faithful in every study, and was a close student. One of her instructors says that rarely has he seen a brighter or more interesting Miss. Her father had means to gratify her youthful inclinations. She obtained an excellent education, and at the age of 17 years was ready to graduate. About that time, in a horseback ride, she fell and several of her ribs were broken. From the injury she quickly recovered, only to meet with another, and more serious accident. As she was alighting from a horse car, the conductor, thinking that she had stepped to the ground, rang the signal to start, and turning from her, walked to the front of the car. Miss Fancher's dress caught on the step, and the starting of the vehicle threw her with violence to the pavement. She was dragged a long distance before her situation was perceived. Her spine was seriously injured and her body and head fright- fully bruised. In a short time she went into convulsions. She was carried to the residence of her aunt, Mrs. Crosby, in Downing Street, and put into the bed whence she has never been removed since, save for a few minutes at a time.

This was early in 1865. Very soon after the accident she underwent most astonishing physical changes. Her nervous system was uncontrollable whenever she was in any manner excited, while she was absolutely paralyzed at other times. In succession she was bereft of vision, speech, and hearing. From violent spasms she drifted into a trance-like state, from which it required the unremitting efforts of physicians and friends to arouse her.

At the expiration of twenty days her faculties were all restored. For half an hour she saw, articulated, and listened. Then these three senses deserted her again, and within ten more days her fingers became clenched, her jaws locked, her limbs twisted. Spasms were thereafter more frequent and violent.

Life Without Food.

The days slipped away into weeks before she was able to keep any food on her stomach, and it was just short of two months that she was without nourishment. Then very light food was one day given her with seemingly beneficial results. She has eaten altogether since that day—nearly thirteen years ago—not so much food in the aggregate as an ordinarily healthful girl of her age would eat in forty-eight hours.

Three months and a half after the accident she went into a rigid trance for twenty-one hours, and then passed into a relaxed trance that lasted for three days. Her throat became paralyzed, and she could neither swallow nor utter a sound. Her right arm doubled up back of her head and became fixed there with the rigidity of death. A year later this condition was followed by absolute rigidity of body, with the exception of the left arm and hand, which she was able to use. This latter condition, lasted for nine years, in all of which time she was continually drifting into and out of trances. She continued to be blind, the pupils of her eyes being rolled upwards, and the whites only visible when the lids were parted for examination. Very tightly indeed were the lids sealed, and with difficulty were they opened. She had the power of speech, however, almost all of the time, although it left her at intervals.

Three years ago the rigidity of her body relaxed and sight and hearing were restored. Memory of everything that had happened in the nine years disappeared. She could not recognize friends whose acquaintance had been made in that period. Her thoughts went back to events that were happening when she sank into the nine years' stupor, and she began to talk of them as though they had occurred an hour before. In all the nine years she had been in a semi-unconscious condition, possessed, however, at times of astonishing mental vigor and of mechanical ingenuity. She refused food when offered to her, saying it made her sick. Dr. Speir and Dr. Ormiston forced food into her stomach with the pump, and, after paralysis of the throat came on, tried to feed her through a silver tube inserted in the neck. Food sickened her, however, and, eventually, all efforts to induce her to take nourishment were abandoned.

At long intervals she expressed a wish for the juice of some fruit, for a bit of candy, but she rejected solid matter, and for weeks and months, according to her own assertion and that of her attendants, she swallowed nothing. Her physical condition was constantly changing. One day she was without sense except touch; the next she could hear, and taste, and talk. But her eyes did not open until at the end of the nine years.

Cold, As Though In Death.

At intervals during these nine years the body frequently became as cold as though in death, no warmth being detected except in the region of the heart. That organ kept up a slow, measured pulsation, except when she went into trances; then its beating was often imperceptible. Her head and shoulders retained their normal condition, but soon after each of these attacks her legs would be drawn up and contorted, her feet contracted. At the same time, to quote the language of her physicians, " her intestines shriveled and wasted away, leaving little more than a coating of skin over the back bone in the cavity they had occupied. They became almost entirely inoperative, and for years were completely so." She was so sensitive to heat in the nine years' period of rigidity that fire was not lighted in her room, nor was the temperature raised in any manner. In mid-winter her only covering was a single sheet, and the window was kept partly open. In all these years her right arm remained bent behind her head, and when relaxation returned at the end of that period, the member was not released from its tension, as was the rest of the body. The arm remains still in the same cramped position.

For the last three years her physical changes have been frequent and painful, and she has successively lost and regained several of the senses. From the first she has not slept, except while in a trance. Several times in the earlier years it was thought she was dead, so cold had her body become, so rigid her limbs and flesh, so motionless her lungs and heart. But vigorous rubbing with stimulating liquors, and persistent attention, brought her again to consciousness. While in the nine years of rigidity she suffered intensely from neuralgic pains. These the physicians became convinced were increased by the bad condition of her teeth, that suddenly had begun to decay. A dentist was summoned to extract them, but the jaws were so locked that it was not until chloroform was administered that her mouth could be opened. Then nearly every tooth was removed. On recovering from the influence of the chloroform she went into the most violent of all the spasms she had.

POWERS OF SECOND SIGHT.
Sealed Letters Deciphered—Distant Friends Seen and Their Surroundings Described—Works of Art Fashioned by a Blind Girl.

No sooner had Miss Fancher emerged from her first trance, soon after the accident, than she astonished her relatives by an extraordinary description of what she had seen while in that condition. It was unmistakable second sight. As the trances continued the manifestations increased. She watched and related in detail the movements of the family's friends in different parts of the city, and ultimately narrated what was happening to those who were many miles away. She read letters that were enclosed in envelopes and kept in the pockets of those about her. She recognized persons who rang the door bell, while they were still outside the house, and, of course, not visible to her. She read books whose covers were closed, and newspapers that were folded. Every day brought some new and astonishing development of this power.

Yet with all this was the most sensitive repugnance towards letting her condition become known to the general public through the newspapers, or towards being a subject of talk or gossip by strangers. Her friends were always welcome to her bedside, but it was long before a stranger was admitted, and yet longer before she could be persuaded to show her powers to any but the most intimate friends. This sensitiveness continues even to the closing of the thirteenth year of her illness. She will not consent that her friends shall give any information concerning her that is intended for publicity. And they have so far acceded to her desires that, although repeatedly sought for, it is not until very recently that any details of her curious existence have been obtained.

She numbers among her frequent visitors, clergymen, physicians, scholars, and men of science, many of whose names are mentioned in this article, and all of whom are instantly attracted by her marvelous condition. She lies in a modest yet comfortable home, surrounded by the fashionable Avenues of that part of Brooklyn known as the Hill. Her intelligent and lady-like bearing, the unquestionable position of those with whom she is surrounded, her unmistakable truthfulness, the abhorrence with which she regards publicity, and the absence of any motive for enriching herself or her friends by the use of her gifts, seem to those who have studied her case to preclude the possibility of intentional deception or imposition.

Her Appearance in Trance.

It is in the condition of trance that Miss Fancher makes her most astonishing revelations. At these times she suddenly starts as though charged from an electric battery, and instantly becomes rigid in every joint and muscle. Her face takes on sometimes a most painful expression, at others one of positive pleasure; yet oftener it is as the face of one who is dead. To those unaccustomed to seeing her, the conviction that she is indeed dead is irresistible. A deathlike pallor creeps over the already pale face. Not the slightest movement is perceptible in any of her muscles. She ceases to breathe. Her body becomes cold. Her heart gives out no pulsations that are easily detected, although her physicians have not convinced themselves that it does not beat. The initiatory start often raises her up into a half-reclining position, in which she remains as immovable as though she were of marble. Every one who has seen her in this condition speaks of the beauty and pathos of the scene—the ashen complexion; the brown, fine waving hair streaming toward her shoulders, yet not reaching them; the faultless features, neither wrinkled nor drawn nor wasted, and yet not rounded and ruddy as in her school-girl days; one hand and graceful arm transfixed in its position at the instant of attack, perhaps pointing upward, perhaps extended to receive a visitor's salutation, perhaps folded over her breast; the other arm bent behind her head as though she were resting upon it; the eyes closed.

She remains thus sometimes for half an hour, some- times for half a minute. She has remained so for twenty-four hours. After she recovers, the breathing for a few seconds is very labored, and she is exhausted, the muscles relax to their former condition, and she settles back upon her pillow with a very marked expression of either acute sorrow or great pleasure upon her face, for her experiences in the trance give her one or the other of these sensations.

The trances are the only rest she obtains. She never sleeps. Day and night are alike to her. She can distinguish persons, forms and colors with as much accuracy at midnight as at midday, although it is established beyond question that she has not the sight of her natural eyes, nor has she such normal sight save in the interval mentioned since the beginning of the attack.

"MAD" MOLLIE

The Effect of Excitement.

Any undue excitement throws her into a trance—a thunder clap, the firing of a cannon, the unexpected intrusion of a stranger into her room, worry over an absent member of the household; and the trances are repeated with rapidity until her mind is again in repose. Often-times, when worried over the absence of some loved one, she has said, "I must search for her," and has gone into the trance. On emerging therefrom, if asked whether her search was successful, she answers promptly if in the affirmative; " Yes, I saw her in Street; she will soon be home," and very soon in walks the wanderer. Sometimes she is not successful in several attempts, but she ceases not until satisfied. At other times her vision wanders. It has gone to a summer seat on the Hudson, where were several of her friends, and she has afterward been able to describe minutely the houses, the barns, the meadows, and fences, the water in front of and the woodland in the rear of the dwelling, and with a fidelity that is instantly recognized by those familiar with the region.

When scientific men and physicians have produced some extraordinarily difficult tests she has been obliged to wait until the trance condition came upon her; for it does not seem always to be voluntary. But if it is a simple question of reading an ordinary sealed letter, or announcing the arrival of a person at the Street door, she easily solves the difficulty without recourse to the trance. As she rests continually upon her right side, her face is averted from the entrance to the room. Yet she often- times knows who enters, although unable to turn her head, and is quick to discern any peculiarity or change of dress. If a gentleman friend puts on a white necktie in early spring, after having worn a black one, she is quite likely to cry out, her face averted: "Good afternoon, Mr._____ ! Where did you get your necktie?"

It has been deemed necessary to darken her room, and the shades are tightly drawn; yet the darkness does not affect her vision. She is ever busy in the darkness, reading or at needle or wax-work, or casting up the accounts of the family, for she keeps a record of every expenditure. She writes letters with astonishing rapidity, in a neat, legible hand; although it is certain she cannot see with normal sight, and, mindful of the interest that her condition may excite among scientific men, she has kept a complete record of her feelings, her sensations while in trance and out of it, her religious beliefs as strengthened or shaken by the revelations of her peculiar state, and of everything that she thinks will interest her friends. This record she guards with care. She is willing that it may be given to the public after her death, but not until then.

"MAD" MOLLIE

Her fondness for dogs and cats, birds and squirrels has amounted almost to a passion, yet, strangely enough, her pets do not live long. Whether she draws the life from them has been an interesting study for some of the men of intelligence who have visited her.

Persons who have entered the room have found her apparently doing nothing, and have asked her why she was idle. "Oh, I am reading such and such a book."

"Well, where is it?"

"Under the bedclothes, here," and she produces it and talks of its contents.

Blind, Yet Discriminating Colors.

While Miss Fancher's eyes were absolutely sightless, the eyelids being closed and the eyeballs fixed as though in death, she was able with facility and without seeming effort, to make marvels of fancy work. For her gentlemen friends she embroidered suspenders and worked slippers and watch pockets, and for companions of her girlhood she made needlework of all kinds, pin cushions and wax flowers. Every stitch was in proper place, every shade of colored thread and worsted was correctly drawn.

Her handiwork was as near perfection as could be. Some of it was sent to fairs, where its maker being unknown it was pronounced superior to all others of its kind exhibited.Sometimes she worked from paper patterns purchased at a fancy store, sometimes from other fancy work, but oftener she originated her designs. It was impossible to deceive her in the quality or shade of the materials with which she worked, her rare power of so-called second sight enabling her to detect any flaw with greater accuracy than did the natural vision of her friends.

Once, when a peculiarly delicate effect in a piece of worsted work called for an especial shade, it was necessary to ask a gentleman friend to procure it for her in New York city. Miss Fancher evinced considerable anxiety lest an error should be made in the selection, and gave more minute directions concerning its purchase than was her practice. In due time her friend returned with the parcel. "You've bought the wrong shade, I am sorry to say," was the greeting she gave him before he had so much as spoken to her, and while the worsted was yet in his pocket.

"It's just according to sample, Miss Mollie. The salesman was very particular to compare them."

"Yes, he may have thought so, but it's a shade too light, and it will not do."

The worsted was produced and the pattern from which the work was to be made was put by its side. Those in the room could not detect a difference. The sick girl insisted that it was too light. "Take it back, please, when you are passing, and the expert will convince you that I am right," she said. Back went the gentleman with the worsted.

"You gave me the wrong shade," said he to the clerk.

That young man examined and denied.

" Call your expert," said the ambassador, and the expert came.

"It is a lighter shade than the sample," was the expert's decision, and he quickly produced the proper one.

"This is just right," was Miss Fancher's greeting, as the second parcel was handed to her unopened.

Marvels in Wax Work.

Yet more astonishing are her effects in wax work. She fashions in wax beautiful designs—windows filled with flowers and vines and butterflies, bouquets, crosses and anchors. Once asked how she was able to do all this, she answered: "Oh, I see the leaves and then make others like them."

All this wax work making and embroidery and needle- work on canvas is made while one hand is rigidly held back of her head. With this hand she holds her work and plies the needle with the other. Even though she had the sight of her eyes, it must be impossible for her to see the work in the position in which she is compelled to hold it. She works monograms of her own fancy into the silk handkerchiefs of her gentlemen friends, and puts butterflies and leaves and birds upon them with rare taste and skill. One of the most beautiful of her wax work productions—an exquisite and delicate bower of roses and creepers, adorns the parlor of Prof. West's Brooklyn Heights Seminary, 126 Montague Street. She has not neglected any of her friends; all have some little gem of her own fashioning.

"MAD" MOLLIE

Watching Her Distant Friends.

The faculty that the young lady's friends have most frequently noticed in her is that of following some of her acquaintances—those who are dearest to her as a rule—from place to place. Hundreds of times she has done this with scarcely an error as to place or occurrence. For example, one afternoon she suddenly said:

"I see (mentioning the gentleman's name) in his office. (The office was in New York.) He is closing his desk. (After five minutes' pause.) He is walking down Fulton Street. (Another pause). Now he is going upon the ferry-boat; now he is getting into a Fulton Avenue car. With him is a tall gentleman with black eyes, black hair and mous- tache; they are talking and the car has started. Now they are passing the City Hall. There, the tall gentleman has got out of the car at St. Felix Street and is coming on alone. He, too, has got out of the car and is coming this way; I guess he is coming here. Yes, he is; here he comes around the corner; look out and you will see him," and looking from the window the gentleman referred to was indeed approaching at a rapid pace and was soon in the room.

" Whom did you ride up with?" was asked by one of the persons to whom Miss Fancher had been describing the ride.

" Mr._____."

" Describe him."

" Tall, black hair, moustache, and dark eyes; he left me at St. Felix Street—why?"

"Mollie has been watching you for three-quarters of an hour or so, and has been telling us about this tall man. You had better be careful how you carry your-self," was the reply.

Her Sight Not Omnipresent.

It may be of interest to those who would seek searching inquiry into the girl's powers of sight-seeing to know that she cannot follow two persons who take different directions. This was proved unintentionally by an accident a few months only after the remarkable power was first developed, and one that was at that time considered the most astonishing of her performances. An intimate lady friend was convinced that Miss Fancher's powers were identical with those possessed by clairvoyants, and she wished to consult a clairvoyant that she might compare the two. Miss Fancher had, from the first, disclaimed any connection with so-called clairvoyants. To be classed with them or to be suspected of employing their methods, so far as she knew what their methods were, gave her mental pain. Her sensitiveness upon the subject made her unhappy.

Seeming to divine that her powers would certainly be called by some clairvoyance, she took especial occasion to beg that no clairvoyant, or spiritualist, or second-sight seer be permitted to see her. She wished to have nothing to do with them. This feeling, therefore, led this intimate friend to make no mention of her desire to consult a clairvoyant, knowing that it would pain Miss Fancher to know of the visit. Before starting, the lady called upon the girl and, after a half-hour's stay, started to go. At the same time a gentleman friend present arose to go. " See if you can follow me where I go," he said, as he left the room with the lady. The gentleman went to New York and the lady to a clairvoyant's house, where, having tested the clairvoyant's powers to her satisfaction, she drifted off into a general talk in which Miss Fancher's case was mentioned, and at length departed. Thoroughly interested, the lady decided to go again to see her. She found the girl sobbing as though heart broken.

"What is the matter, dear," the visitor asked soothingly.

"You have been to see a clairvoyant about me, and it makes me feel, oh, so badly," was the reply, and Miss Fancher proceeded to narrate in exact detail through what streets the lady had walked, and at what number she had rung the bell and been admitted. The details were absolutely correct. It was an incident that had interested the girl more than any other as yet coming within her notice since her changed condition, and is regarded by many as proof that things that most directly concern her are things which her powers of sight-seeing most clearly define. The next time that the gentleman friend called, he asked: "Did you follow me the other day, as I asked you to?" to which she answered: "Yes, until your car reached Cumberland Street; then I saw that Mrs. (mentioning her lady friend's,name) was doing something that very much interested and pained me, and I could not go with you any further, but had to go with her." She seems to have been enabled to follow both in their separate paths for a short distance, although they took different routes after a few steps together; but after her mind became fixed upon the lady's movements, in which seemingly greater mental effort was used, whether required or not, her gentleman friend was lost to view.

Two Curious Instances.

The two stories of Miss Fancher's powers of sight- seeing that her friends tell of with the greatest interest are of the return of her uncle Isaac from California, and the welcome home, some time afterward, of her lost pet dog. Her uncle, Mr. Isaac Crosby, went to California before the accident to Miss Fancher, and while she was a comparatively little girl. He was strong, healthy and robust, with a full face and a big chest. While in Califorma he contracted consumption, and nine years after his arrival there, returned to Brooklyn, and first of all sought Mrs. Crosby, with whom Miss Fancher lives. Prof. West, her old instructor, and Mrs. Crosby, sat in her room when the door bell was rung. Mrs. Crosby started to answer the summons, and as she stepped from the room Miss Fancher exclaimed in astonished tones, "Why, its Uncle Ike !"

" Who is Uncle Ike?" asked Prof. West.

" Uncle Ike! Why, he went to California before I went to your school. How he has changed—how sick he looks." And Miss Fancher entertained the Professor with a description of the uncle's departure for the land of gold, how he then appeared, and his contrasted physiognomy on his return. Meantime Mrs. Crosby had opened the door, and, not recognizing her brother, asked the visitor's business. Mr. Crosby had indeed so changed that it required some little talk to convince the sister of his identity. After a half hour she returned upstairs and saluted Miss Fancher with "Who do you think is down in the parlor?" and Miss Fancher very promptly answered, " Uncle Ike, of course, and he is very sick." The girl had instantly recognized him, while, of course, it was impossible for her to see him.

Miss Fancher's pet dog had contrived to find a warmer place in her heart than had her other pets. He rarely left her, and he was much of a companion in her long hours of wakefulness. But one day the dog disappeared from the house and was seen again no more for some time.

Miss Fancher mourned for him, but she insisted that he would soon return again, and she seemed to be constantly looking for him. It was about 2 o'clock one rainy, tempestuous morning that she aroused Mrs. Crosby. "Get up, get up," she cried, "the dog is coming home, I see him way down the Avenue. He is coming this way and he will soon be here." Mrs. Crosby did not hurry and Miss Fancher broke out once more, "Here he comes nearer. Go down and let him in; he'll be here by the time you get to the door; there he is across the Street—now he's on the step." Mrs. Crosby went down and there was the lost dog, gaunt, hungry, but happy to get home. He was taken to Miss Fancher, and in the silent hours preceding the break of day she fed him with the best the house afforded.

A gentleman who had been a frequent visitor entered her room one afternoon and, laughingly tossed a wallet in the air, saying, " Tell me how much change is in there and will give it to you."

" Sixty-seven cents," was the girl's reply.

The gentleman did not know himself how much money the wallet contained, and counted its contents. Miss Fancher's declaration had been correct.

Her powers of vision seem to have no limit. She has not only seen and described the appearance and actions of friends in other cities, but has been able to picture the doings of very near acquaintances who, for a time, lived in the Bermuda islands.

DR. DURYEA SUGGESTING A THEORY.

The Mind Freed from the Bondage of the Body—Possibly Governed by New Laws—at all Events Quickened and Enlarged.

"I have known of Mollie Fancher for several years," said the Rev. Joseph T. Duryea, pastor of the Classon Avenue Presbyterian Church. "I have seen her, and I have bestowed some study and considerable thought upon her. After I had become convinced that she really did the strange things that were told of her, I mentioned her in some of my discourses. Mr. George W. Benson, who is well known here in Brooklyn as the Chairman of our Committee of One Hundred that undertook to purify city politics, and who is this week out of town, saw her day after day for years, and was absolutely amazed at her powers. I had known of her some time before I went to see her, and in passing the house I had once or twice stopped to speak with her aunt when she happened to be at the door. The afternoon I called upon Miss Fancher, I was with Mr. Benson. He entered the room in advance of me and motioned me to silence. After he had conversed with her a few sentences he said: 'Mollie, who is this?'"

She answered: "I don't see anybody, except you."

"Look sharp," was the rejoinder, and then the girl made a movement as though in mental effort, and after a moment answered, "I see him now; it's Dr. Duryea."

"Did you ever see him before?"

"Yes, down at the gate, talking to aunt."

"How long ago?"

"About three weeks—the day aunt went down to call in the dog."

"Now, how can you prove to Dr. Duryea that you saw him there?"

"He wore a rubber coat."

"Then," added Dr. Duryea, "I remembered that it rained, and as I had to go to the church and then to a funeral that afternoon I had slipped on my rubber coat. I remember it more particularly for the reason that it was the last time I ever wore the coat. I gave it to the driver as I entered the coach after the funeral, and he hung it up to dry by a stove in the livery stable on his return and it was burned up. It was on my way from church to the funeral that I stopped for a moment only, to talk to Mollie's aunt. Mollie's Spitz dog was out on the step barking at boys that were teasing it, and the aunt had gone out to take it in. The girl described us perfectly."

"Being convinced then that Miss Fancher practices no deception, how are her powers to be explained?"

"It is impossible to satisfactorily account for them. That she has most astonishing powers of seeing friends in different parts of the country and city, and of doing other almost incomprehensible things, I have not a doubt. The child cannot deceive; she is beyond that; she does not wish to practice imposition. But her physical changes have in some manner released her mind from the imprisonment of the body, and she does with it what other mortals cannot do with theirs. Here she is deprived first of hearing, then of sight, then of speech, her throat paralyzed—sealed up so that nothing could be passed through It—in such a state that you might as well expect her to swallow a ramrod as a piece of bread; her abdominal organs in the same condition. The mind or spirit was absolutely confined. May it not with a mighty effort have burst away, and, once partly freed from the confines of the physical body have been governed by other and higher laws than those that control it while under the bondage of the body? That men's minds are largely subject to their physical condition is well understood.

"Occasionally, as in this instance, under peculiar conditions, we find this power, which we call second-sight or clairvoyance. What it is we have not yet ascertained, for the reason, possibly, that so few of the cases have been scientifically investigated; no critical comparisons of one case with another have been made to discover the analogies. I think such instances should have the most widespread publicity of descriptions of their mental and physical phenomena. The more we know of them the sooner we shall solve their mysteries."

"Miss Fancher sees the images of those who have gone before her to the spirit world?"

"Miss Fancher unquestionably thinks that she sees them and communes with them. Yet this is not so incomprehensible as some of her other acts. She has known their faces upon earth. With increased mental powers naturally comes increased imagination. I can readily understand how little increase of imagining it would require for you or for me to think in our dreams, or out of them, for that matter, that we are talking with those who are dead. Men imagine they are sick while they are well, and imagine they are well while they are sick, imagine almost every conceivable thing; nevertheless, they always have had something from which to work. Miss Fancher may think she is in heaven, yet she has read enough in her Bible to give her a basis for making a picture of heaven in her mind. While I do not say that she has not seen so-called spiritual sights, I can see an explanation of why she thinks she has seen them. It is her power of sight of things upon earth that are concealed from the sight of others that puzzles me. Tests are made of the power in which she has absolutely no foundation from which to work. How does she arrange and decipher the contents of a letter that has been cut into pieces and sealed within an envelope—a letter the contents of which those who gave it to her had not the slightest notion? Let's settle that before we get into the merits of what it is possible may be produced by a heightened imagination; it's the more astonishing performance."

"Miss Fancher's case is known to many in the neighborhood, is it not?"

"It is; I very often mention it, and I teach its lesson. I like to see such peculiar manifestations of the mind and the body made public. They teach the difference of existence between the spirit and the flesh, and the superiority of the one over the other. I have followed her closely, and always with no more deep wonderment at her peculiar manifestations than admiration of the sweet, contented cheerfulness of her disposition, the purity and simplicity of her life, and her steadfast hope."

PROF. WEST'S REVELATIONS.
A Well-known Brooklyn Man Who Has Spent Hours at Her Bedside—A String of Anecdotes—New York Preachers Interested.

Prof. Charles E. West is principal and proprietor of the Brooklyn Heights Seminary, at 138 Montague Sstreet, and he is widely known throughout the city as a scholar, a man of science, and a Christian gentleman. It was in his institution that

"MAD" MOLLIE

Miss Fancher obtained her education. Immediately upon hearing of the accident to her, a favorite pupil, he went to see her, and barely a week has elapsed since that time in which he has not visited her. She has ever been delighted to greet him, and has confided to him, as much as to any other, her sensations, her joys, her sorrows, her religious beliefs, her secrets. " I have been there by day and by night; have called unexpectedly; have remained there for hours at a time," he said yesterday, " and I have kept complete memoranda of what I have seen and heard. I never knew a more truthful, sincere, and intelligent girl than she has proved herself from the very first of our acquaintance. I have spent my life in study, and I have devoted very much of it for the past twelve years to Mollie Fancher's case. She has been a revelation to me. I think I have recorded every change in her mental and physical condition. I have all the results. It would take you half a day to read what I have written about her, and even then the wonderful things she has done are scarcely touched upon. I have been very anxious that a commission of such men as Tyndall and Huxley and Agassiz be made up to prosecute a most searching inquiry into her condition.

Indeed, I had arranged with Prof. Wyman of Harvard University to come to New York, and, with some one else—we had Agassiz in mind—spend weeks with her. As he was about to start, Mollie was taken worse. She was then in the most death-like condition that we had seen her, and we all thought that she must soon pass away. It was deemed better to postpone Prof. Wyman's visit until she was better able to have an investigation made. But in a few weeks the professor died, and Agassiz also soon was gone. She outlived both.

"I have taken clergymen and physicians to see her. She mystifies every one. They are charmed by her cheerfulness, her vivacity, her Christian faith. It is impossible not to admire her; yet when they see the beautiful works of art that she fashions without the aid of the natural eye, and when they get a glimpse of her wonderful power of so-called second sight, they become mute. I have seen persons who were afraid of her as they might be of a veritable ghost or supernatural apparition. None in all the hundreds whom I have seen at her bedside have I heard express a suspicion that she is an impostor. To see her seems to carry conviction. There is no more doubt that she does these wonderful things than that we sit here. I have seen her do them. I have sat in the twilight of a summer evening and watched her make fancy-work articles in colors, her right arm bent back of her head and resting upon a pillow, the hand capable of being slightly bent at the wrist, her fingers clenched and almost immovable. To this hand she carried the work in her left one, of which she has had the full use, and then the needle danced in and out of the canvas, drawing every thread to its proper place and tension, every color to the exact spot. I knew she was absolutely blind; but even though she had vision

150

she could not have seen her work while it was held in that position."

The Difference Between Black and Brown.

"She distinguished colors with an accuracy that made the rest of us ashamed of ourselves. One evening a physician was there, and he boldly said that he believed she could not detect the different shades. Mollie had a ball of worsted thread, in which were probably ten or twelve colors. She asked the physician to select one, and he pulled out a piece. Mollie's face was turned from him, but he had no sooner separated it from the others than she cried out 'brown.' It was dark in the room, and he went to the window, pushed aside the shutter, and examined the worsted.

'You are wrong,' said he, ' it's black.'

'It's brown, most assuredly,' reiterated she.

"The physician supposed he was right; so he said with the utmost confidence, ' For once you are wrong; it is certainly black.' Miss Mollie quietly reached for the ball of many colored worsteds, and pulling therefrom a thread said: 'Here is a piece of black, that you have is dark brown.' The physician compared the two, and then saw that he was in error and that she was correct.

"I sat in the room another night," went on Prof. West, warming up with enthusiasm, "after it had become dark. Mollie had lost a pet bird—somehow all her pets die very soon; she seems to draw the life right out of them—and a friend had sent the skin to be mounted by a taxidermist. The stuffed bird was on the mantlepiece. We opened the door of the cage in which was a live bird, and as Mollie called to it, it flew to her. She fondled with it for a few minutes, and then it flew from her. We paid no attention to it, but very soon the girl called out to us that the live bird was on the mantel, curiously inspecting the dead one. It was so dark that we could not see it at all, and Mollie's face was turned from the mantel. We made a light, and sure enough the canary was in a brown study over the bullfinch. The girl was absolutely blind, you must remember. The light was extinguished— for light seems to make Mollie uneasy, and our conversation went on. After a half-hour I asked her what had become of the bird, and she answered, 'Why, don't you see him there on the mantel, fast asleep?' We lighted up again, and there the bird was, its head under its wing."

"MAD" MOLLIE

Photographs Recognized.

"She does all sorts of little things that fill you with astonishment. Sometimes I have carried to her a photograph of some one whom she knew before the accident. She always saw and recognized it before it was taken from my pocket. I know of many instances in which she has read letters while they were in an envelope in the pockets of gentlemen. As for books and newspapers, she reads them readily, no matter what part of the room they are in. When first taken she seemed to read by sense of touch, which, by the way, was for many months the only sense she possessed. Drawing her thumb over the printed lines with great rapidity, she was able to tell for a long time thereafter just what the text was. Her memory of things that happened while she was in that rigid condition was astonishingly accurate. I took her a book one day, and she drew her thumb rapidly over the title page and began to laugh. Of course I asked the cause of her merriment, and she answered that—, mentioning the name of a very dear friend, had two years before given her the same book; and with that she gave me a running sketch of its contents in a highly intelligent and surprisingly accurate manner.

"She soon ascertained, however, that it was not necessary to touch the words to understand their meaning, but absorbed the contents of printed or written matter. She knows whenever the newspapers print anything about her before it is read to her. The two things that she seems most to dread are, first of all, any notoriety through public prints or through the gossip of her friends; and second, the being classed in any manner with clairvoyants or second-sight seers or spiritualists, and these dislikes alone should go far toward making the public believe that she does not attempt imposition. Her excessive sensitiveness to all notoriety, and her sincere desire to keep all knowledge of herself from the public, remove every motive for deception. To my knowledge she never has made a penny by her gifts, although having many opportunities to do so. Many persons thinking that she is a clairvoyant, have called to consult her, and many young men and young women have desired her to tell their fortunes, but she has not allowed them to be admitted to the room. She knows who her visitors are long before they are ushered into the hall below, and she allows them to see her, or refuses, just as the whim takes her. I took Kossuth's sister there just before her departure for the Old World. Miss Mollie refused to see her. Afterward I asked Mollie for an explanation. "Why, I didn't like her looks when she entered the door,' was the reply. The door is on the floor below. Another time I took a gentleman of reputation as a scholar. She directed that he be kept from her room, for the same reason; she did not like his looks. While she was blind I took a large man with a great black beard to her, and said, ' What do you think of this little man with a smooth, sharp chin? ' and without turning her face, which was from us, she answered, ' He is very large and has full whiskers. I can see him.'

"She knows what is going on all over the country, but whether from her marvelous sight-seeing or because she reads it, I am unable to say. She is not willing to talk to visitors about her gifts. The topic is painful to her. To her friends, however, she is more free, and she is quite willing at times to explain her sensations. She tells them where she goes and what she does.

"She has revealed things to me of which I had no conception—mainly while we were talking upon religious topics. She is as earnest a Christian as I ever knew. What she sees only makes her faith the stronger; and I believe that her reason for longing to die is that she may go to heaven. I think she has glimpses of the other world, if she has not indeed been there. I cannot tell you that strangely interesting part of her experience. After she is dead it will be known; but it's more of a revelation than that seen by John from the Isle of Patmos."

"Does she see friends who have gone before her?"

"Yes" (speaking with great reluctance). "She sees many of them. She sees her mother. She longs to be with her mother. She says her mother comes to her." And the Professor wiped his eyes, nor did he speak thereafter for many minutes.

A Committee of Clergymen.

"Tell me more of the strange things she does."

"Why! bless you! they would fill a book. The trouble with your printing them is no one will believe them. I have told this girl's history to hundreds; they laugh at me. I told it to Dr. Irenaeus Prime. He laughed at me. But I brought him over to Brooklyn to see Miss Mollie, and he went home convinced, yet mystified. At the next meeting of the Chi Alpha, the secret society of New York clergymen, Prime, after things began to lag, said, 'Do you want to hear an improbable story?' and they all shouted, 'We do.' Well, Prime began to tell them the facts about Mollie Fancher, and he had not more than fairly started before they cried 'Hold—enough—that's too much.' 'Hold! yourselves,' cried Prime, 'didn't I say I was going to tell you an improbable story,' and he made them hear him through. Then they discussed it at great length, and appointed a committee to investigate.

"Over to Brooklyn came the committee, and straight to me, and I read them from my memoranda for an hour and a half, and then they went up and saw Miss Mollie. They reported to the Chi Alpha that all the wonderful things Prime had told them were true, but it was a case beyond their understanding.

"I don't blame folks for not believing; it's past belief."

Why, Dr. was forever making fun of Dr. Speir and myself for believing what the girl does, so one day I took him up to see her. ' I warrant she will perform none of her miracles while I am here,' he said, while on the way. We were not fairly seated before the postman's rap was heard, and down went Mollie's aunt, Mrs. Crosby, for the letter. ' It's from my friend, So-and-so,' said Mollie, when her aunt was half way down stairs. Back came Mrs. Crosby with the letter, and Mollie began to tell what was in it. "Take the slate,' said I to the unbelieving physician, 'and Mollie will dictate the contents of the letter.'

Mrs. Crosby held on to the epistle, and the doctor took the slate, and Mollie began to repeat the letter. She did not take it in her hand, and she was not within eight feet of it. After the Doctor had filled the two sides of the slate, Mollie asked Mrs. Crosby to open and read the letter aloud. This she did, while the Doctor examined what was on the slate. The letter was exactly the same as Mollie had dictated. The Doctor went home convinced of the girl's marvelous powers.

"Yes," said Prof. West, in concluding, "I want to see a commission of the scientific men of the country investigate this strange case. The girl is simply a miracle. She says she is a miracle, and I know she is one. The entire scientific world should know all about her, and I hope the time will come when it will."

CHAPTER XXI.
STATEMENT OF DR. S. FLEET SPEIR.
Relative to the Case of Miss Mollie Fancher,
Taken July 26th, 1893, at Her Residence, 160 Gates Avenue, Brooklyn.

I have treated Miss Mollie Fancher professionally since the 6th of April, 1866, and then learned the history of her case up to that time. At that time I took charge of it, and had in consultation with me Doctor Robert Ormiston of this city, and in connection with him I continued from time to time in attendance down to the present day.

I have read, and carefully considered a letter written by Prof. Charles E. West, dated October, 8th, 1878, in which he describes the condition of Miss Fancher up to that time. I fully concur with the statements made by Prof. West in his letter concerning the case of Miss Fancher, with a few exceptions.

As to her having been paralyzed up to the time of Dr. West's statement, as a matter of fact, Miss Fancher has never been paralyzed, in the sense that the word is usually understood. She has lost the use of her limbs, and at times has lost the power of sensation. As nearly as I can recollect, for a period of about nine years, her lower limbs were in a three twist. The result to the limbs has been that instead of being the natural hinge-joint to the knee, it approaches the condition of a ball and socket joint; her limbs are drawn up backwards, the ankles bent over, and the bottom of the foot bent upwards, and remains in that condition. This is so of both feet. The limbs cannot be straightened out; they are contracted underneath.

For a period of about nine years, day and night, she was subject to trances, spasms and catalepsy. During that time the most constant care and attention were required to prevent personal injury. In these spasmodic conditions she was liable from time to time to be thrown upon the floor, and the greatest attention was required, and barricades were placed around her bed to prevent her doing so. Her spasmodic conditions were so violent that she was thrown backward and forward with great force and rapidity. There was a back motion which is hard to explain, by which she seemed to be thrown into the air, rising from her bed. At times her body would become rigid, and upon one occasion one portion of her body was turned to the right, and the other to the left in a distressing manner, and remained so for quite a time, she being in a rigid condition.

To be certain that Miss Fancher was living without solid food for the long period of time which has been stated, I resorted to giving her emetics, and the result was that nothing was thrown from the stomach, showing conclusively that her stomach was empty. During the period of nine years the quantity of food which she took into her stomach was so little that it was a matter of great astonishment how life could be sustained.

With reference to the condition of Miss Fancher's eyes:—When I first attended Miss Fancher it seemed to me that her eyes were in such a condition that she could not see by the use of them. When I first saw her, her eyes were glaring open, and did not close; did not close day or night, and there were no tears or secretion in them. I made the usual test for anaesthesia, even going to the extent of touching the ball of the eye with my finger, without receiving any response. During the first part of her troubles they were considerably dilated, and not changeable by impression of light. The pupils of her eyes are still considerably dilated, although not so much as formerly, and do not respond to light. The pupil of the eye does not change at the approach of light.

We have caused a careful and critical examination to be made by a competent expert—an oculist— in whose skill we have great confidence, and agree with him that she cannot see by the use of her eyes—at least as a person ordinarily can see. She has the power of seeing with a great deal of distinctness, but how she does so I am unable to state. This condition as to her eyes has been substantially so since I first began to attend her. This feature of Miss Fancher's condition relative to her power of sight has attracted a great deal of comment. At one time she did all her work, crotcheting, etc., back of her head.

When she selected worsted or color she put it behind her head to see it. For nine years her right arm was behind her head, where she did her work by bringing the left hand up to the right hand, which was back of her head. I recall one instance where Dr. Ormiston and myself being present, Miss Crosby received a letter from a postman. I took the letter in my hand; it was sealed, and Miss Fancher at the time being unable to speak, took a slate and pencil and wrote out the contents of the letter, which on being opened and read, was found to correspond exactly with the letter. During that time she maintained conversation with her physicians and friends by the use of the slate, she being unable to speak.

On another occasion she gave me warning that I was likely to be robbed, and told me to be on my guard. The sequel was that immediately after I was robbed of a valuable case of instruments. On another occasion I had invited a number of doctors to call at Miss Fancher's house, and we were waiting for one to arrive, when Miss Fancher said, "He is coming; I see him coming now," and told where he was, which was correct. On another occasion I prepared a paper which I read before a medical club regarding the case of Miss Fancher, and which excited the ridicule of the gentlemen present, when I invited them to visit her and see for themselves. It happened upon that evening that one of the gentlemen present had been reading a clipping of a newspaper which was a very proper thing to be read before, and considered by a medical club, but not quite the thing to be read by a young lady. He replaced it in his pocketbook. On the next day he accompanied us to the house of Miss Fancher, and being very skeptical, advanced to the bedside of Miss Fancher, saying, "What have I in my pocketbook? " She instantly replied, "Something which you ought not to have there."

He started back, and said, "Well, I guess that is so," and gave place for some other gentleman to see for himself.

During my acquaintance with Miss Fancher and her aunt, Miss Crosby, during her lifetime, the actions and conduct of both entitle them to what they always had—our highest respect and esteem.

One remarkable feature during all these years she has been confined to her bed is, that she has never been afflicted with bed-sores, although her right hip, from constant pressure, is flattened, and the flesh is gone, so that the bone is merely covered by the integument. She has always explained, when asked how she saw without the use of her eyes, that she saw out of the top of her head.

Miss Fancher's condition is materially changed from what it formerly was. From being exceedingly thin and emaciated, she is now quite fleshy. She experiences the sense of touch in all her limbs and parts of her body, although at one time, about six years ago, there were indications of paralysis of the left arm which continued for nearly two years, but which have since disappeared. There is a little numbness in her fingers at times even now.

Miss Fancher experiences quite remarkable conditions from the action of her heart. At times the chest over the heart seems considerably enlarged; it presents something the appearance of aedema, but responds to pressure in a different manner. It seems more elastic, and every day she raises about half an ounce of blood, which comes from the mucous membrane of the throat and bronchial tubes. The upper portions of the body are quite fleshy. Her food at the present time is very light, consisting of jellies, fruit, and she drinks great quantities of water.

When she lost the use of her hands, she wrote with her toes, taking the pen between them.

Upon one occasion, when she had lost the power of speech, I was present when some one made a remark, to which she took exception. She took a pencil in her left hand and rapidly wrote a reply, which at first none could read. She had written backward, commencing at the end of a line and end of a word, and so to the beginning. By holding a looking-glass we readily made it out. It was a sharp caustic reply.

S. FLEET SPEIR, M. D.

Statement of Dr. Robert Ormiston.

I have been present at the making of the foregoing statement of Dr. S. Fleet Speir. I am familiar with nearly all the facts to which he has referred, and in so far as I recall them they are correctly stated by him. I also agree with Dr. West in the main, in what he has stated in his letter referred to by Dr. Speir. I have seen Miss Fancher quite frequently since I was first called into her case, and regard her as a lady of integrity.

ROBERT ORMISTON, M. D.

The Eye.

From time to time examinations have been made of Miss Fancher's eyes, and it has been my purpose to insert, in one of the chapters, a more complete statement of their appearance and condition at different periods during the past twenty-eight years of her confinement to her bed.

The death of Miss Crosby removed the one who could have given the most consecutive statement of this important feature of her case. Those who only saw her occasionally can inform us of what they observed when present. Therefore, I shall here set forth what, to me, amounts to the most reliable information of the appearance of her eyes, and of the use she has made of them.

But first, let us speak of the eye itself as an organ of vision.

This wonderful organ is probably the most sensitive of any we possess. A study of its structure and methods, by which its office is performed, impresses the student with the marvelous cunning of the Creative intelligence, which we denominate Deity. Most of the great optical instruments have been fashioned from studying the structure of the eye.

The cornea is the most prominent part, and is most exposed to injury. Any injury to the cornea is likely to result in impairing the sight, as through this part of the organ light must be transmitted to the inner part, which connects with the brain. It is transparent, concavo-convex in form, and composes the interior fifth of the globe of the eye, and is accurately fitted into the sclerotic or fibrous coat, forming the posterior portions of the organ.

The degree of convexity varies, being usually greatest in children, and near-sighted persons. Nature has carefully provided moisture for the eye from the surrounding parts, that the outer surface may be constantly washed or moistened by the action of the delicate inner surface of the eyelid. The eyebrows and eyelashes serve as protectors to the organ itself, which is sensitive to very minute particles of dust. Back of the cornea is a circular vertical membranous curtain, designated the iris, pierced in the middle by the pupil. This curtain hangs in the aqueous humor, separating it into the anterior and posterior chambers of the eye. The iris is variously colored in different individuals. It is provided with delicate fibers for dilating and contracting the surface of the opening constituting the pupil. The cornea is filled with aqueous humor. The crystalline lens is back of the iris, and back of this the vitrious humor, and back of this is the retina, which is connected with and seems to be a part of the optic nerve, which connects with the brain, with which all the nerves are ultimately related. Many have supposed that in some part of the brain there is a point denominated the sensorium, where sensation becomes manifest: the so-called " seat of the soul." That there may be such a point seems quite reasonable; that the exact place has ever been determined is very uncertain. The muscles of the eyeball, to a limited extent, control its action, and cause it to be moved in any direction. There are minute arteries and veins coursing through various parts of the eye, which feed and sustain it.

For at least nine years from my first acquaintance with Miss Fancher, with the exception of the occasion when one of her strange personalities was conscious, I had never seen Miss Fancher's eyes, so as to distinguish their appearance. If they were not entirely closed, they were so nearly so that only a whitish line could be observed at the lower part of the eyeball between the eyelids. When addressing persons in different parts of the room, the eye-balls did not seem to turn under the eyelids as is the case with other persons. When I was able to see her eyes fairly, to me they did not present the appearance of the eyes of any other person whom I had ever seen. There was and is a peculiar appearance about them, which did not indicate that they were in a normal condition. There is another peculiarity about her, which is worthy of careful consideration. If a person should present before her a sharp knife, and make a movement as if to thrust it into her eyes, she would not recoil or exhibit the slightest consciousness of fear or apprehension of danger. She acts precisely as would a person totally blind under like circumstances. It will be hard to find any person who is not blind, who will not flinch when the attempt is made apparent to thrust a sharp instrument into the eye.

Competent persons from time to time, have made careful examinations into the condition of her eyes, and have become satisfied as the result, that her eyes are sightless. The arteries and veins are scarcely perceptible, and indicate that an insufficient supply of nourishment is afforded to the organs of sight to give them strength for ordinary use.

The optic nerve is said to be grayish in appearance, indicating gray atrophy, which would render it incapable of transmitting the sense of sight to the brain itself. She can turn her eyes upward only a little, and then with great effort. But it is common, when she goes into the rigid trance, for the globes of her eyes to be turned very much upwards, so that only small parts of the cornea are visible. At such times, the range of vision of the two organs is not the same, but divergent. She evidently has better action of the muscles controlling the eyes than she did a few years ago.

I recently questioned her as to what had produced the change in the condition of her eyelids, they being open a considerable portion of the time. She replied that she was inclined to attribute it to the coming of the several other Mollie Fanchers who have been previously described, and who also come with open eyes.

This has been going on for quite a number of years now, and it is very evident that with the appearance of each of these peculiar individuals, some of the dormant nerve forces are awakened and brought into action, and cause the opening of the eyelids. This frequent action has tended to bring them more into a normal condition, so that the individuality that we ordinarily see, called "Sunshine," or Mollie No. 1, is regaining to a considerable degree, the use of the eyelids and muscles connected with the eye. Whether this will result eventually in a restoration of the sight of Miss Fancher to a normal condition, is exceedingly problematical.

Disclaiming any more than a cursory knowledge of the structure and disease of the eye, it would not be appropriate for me to conjecture upon the subject.

I notice that some statements have been made, which are herein contained, indicating that for very long periods of time, Miss Fancher's eyes were continuously open. Careful inquiry enables me to say, that when the word "continuously" is used in that connection, it is not to be understood that in the changes produced by her trances and spasms, that at no time were the eyes closed; but that they remained open for a very long period of time; and that a finger could be inserted, and in fact was inserted under the eyelid, and rubbed against the ball of the eye, and would have produced instant pain and inflammation, had her eyes been in a normal condition and sensitive to touch. Even now she can do strange things with her eyes, which indicate to a great degree, absence of sensation.

The fact that a strong light in her room is painful to her, and is seldom permitted, indicates that the optic nerve is not wholly devoid of sensation; but the other fact, that a strong light may be focalized upon this nerve without producing any evidence of pain, in some degree rebuts the presumption that it retains any life whatever. I have known a deaf mute from childhood, to be thrown into spasms of agony from the firing of a cannon close to his head. So also, may it not be possible for Miss Fancher to be distressed by a strong light thrown upon her head and face for a long time, and not be affected by concentrated rays directed into one of her eyes, for a short time?

Light, color and sound are found to be wonderfully related. In her most sensitive conditions Miss Fancher has been found able to distinguish colors, even to the most delicate shades, when absolutely concealed, not only from her normal sight, but while in the pocket of another, and when the experimenter did not know the color of the article to be described. Then, at times, by the mere touch of her fingers to a garment or other article, with her face turned from it, she could correctly describe the color. At other times she has failed to be absolutely correct, all depending upon her physical and mental condition at the time. Those who have made psychology a study by experimenting with sensitive and clairvoyant persons, will understand why good manifestations of abnormal powers cannot always be shown. Such sensitives, when urged to give some manifestation of abnormal powers, become nervous, and as a rule will fail.

Confuse a nervous child and it cannot recite a lesson which it has learned. Persons seeking for knowledge of such matters, should have these considerations in mind, and be gentle, and not themselves too anxious. As an illustration of this important consideration, reference is made to the unexpected visit of a number of medical men with Dr. S. Fleet Speir to Miss Fancher's chamber, when she was required to display before them some of her marvelous powers. At first, she says everything seemed dark, and the doctors were more incredulous than ever; but her clairvoyant sight soon came again, sufficiently strong to enable her to discomfit the foremost of her doubters by informing him that he had something in his pocketbook improper for him to carry.

CHAPTER XXII.

An interesting feature of Miss Fancher's case, which needs more special mention, is her power of discerning colors by the sense of touch. Of course when we have established the fact that she possesses clairvoyant sight, we are left largely to the truthfulness of her own statements as to the possession of the powers of distinguishing colors by the sense of touch, for the reason, when it is shown, that she can see so as to describe what is beyond the range of ordinary vision, it follows that she may be able to see colors, and describe them in the same manner. But those who know her best, do not question her power to sense colors by the passing of her fingers over them. She describes them as conveying different sensations to her. Some are much more pleasing than others. She has her favorites and interblends different ones in her work most exquisitely.

When the day is gloomy, she is depressed, and her clairvoyant sight is imperfect. She is at times largely guided by the sense of touch, in selecting the colors for her work. She is very industrious, and were it not that she can concentrate her thoughts upon some object aside from herself, she would clearly go mad from the contemplation of her own misfortunes and misery.

Miss Fancher exercises some of the gifts of nature more keenly than ordinary persons do. She has a large and well balanced brain. She has excellent business capacities; and is naturally very ingenious.

During the nine years of which we have so frequently spoken, with her right arm carried upward and back under her head, and her hands, with the exception of the thumbs and index fingers, being firmly closed, she did a vast amount of very delicate work. Of course to do her embroidery and work in colors, it was necessary that she should make use of both her hands, so that kind of work was performed above her head, and beyond the range of her natural vision. And yet, it was done with as much precision and nicety, as if she had the ordinary use of her eyes, and was observing by their use every stitch as the work progressed. That she did see, could and can see from the top of her head and from her forehead, cannot permit of a reasonable doubt.

She reads letters placed upon her forehead, and has done so hundreds of times. In doing her work in wax, she was provided by a professor of Harvard College with a peculiar knife, with a rounded blade for cutting the leaves for the flowers. The handle was so constructed that it could be slipped into her closed left hand, and there held while she guided it over the sheets of wax, cutting it in the desired forms, upon a board placed upon her bed. These flowers were delicately tinted by her own hand, with appropriate colors, and many specimens of the work which she did during that long period, are now in the possession of, and are much prized by numerous friends.

She has within the past few years become interested in the work of the George F. Sargent Company, of New York, which is engaged in the manufacture and sale of numerous articles for the comfort and convenience of invalids. It is hard to conceive of anything that an invalid may require, from little wagons, chairs on wheels and reclining chairs, to adjustable tables, beds, and numerous devices, to make the existence of invalids as comfortable as possible, which this company does not manufacture. As might well be supposed Miss Fancher has taken a great interest in the success of the company.

She holds a few shares of its stock, and has been Secretary for a long time, and with her own hand addresses annually thousands of circulars, advertising the wares of the company all over the world.

She sells the articles which she embroiders or crochets to those who call upon her, and desire some memento of their visits. She is naturally proud in spirit, and desires to give something in return of a substantial value to those who may patronize her.

We will in the following chapter give expression to a few thoughts touching upon the range of her clairvoyant powers.

It must not be inferred from what has been said, regarding Miss Fancher's clairvoyant powers, that it is claimed that this gift is exceedingly uncommon. In all ages, of which we have any authentic history, mention is made of persons possessing or claiming to possess this power. Paul possessed it, and in the first chapter of John, from the forty-third to the closing verse of the chapter, is an interesting account of the conversion of Nathanael, who was being brought by Philip to Christ, as being the Messiah. " Jesus saw Nathanael coming to him, and saith of him, behold an Israelite indeed, in whom is no guile.

Nathanael saith unto Him, whence knowest thou me? Jesus answered and said unto him, before that Philip called thee, when thou wast under the fig tree, I saw thee. Nathanael answered and saith unto Him, Rabbi, Thou art the Son of God; Thou art the King of Israel.

Miss Fancher has many times read the contents of sealed letters, and when the fact is established that she cannot see by the use of her eyes, if she can read at all, and discern things so as to describe them correctly around her, it necessarily follows that it must be by the clairvoyant power, or some other equally mysterious gift. Upon one occasion I visited her in company with my wife. We entered the front room, and the doors leading to her chamber were closed. The room was cold, and Mrs. Dailey shivered as she entered. A few moments afterwards the doors opened and we entered Miss Fancher's apartment. She at once remarked, " Mrs. Dailey, are you cold? I saw that you shivered when you came in." There is no way that she could have seen it, without being able to penetrate, or see beyond the walls of the room. She has sent me to get something which was beyond her reach, in her room, and which was entirely hidden from the line of her vision by intervening objects, and when I did not find it readily, she minutely described its position so that I could find it.

CHAPTER XXIII.
"Without the Clap-Trap of Clairvoyance."

To persons who have for years been interested in the study of psychic phenomena, and understand that the term "second sight," as used in the case of Miss
Fancher, is synonymous with "clairvoyance," such expressions as are found in the
headings of some of the newspaper articles, which are in whole or in part here
reproduced as historical matters, are amusing. The term " second sight " has often been used in referring to the fact that old people, whose sight has become
impaired, do some- times regain at very advanced ages, their vision, so as to be
able to dispense with the use of glasses, which they have been accustomed to
wear, and thus to see again as distinctly as in youth. Such cases are not at all uncommon, and the regained power is commonly called " second sight." But these
people only see as do others, in their normal condition, the material and substantial objects by which they are surrounded. They do not perceive those things which
are intangible to the senses of ordinary mortals; they do not see as did the prophet
Elisha, when compassed about by horses and chariots and a great host, which
had come to capture him, the mountains full of horses and chariots of fire, which
were round him to protect him (II Kings, chap, vi, verses 14-17). The power or gift
of sight which the prophet exercised, was not possessed by his servant, until his
eyes were also opened to the entrance of spiritual sight; and then he beheld for
himself, and saw what was to others invisible—forces able to smite and overthrow
the enemies of the prophet.

This is the true second sight, which such cases as this of Miss Fancher tend
to prove will be sometime possessed by all, as the natural result of the change
produced by death from which we shall be raised, as described by Paul, with a
spiritual body, and we shall with our spiritual sight, behold the glories and won-
ders of the spiritual world, of which Paul himself had through the exercise of this
clairvoyant power obtained knowledge (15th chapter, I Corinthians). In the 12th
chapter of I Corinthians Paul says:" Now there are diversities of gifts but the same

Spirit, and there are differences of administrations but the same Lord; and there are diversities of operations; but it is the same God which worketh all in all. But the manifestation of the Spirit is given to every man to profit withal; for to one is given, by the Spirit, the word of wisdom; to another the word of knowledge by the same Spirit; to another the working of miracles; to another prophecy; to another, the discerning of spirits; to another divers kinds of tongues, to another the interpretation of tongues; but all these worketh, that one and the self-same Spirit, dividing to every man as he will!'

In view of the power of second sight, so unmistakably possessed by Miss Fancher, her statements that she discerns spirits, should not be considered in the least as preposterous by those persons who give to Paul their confidence. He was the leading apostle and most conspicuous writer of that age, when the foundations of the Christian church were being laid, and he nowhere claims that he spoke for that age alone. He certainly was speaking to the church at Corinth as a body, and urging the members of that church to seek most earnestly for the highest spiritual gifts, and not in a boasting spirit did he say: "I thank my God, I speak with tongues more than ye all." I Corinthians, chap, xiv, v. 18.

Thus, that which writers have glibly termed the " Clap-trap of Clairvoyance," has, with other gifts which Miss Fancher has at times possessed and exercised, the highest authority of the Christian Church, and should no more be despised or condemned than the exercise of any other gift of God to man. People possess, what we term natural gifts, in unequal degrees. The souls of some persons are strangely affected by the sounds of music. Some are wonderfully gifted in the fine arts, and their works have been the admiration of the lovers of art in all following time.

It is a very common occurrence for people to advance as an argument against the possession of clairvoyant or clairaudient powers by others, that they possess no such gift themselves, and seem to consider that as conclusive proof that it exists in none. It might as well be advanced by a person, that no such thing as tune exists in music, because he has no ear and cannot distinguish one air from another.

Poor blind Tom! Sightless, uneducated, a black son of Ethiopian parentage—who could have suspected that he would have become a prodigy in the musical world? The vibrations of sound left deep impressions in his very soul. He caught the most intricate compositions as they were given expression under the touch of accomplished per- formers, and repeated them, to the astonishment of thousands. The gift he possessed was abnormally developed. Nature, always kind, and striving to repair one misfortune, may have striven to compensate this poor boy for his loss of sight, by attuning his soul to respond to the divine harmonies of sound, until it was full of ecstacy, and overflowed, to the astonishment and pleasure of others.

People who have lost their sight become exceedingly sensitive to touch as well as to sound. An English clergyman was sick with yellow fever in the West Indies. He related to me that when very near death, he was lying on his cot in a hospital ward, when the walls of the room seemed to melt away, and he saw beyond them, and discerned what was being done in other wards from which he was separated by partitions of wood, and brick and mortar. He saw his wife and daughter, who were miles distant, in a carriage, coming on their way to visit him. These pages could be filled with thousands of similar experiences to sustain the statements herein made, as to the powers possessed by Miss Fancher.

On the evening of June 15th, 1893, I visited her; and finding her alone, gathered the following in answer to my questions, which I give as nearly in her language as I can recall:

Question. Will you explain more fully all your sensations of sight?

Answer. Well, as I have said, my vision is not always the same; much depends upon how I am feeling, and the weather conditions. Sometimes the whole top of my head seems on fire with the influx of light; my range of vision is very great, and my sight astonishingly clear. Then again it seems as if I was seeing through a smoked glass, and my vision or consciousness of things is dim and indistinct. Sometimes I can see all through the house. When my aunt was alive it was the most common thing for her to mislay her portmonaie (purse), veil, or gloves, and not know where to look for them, and to come for me to find them, and I would go rumaging through the house, and finally tell her where to go for them. I have the same powers now, but not at all times. Were some one to come suddenly and ask me to do such a thing, I might not at the moment be able, but after a little, when not anxious to see, I can see most clearly.

Question. Do you when not entranced see your friends in the other world around?

Answer. At times I do. They seem very real to me. Let me explain if I can make myself clear how it is. I can compare my sense of sight as much to a camera as anything. Sometimes a face seems close to mine, and then it shuts out the view of surrounding objects the same as the objects would close to the camera. Then again the central object is further away, and my range of vision is greatly enlarged. Do you understand?

Question. Now, tell me more particularly about what you say and do in your trances?

Answer. Well, when I go into my trances, I am usually conscious of being in existence, but they are not like dreams. They are like indistinct wanderings; something like the dreams I used to have when asleep, before I was injured. When I come out of my trances, they at times leave quite distinct recollections, or impressions upon my mind. Sometimes they are dim, and are slowly recalled, and then become very distinct. Now, as a usual thing, when I go into a trance, I go out and around, and see a great deal. Sometimes I go into a house and view the condition of the rooms, and do not see any one in the rooms. Sometimes I see persons and nothing more. I very seldom speak of where I have been, and who I have seen. At the time that Mr. Sargent was incorporating this company, I am connected with, he was at Muskegon, Michigan. I went into a trance and was gone for hours. My friend, Bert Blossom was present in the room; when I came out of the trance, he was greatly alarmed, thinking I was dead. I told him I had been away to where Mr. Sargent was, and saw him on a stage, and he was singing to an audience of people in a large room. I had seen and heard him. Mr. Blossom said that that was most unlikely; but within the next three days I received from Mr. Sargent a letter, informing me of the fact that a Mr. Chase, at Muskegon, had opened a large piano factory, and that they had celebrated the event by a concert, at which he had taken a part in singing; and he also sent me a newspaper giving an account of the affair, and I subsequently learned from him that I had correctly described the event and scene.

I have upon two occasions blindfolded her, and upon each she described objects in the room, and what persons present were doing, with the same exactness as before my having covered her eyes.

I have repeated very little of conversations had with Miss Fancher, concerning her statements to me of her having seen spirits. Upon one occasion, I said to her " People speak of your thinking you see spirits." She re- plied, "Well, I see spirits if I see anything. I know what I see as well as other people know what they see."

Quite recently Madame LePlongeon, a personal friend of both Miss Fancher and myself, informed me that she had just had quite an experience with Miss Fancher. She had called on her, and she complained of great nervousness, occasioned by the presence of the spirit in her room of quite a distinguished man—an editor—who had recently passed to spirit life. She said this spirit came to her early in the preceding evening, and had given his name, and had endeavored with great persistence to make known something, which he wished, evidently, to communicate to his wife. She could not make out his message, and desired him to leave her, which he did not do at once, but continued his efforts until the following morning, when, like the ghost of Hamlet, he stole away.

At one time he brought his wife before her, and showed Miss Fancher some paper, from which she inferred that these were papers he wished his wife to have. His wife is still living.

Miss Fancher had never seen this man or his likeness before. Madame Le Plongeon then went to the Brooklyn Library, and found, after considerable search, a likeness of this man among a large number of others, which she brought in a large publication and covered the name under each, before she presented it to Miss Fancher. Miss Fancher rejected several until the correct likeness was presented, which she at once recognized, saying, "Now, his hair is gray, in the picture it is black."

The picture was one taken in the gentleman's early life, when his hair was dark. At the time of his death it was gray. In the presence of Dr. Ormiston and Dr. Speir, I asked Miss Fancher about this occurrence, and she corroborated the statement of Madame Le Plongeon quite fully.

CHAPTER XXIV.
A PEN PICTURE.
By Miss S. C. Clark.

During long years of personal invalidism, the writer had heard much and thought often with deepest sympathy of the remarkable invalid of Brooklyn, from whose couch of phenomenal suffering physicians sometimes came to her own. How many inquiries were made of them regarding her, how sad the stories told, how natural the longing thus encouraged to see this beautiful, patient girl. Released at last herself from painful bondage to the flesh, and years later visiting New York, the old-time desire sprang forth once more to see Mollie Fancher, a wish prompted by no motives of idle curiosity but from friendship already warm and true, from yearnings of sympathy and compassion born of that strong kindred tie—the fellowship of suffering, even though her own had been of a type not to be mentioned in comparison with this modern miracle.

A friend, whose privilege it had been to make Mollie's acquaintance, volunteered the office of conductor to her bedside, receiving in response to the query sent her by mail, the usual gracious assent vouchsafed to the many thousands who year after year have coursed through that chamber, which is at once prison-house and shrine.

Arriving at the little three story house, set squarely upon the pavement at the corner of two quiet Brooklyn streets, a pause was first made in the fancy goods store, on the Street floor, where so many and such varied specimens of the sick girl's beautiful handiwork were displayed on sale. Paintings on silk, velvet and other textures, embroideries of rarest excellence, whose flowers bore the touch of inspiration upon them, even the fragrance breathed forth from the artist's pure soul; there were divers articles of worsted work, and souvenirs of every choice and quaint design. It was a most pathetic display, as if the heart's blood of the patient sufferer had been crystallized into many colored gems, a kaleidoscope of genius born of pain—that crucible of power.

The lady in attendance, lifting the mouth-piece of a speaking tube, signalled to the quick ear chained to its pillow in the room above the arrival of expected guests, and the order was immediately given that they be allowed to ascend to the parlor on the second floor, from which wide folding doors led to Mollie's room— that chamber with its tragedy of twenty-eight years' conflict, under the burden of a life which has come to its possessor as a crown of thorns, the scene of many vain yearnings for the Angel of Death, so pitifully reluctant to approach with his oft-time coveted release.

Who could enter this place but with reverence, or fail to step lightly as if upon holy ground? The pale afternoon's rays of a winter's sun fell with caressing touch across the farther corner of the room, whose light was dimmed by the draperies that partially concealed the pane. Against an opposite wall arose the back of a high pointed bedstead, across which were arranged large linen pillow-shams, as if the couch were unoccupied, while low in front of these a snowy bolster lay across the bed, and upon this, at one side, a tiny, thin pillow held the dear, curly head, from which flashed a smile of welcome, lighting up the whole face with radiance, despite the closed lids and sightless orbs. The hands were extended with warmest friendly grasp, and seats were assigned near by, the courtesy not neglected of request to lay aside bundle, hat and cane, an attention which a hostess less blind might easily omit, for it is always the warm heart that forms the mainspring of true politeness and not the acquired finesse of social mandates.

And what was the vision that then enthralled the gaze? What did this girl look like who for years had been torn by spasms, convulsions and agonies inconceivable? Where was the trace of this supreme anguish? Was the face contorted and misshapen, the flesh shriveled and wrinkled as one might readily suppose? Ah, no! The face might easily have represented that of a maiden still in the bloom and freshness of youth with the texture and hue of health. Round and full and pink and white, every line and contour of face or feature expressing a sweet serenity of disposition which could easily ripple into mirth. No trace was there of most excusable impatience, no wrinkled record of frown or scowl. A small pretty mouth accustomed to smile, and above the closed blue eyes and the placid white brow arose a crown of auburn hair, glinted with sunlight caught from some other realm than this, whose solar radiance she has not seen for so many weary years. The hair is short and parted on the side nearest the pillow where from its constant friction it is much worn, but the tightly curling rings are tossed jauntily upward on the top of the head as fitting aureole to the gentle, sunny face.

172

"MAD" MOLLIE

A dainty dressing sack of delicate pink, embroidered by her own needle, left the plump white throat exposed, and the loose sleeves fell back from a perfectly moulded arm and beautiful hand at whose juncture tiny circlets of gold almost cut into the dimpled wrists. As she lies in bed, she looks hardly the length of a child, as from her knees her limbs are turned sharply back, and, when in merry vein with her attendant, she sometimes revolves them in their sockets as if turning the handle of a street organ.

Yet pathos enough fills her heart as she engages in conversation, discussing freely her peculiar and pitiful history, and tears flow in spite of her efforts at self-control when she speaks of the dear aunt who for twenty-six years laid by her side at night, and watched her hourly with tenderest care. When asked if with her wonderfully clear vision she cannot still enjoy her dear companionship and see also other dear ones who have been so strangely taken from her; "O, yes," she said, "I see them constantly, but I want them here. I long for the sound of their voices and to feel the dear touch of their hands."

Ordinary words of comfort and cheer fall powerless here in the presence of this overwhelming burden of suffering increased by loneliness, poverty, and the loss of almost every earthly tie. The situation is one that the strongest heart could not behold unmoved, it is a test of endurance under which the best balanced mind might falter and weaken. Yet clear is every mental faculty, unimpaired and fine the intellect, the affections warm and spontaneous in their expression. The narrowness of the habitual invalid, shut in perforce between four chamber walls, finds here no place; her interests are wide and varied. The patience with which she has endured these long, pitiless years is superhuman, and has its fount deep within a soul that must be known to be appreciated.

It is said that no man is ever a hero to his own valet, and yet an attendant who has watched over Mollie in the dreary, agonizing night struggles, when for many an hour the heart has stopped its beating, and who has seen her in every painful experience, exclaimed to the visitors as they took their departure that wintry day, "O, yes, she is beautiful, but then you can't begin to know her in a brief call. You have to see her day after day and month after month to realize quite how sweet and lovely she is."

Strange and awful mystery of a life that has no parallel. Who can unfold its wonderful secret, its cause and purpose? If, as is claimed, astrology holds the key to human destiny, why among the myriad births which must have occurred on the planet at the hour of Mollie's advent, has no repetition been found of this life of torture and slow release? Beneficent stars are found in every other horoscope.

173

"MAD" MOLLIE

The explanation has been offered that no babe born at the hour of Mollie's nativity could have survived its sixth year. She also should have gone there. Her mother departed instead, and consequently being no longer properly related to the planet, this girl is unlike anything upon it, and therefore not amenable to the usual measures of relief effectual with other sufferers.

Again, the not irreverent but awesome question arises, what is the divine purpose in this strangely blighted existence? There is a divinity that shapes our ends. Chance is not supreme ruler. Then why this prolonged suffering when purification seems already out-wrought? Are there deeper lessons in spiritual truth yet to be learned?

Was there a prior life-record of which this strange and terrible experience is the sequel? In what other way than by the acceptance of the fact of a re-embodiment can the reputation of Deity be saved from reproach? A human monster of injustice and cruelty would not inflict this prolonged torture or behold such resignation unmoved. Has the hazardous gift of free agency brought sometime to this soul mistakes which can only be overcome and outgrown by a mighty atonement?

Problems all to the human mind which often forgets that "while wisdom and sight are well, still trust is best;" a trust so unflinching that it never falters, but grows brighter under every test, exclaiming with the psalmist, "Though He slay me, yet will I trust in Him."

The present hour is hard to bear and difficult to comprehend; but of dear Mollie's future, when freed from the body of this death, there can be no doubt. Her truest friends can anticipate in her joyful release, the weight of glory which will be hers when every pain shall be transformed to a radiance with which few newly emancipated spirits can be clothed, even the "white robes" only worn after "great tribulation," and every tear this crucial discipline has cost will but add brighter jewels to her fadeless crown.

CHAPTER XXV.
MOLLIE FANCHER, THE WOMAN.

To such as enjoy the privilege of intimate acquaintance with Mollie Fancher, it is probable that the idea of phenomena connected with her life, rarely occurs to them; unless indeed, it be the fact that a life schooled to such suffering can exemplify so perfectly the analogy of the gold of the refiner's fire. We therefore beg permission to drop the curtain for awhile, on the more dramatic scenes and incidents of her phenomenal existence, while we attempt to give a few glimpses of Mollie Fancher, the woman.

On the same side of the same bed, the earnest, patient face has peered out from beneath the snowy coverlid, and the aching head has pillowed itself on the same resting-place, through all the weary years of suffering. And yet the pittiless blade of pain has plowed no furrows in her placid brow; no silver threads among the silken curls bear evidence of King Time's march; and the tiny, shapely hands, with their pink, taper fingers, are no tell-tales of the prodigious product of their cunning.

Her bed is placed with the pillow to the east. At her right is a low piece of furniture—half stool and half chair—with back and side-arm; underneath the (lifting) seat of which is an ample compartment. This serves as a seat for her friends as well as a receptacle for such articles as she may wish close at hand.

To the right of the bed, placed against the wall, is a dainty device of her own invention, answering the double purpose of bureau and cabinet. It has curtained shelves below in lieu of drawers, the canopied top forming a recess above filled with bric-a-brac, etc. All of this is artistically arranged and tastefully draped. These articles of furniture, to the casual observer, would seem to be merely the caprices of architectural design; but from the quantity and variety of articles she is able to produce from them, one would almost imagine that there was a warehouse just beyond.

There is a marked personality about all her belongings, as about every thing she does. Order is a part of her nature. What she needs and uses most frequently is always within reach of her hand. She directs the disposition of every article of the house, whether above or below stairs, and never forgets where such and such a thing is; even to the interior of a bureau drawer, or a closet, from garret to cellar.

Her own apartments have that peculiar unstudied air of restfulness which causes the visitor to wonder at the effect produced; and yet, if we attempt to individualize any single article in the rooms, nothing could be found that might be considered especially elegant or luxurious.

The furniture is practical and comfortable. Pictures, dear to her more from association than from artistic elegance, embellish the walls. Here and there are unique pieces of bric-a-brac, a screen, or odd pieces which have been presented her. A sweet little window-garden, and an aquarium, fill the south window. One or two birds within their cages, are singing, or hopping from perch to perch, and usually there are to be found flowers and fruits, that at the same time exhale sweet odors, and charm the senses.

Miss Fancher is decidedly unlike any other invalid. If the reader has a preconceived idea of her as one of the sanctimonious sort, with long-sleeved, starched night-gown, and ruflled collar and wristbands, lying, with hands folded, apparently waiting and listening for the dip of the ferryman's oar, we must disabuse him or her of that fancy.

To look at her, you forget the invalid. She has a noble face, but withal one that is exquisitely sensitive in expression to the emotions that sway the heart. Her head is finely shaped; with hair conveniently short, parted jauntily upon the right side, and, as Tennyson expresses it, " running over with curls." Around her shapely throat, she wears, as she has done for years, a string of silver beads; and a few simple rings ornament her fingers.

Without vanity, she is a lover of the beautiful, and has an eye for the artistic, hence, her personal appearance is always attractive. The sacks that she usually wears, are of dainty tints, and tastily embroidered; and are of her own design and handiwork.

The side of the bed upon which she lies, is a separate section, occupying but half its space, and has an adjustable head or back, which enables her to rest in a position slightly reclining. When at work, at her feet, within easy reach, is a willow basket, containing the implements of her industry, writing materials, etc.; while the other side of the bed serves as a table for unfinished work.

Mollie Fancher is every inch a woman. A healthier mind never made its dwelling-place within a mortal body; and though physical suffering is an ever present attendant, and while she is ready at any and all times to follow the beckoning finger of "Death's bright angel," all of that gives her no concern. The unfaltering faith that has held her through sufferings equivalent to an hundred physical deaths, still seems as an anchor for the tempest-tossed barque,—ready to be cast for permanent mooring, when the voyage of life is ended.

She is keenly sensible to the responsibilities of living, and ever ready to follow in the procession, bearing her share of life's burdens in common with her fellow-travelers, in the belief that the more thoroughly life's lessons are learned, the larger the measure of joy that will be meted out in the nobler and more extensive sphere of useful activity in the existence beyond.

We have described her rooms and surroundings; picture, then, Mollie Fancher the woman, at work. When it became apparent that there was no escape from the fetters of infirmity that were to bind her as long as life should last, she set at work to adjust to her shoulders the yoke upon which the burdens were to be placed, without a murmur.

The active, intelligent brain took the lead; it conceived things of beauty susceptible of execution in needle-work, flowers of wax, etc.; and the willing fingers obeyed the mandates of the mind. No obstacle was so great, but the way was found to overcome it. Her nine long years with one arm drawn to the back of the neck, and the other hand with the four fingers clenched to the palm, the thumb alone being free for active use, were still years of industry; and with sightless eyes, through all available conscious hours, day and night alike, until the mental images were transferred into fabric, startling in originality, vivid in color, and reproducing Nature to an extent hitherto unequaled.

The world will never know how much of pain there was interwoven with these stitches, nor what became of the proceeds of that labor. She had a way, 'tis said, of not letting " the right hand know what the left hand doeth," and the nine years referred to are a blank in the memory of the Mollie Fancher of to-day; but in a variety of ways, it has leaked out, that at about this time, there were hungry mouths fed and shivering children clothed, that never knew who was their benefactress. Although the flowers of wax that were fashioned by those crippled hands, exhaled no odor, we feel that, inasmuch as the Mollie Fancher of that period is dead, it is appropriate to her memory, to render, in behalf of the forgotten beneficiary, this tardy tribute; that from the spirit that inspired the making of these flowers of wax, was emitted a perfume as fragrant as the sweetest incense ever in censer, before sacrificial altar.

Ample and well-authenticated statements are elsewhere in this volume made, pertaining to that period of nine years, around which, like a parenthesis, have been drawn the marks which separate it from her life before and after.

Occurrences of that time, are still referred to, both by herself and her friends, as contemporaneous with the life of "The Other Mollie." That individuality did, actually, die, so far as any subsequent developments up to the present time have indicated. There has been no reappearance of that identical personality. The physical life, however, was continued, and Life's burdens had to be taken up at the point from which they were dropped, nine years before. With this digression from the thread of our subject, we will take up the broken chain of her life, at the threshold of her (so-to-speak) renewed existence.

If the "Other Mollie" has ceased to exist as a personality, she surely bequeathed the spirit that animated her limited life, to the Mollie that succeeded her. And al- though it was bewildering to her, at first, to follow the trend of her thought and action, yet by degrees the situation was mastered. Methods of work that were devised by the "Other Mollie," were studied by the "New Mollie."

Work that was left unfinished by the former, was completed by the latter, according to lines laid out; and thus, in more senses than one, were the broken threads of life spliced so deftly, that the knot uniting them was scarcely discernible. The acquaintances that were formed by the one, were re-introduced, and became the friends of the other; and by the aid of papers, memoranda and letters, left by the "Other Mollie," together with the information derived from friends, the old life gradually so far merged into the new, that the latter became reconciled to carry on, unflinchingly, the effort of her suffering existence—at the same time doing with all her might what her hands found to do.

So much has been written concerning Miss Fancher's ability and capacity for work, that our readers may have been led to wonder if work of such character as has been described, fills up the measure of her life. We assure them that such indeed is not the case.

A mind and temperament such as she possesses, could not be content with anything short of the full development of its every faculty.

Miss Fancher's peculiar condition has in many respects been favorable, and exceptionally so, to the acquirement of a large fund of general information, by which she has striven to profit, and which she has utilized to the best advantage. Physical misfortune, therefore, in her case, as in others, is not without its advantages, and its compensations.

Owing to a wonderfully retentive memory, her mind is a storehouse of practical knowledge; it might be compared to a cabinet of shelves, filled with manuscripts, filed away and labeled, but always ready for production and application as occasion requires. Those who know her best, wonder most at her stable, yet kaleidoscopic character. Stable, in that you always find her the same sturdy, thrifty woman, and kaleidoscopic, in that, no matter how often you meet her, there is always something new to be seen. Her vistors' book displays a record of so many, that it would appall most any ordinary woman to think of entertaining them. Since the beginning of her illness, a careful estimate places the total number of her calls, at between seventy-five and one hundred thousand; and yet, out of this vast number of different persons who have made up the grand aggregate, (with the exception of those who called during that nine years which is a blank in her memory,) there is probably not a forgotten face or name. And it is doubtful if there is any woman living that has made as many friends as has Miss Fancher, during the period of her sickness. Numbered among them, are many of both sexes distinguished in the various arts, sciences, and learned professions; as well as in the financial, commercial and social world.

With the advantages of such personal intercourse, her naturally receptive mind has been developed by the imbibing of information and ideas resulting from such contact, to an extent which falls to the lot of very few. She has also, by the courtesy of the Brooklyn Library, had access to its many volumes; which privilege she has by no means neglected. Added to this, she has been a constant reader of the daily newspapers, thereby keeping pace with the current events of the time. It will thus be seen, that many circumstances, of vastly diverse kinds, have combined to make up a well-rounded character.

Miss Fancher is a brilliant and versatile conversationalist; and, although having decided opinions of her own, she is not inclined to obtrude them. But when occasion demands, she is thoroughly capable of enforcing them with a logic that is not easy to combat. She is sparkling in humor, and caustic in repartee; quick to see the ludicrous side of anything; enjoys a good story, and both the making and the taking of a good joke. Many instances might be related illustrating her ready wit; but it is the lightning-flashes, coupled with her gestures and facial expression, that most charm the auditor; and these, of course, cannot be transmitted to paper.

On one occasion, a gentleman calling upon her, was, as he thought, pressing her into retreat by the force of his argument; but her readier wit discerned his weak point, and she so adroitly turned the tables on him, knocking out the whole underpinning of his argument, that he was himself vanquished. Throwing up his hands, he exclaimed, "Well! you ought to have been a man!" She quickly followed up her advantage by retorting, "I just wish I were a man for about five minutes!" and by pantomimic action, which indicated his personal annihilation, he was left to contemplate what indeed might have been his fate had such really been the case!

On another occasion, a gentleman who prided himself on his superior wit, undertook to chaff her, upon her alleged powers of second-sight. He facetiously inquired:

"When you are away on any of your occult preambulations, do you ever come across me?"

She answered:"Oh, yes; frequently!"

"Well," he rejoined, "that is very interesting. Do you ever see anybody around me?"

"Very often," was the demure reply.

"Ah, indeed!" continued the gentleman, sagely. "And can you give me any idea what they look like?"

"Creditors," was the good-natured but crushing reply.

Among the many phases of her character, there is perhaps none more beautiful, than that which is brought out by questions which touch the heart. Her sensitive lip will always quiver at the recital of a tale of grief or suffering. At such times she seems to forget her own crosses and trials. Her quick intuitions and keen insight into human nature, prompt her to speedy action, whenever she sees the way to aid those in trouble. Her special aversion, is meanness, in any form. She delights to spread the sheltering mantle of charity over any weakness in others, but selfishness, she abhors. She is so punctilliously honest and straightforward herself, that the person who undertakes to perpetrate anything of an opposite nature, in any transaction with her, does not long remain uninformed as to her views of the matter, which she has the faculty of making so plain, that if there is a latent sense of honor in the individual, an acknowledgment will be offered, or the perpetrator will slink away with the consciousness that he or shehas been weighed in the balance and been found wanting.

The old adage that "Satan finds some mischief still for idle hands to do," can not be applied to Mollie Fancher. Her busy brain is too much occupied with her own affairs, to be able to give unsolicited attention to those of other people. A secret confided to her, is as inviolable in her breast, as though it were buried in the grave. An idle gossip, especially where there is in it a taint of scandal—is to her a thing that is loathsome. Her tastes all run to the beautiful, good and useful.

It has always been an ambition of Miss Fancher, to be of use in the world; something, indeed, that should enter into a wider sphere of usefulness, than the making fancy work or embroidery. Some six or seven years ago, an opportunity presented itself in a rather peculiar, though perfectly natural way, of which she availed herself. A lady friend, who is widely known as a contributor to current literature, asked the privilege of bringing to her bedside and introducing to her, a gentleman of her acquaintance, whom she thought Miss Fancher would like to meet, as he was interested in all such cases as hers, he having devoted much time and study to the devising of appliances for the relief and comfort of invalids. Upon his being introduced to her, she said, " Why, you are Mr. Sargent, the Invalid's friend; I have read your advertisements so often, that surely I am glad to meet you." (An account of this interview went the rounds of the press, as may be remembered by some of our readers.)

With subsequent visits, the acquaintance begun at that meeting, grew; and very naturally with it, Miss Fancher's interest in the work in which Mr. Sargent was engaged. It is unnecessary to follow the details relating to the business; but this sketch of Miss Fancher's life would be in- complete, if allusion were not made to the fact that she became identified with the enterprise of which Mr. Sargent was the founder. Known at that time as " The Sargent Manufacturing Company," but recently reorganized and incorporated under the name of " The George F. Sargent Company," this enterprise has for its President, Mr. Sargent, and for its Vice-President, Miss Fancher, with office and warerooms at 814 Broadway, New York.

It should not be inferred, from Miss Fancher's connection with commercial matters, that she is the "typical business woman"—planning and scheming only for the dollar. While any pecuniary benefits that may be derived from her work or interests, she does not pretend to despise, such motives are remote from the real purpose that actuates her.

Had the nature of the business been of a different character, it must doubtless have had no special attraction for her. But in the success of an enterprise such as this, the chief object of which is, the development of devices for the relief of suffering humanity, and the grouping together in such an establishment of all such articles as tend to the comfort of her fellow-invalids, she became deeply interested; and has, ever since her identification with it, been a most important and helpful factor in its fortunes.

In the affairs of the Company, she finds much congenial occupation; and though denied the privilege of the routine work of the office and store, she acquaints herself with their every detail. Each new article handled by the Company is brought to her bedside for inspection, that she may understand its purpose, and be ready to aid by her suggestions, as to faults that are apparent, or improvements that might be made. Through the extensive correspondence, a new world is opened, with which she is brought in touch. The meetings of the Directors are held in her room, and she is a potent influence in their councils. There is a considerable amount of detail work, to which, in her own peculiar way, she finds time to give attention, which to her is at the same time diverting to the mind, and pleasurable in the execution.

In her school-girl days, Miss Fancher was more than ordinarily proficient as a musician. She was the possessor of a sweet though not powerful soprano voice; and as a pianist, the most exacting music offered little difficulty in its rendition. The study of music was not drudgery; music was soul-food, and entered into every fibre of her nature. In later years, notwithstanding the chain of untoward circumstances, that had bound her to a bed of suffering, music has lost none of its charms; it has, indeed, proved the solace of many weary hours. And so, instead of through peevish murmurings, her pent-up sufferings have many a time found a relief in an outburst of tuneful song.

With the Goddess of Music thus enshrined in the heart, the soul can sing, and the lips can smile. It is an inheritance on earth, that bankruptcy cannot touch. It is the ladder by which pilgrims through the darkness climb to the regions of celestial light.

No devotee to the art of music can be indifferent to the other twin sister— poetry. They are the the offspring of the same divine paternity. Neither can plume its pinions for flight, without the other's aid. If one knocks for admittance at the door of a human heart, its hinges must swing back for both. They are God's messengers; sent to attune the heart-strings for rhythmic vibration with the harmonies of heaven.

At Mollie Fancher's heart, their knock was heard, and they were both bidden to enter—and have ever remained —welcome guests.

Should it be asked in what direction lie her poetical tastes, definite answer could hardly be made—only to say, it is a part of the air she breathes. For her, there is poetry in all of God's handiwork. The flowers exhale it; it shimmers in the sunbeams, sparkles in the snow-flakes, sighs in the whispering zephyrs, and weeps in the falling rain-drops. While she bows reverently at the shrine of

"—The grand old masters,
—The bards sublime,
Whose distant footsteps echo
Through the corridors of time; "

She dwells more with
"—The humbler poets
Whose songs gushed from the heart;
Such songs have power to quiet
The restless pulse of care,
And come like the benediction
That follows after prayer."

Yes, with Mollie Fancher, it is the heart-songs that are her treasures; something that has in it strains responsive to the cadences of her own life. She may gather them from the garnered granaries of the greater poets, or catch them from the fugitive verse that covers the skies of current literature; but if there be a ripened berry within the pod, it will be extracted, and find a hiding place within the caskets of her poetic jewels.

Are there not lessons to be learned from the life of Mollie Fancher? We have watched her bravely battling with the giant adversary, Pain; have followed her through the prosaic routine of her daily life; and have remarked her flight, as on eagles' wings, above life's commonplaces. But we have heard no murmur at unkindly Fate; nor do we find record of an idle hour.

Her daily answered prayer, which is given in the following lines in facsimile of her own hand-writing, has been,

Facsimile of handwriting, and original poem by Miss Fancher.

My God, O spare one thing—
To lie with empty folded hands;
I am content to bear my cross.
And will not murmur at the bands
That bind, nor count affliction lost.

But spare, O spare me this;
To lie throughout the livelong day
And through the watches of the night,
Counting the hours. Dark though the way,
With busy heart and hands, my light,

To feel I'm needed not
To live and lie with folded hands,
While others are vouchsafed that bliss,
The need of meeting life's demands;
Spare me, my God, O spare me this.

CHAPTER XXVI.
As a Neighbor.

The following, from a private letter, is published by permission:

Dear M.:
* * * * * ******
You ask if I can tell you any thing about Mollie Fancher. Certainly! In Brooklyn, not to know about this famous lady, is to prove one's self unknowing, whether unknown of not. Mrs. Carleton and myself often visit her.

It seemed very interesting to learn that she was a neighbor of mine; I was not long in sharing the knowledge with her, of which I was not so sure whether it would interest her equally; for she has the luxury of her own likes and dislikes. But a ten minutes' walk brought us together; and I may say truly that we became great friends at once, and have been so for some years.

I confess that, like others, I first sought her from the motive of curiosity. But that all vanished in a moment, before the attractions of her womanly nature, and the genuine warmth of her deep heart. Here was not a curio —or a mystery—or even an invalid, so far as the mind was concerned; but a large-brained, pure-souled woman; physically prone—always prone, God help her !—upon her bed; but mentally and spiritually standing erect in the fullest dignity of her sex, and bidding defiance to every limitation that could afflict the body !

I felt no more liberty to ask her about her peculiar occult gifts, than concerning her private business matters; and not being a scientist, a physician, or a theologian, I have deferred knowing any thing about them from personal information, until she happens to be in a mood to tell me. Then, with her permission, I will give you my views upon the subject.

But as a neighbor, I am free to say, that Mollie Fancher is valuable and charming. A friendly half hour chat with her, is a tonic. She knows all the news, and much history; she can converse about the great events of the world—the only kind of gossip that is not belittling, She shows an honor and honesty in every remark, that leads one to feel that he can throw off the harness of restraint and talk with her as with a friend, and not with a possible newspaper reporter, or social item-monger. She is patient and amiable, and I have never heard a harsh word from her lips, except when talking about something mean and unjust. She is sagacious and sparkling in conversation; her remarks are entertaining enough for the most exacting salon. She is sound of judgment on business matters; her mind is gifted with the vertebrae of common sense.

Her perseverance and industry are marvelous, from all accounts; but for these she claims no credit. They help her forget the pain that comes and comes, but never goes. Her bravery and courage are constantly to the fore, and are needed, in all the various afflictions that fall upon her; for this woman, who for so many years has prayed for death, has wept through the hours of the distant funerals of all of her kin. Her manners and speech are more refined than those of many who have had the opportunity of moving about in the world, with all the advantages derived therefrom. Her personal appearance is not that of an invalid, but of a lady reclining at ease upon the couch of her parlor. Her spirit of love and charity toward the rest of her race is very pronounced, and finds expression in presents to her friends and deeds of charity to the poor.

Stepping into her rooms one day, I saw an old gentleman of between seventy and eighty, taking leave of her. As he passed me, with a word of kindly greeting, he quietly remarked: "I have been visiting here many years, and never went away without feeling that I was a better man than when I came." And that describes Mollie Fancher, in a word, and explains why so many of us visit and value her as a neighbor, and not as a curiosity.
*****

WILL CARLETON.

CHAPTER XXVII.

Conclusion.

With this chapter the task I commenced more than two years since is completed. I fully realize that it is imperfectly done, and that much of interest might be added concerning the life of Miss Fancher. During those two years, events have transpired relating to her which should be mentioned now.

Shortly before commencing this book, I was requested by that eminent scientist, Doctor Elliot Coues, President of the Psychical Congress, held at the Columbian Exposition World's Fair Auxiliary, in Chicago, August, 1892, to carefully investigate, make and report to that body, the facts of the case of Miss Fancher. This was done, and the report was read to a large and attentive audience. It occasioned much comment at the time, through the public press of this country, and also in foreign journals.

As a result, many persons have sought the opportunity to personally visit Miss Fancher, that they might form their own opinions regarding the truth of many of the statements contained in that report. Others have desired a committee of scientific gentlemen to be appointed, to make a personal and critical examination of the lady, and as to her powers, with the expectation that a report signed by such a committee, would forever settle in the public mind the much mooted question, as to whether such powers were ever exercised by any person, and particularly by Miss Fancher. To this effect is an article entitled "The Case of Mollie Fancher," published in the Medico-Legal Journal of New York, June, 1894, edited by Clark Bell, Esq., of New York City. The Section on Psychology of the Medico-Legal Society of New York, appointed a committee, consisting of eminent medical gentlemen, to examine into the case, with whom I was expected to cooperate. For reasons stated to the Executive Committee of the Society, I did not advise Miss Fancher to submit to the desired examination. These reasons were published in that number of the Journal as follows:

"MAD" MOLLIE

"I have seen Miss Fancher quite often for the last thirteen or fourteen years, and I see, what appear to me, great changes in her condition. She is no more the thin, spare girl or woman she was when she did so many wonderful things which have made her life remarkable. She is no longer a fasting woman. While unable to masticate her food as others do, she partakes of the juices and strength of food, and, I think, drinks copiously of water.

"There is a good deal of nourishment in water, people are beginning to learn. She is fleshy; her shoulders are broad, her face is quite large, and usually she has very dark places under her eyes, extending down on her cheeks, as if blood had settled there from a severe blow; this, the physicians say, comes from defective heart action.

"She has the use, so far as I can see, of both hands. She turns herself quite readily in bed. Her eyes, much of the time are open, and move in the direction of the object she is looking for, and I think it is quite apparent, that with the return of other powers, she has regained her eyesight to some little degree. Her lower limbs are still comparatively useless. Her feet are twisted out of shape and the cords under her knees are rigid as steel; her limbs are also exceedingly thin. She gives considerable attention to business matters. She is able to do a good deal of writing, is easily excited, and as sensitive as a person can well be to everything pertaining to her friends and herself. She keeps well posted by reading on public affairs, and has opinions of her own upon all matters which she is able to express in a forcible manner. Recent investigation as to the condition of her sight, shows that there is a change in the appearance of her eyes, but when medical experts examined them carefully with the opthalmoscope, they found the optic nerve presented a very strange appearance, and that her eyes were unlike the eyes of any person, in other respects, they had ever examined. She distinguishes colors by touch; has her trances as she always had them, which serve for her the purpose that sleep does in others. She nightly goes through the various changes of personality described in my report of her case to the Psychical Congress. In my opinion, investigation made at the present time as to her condition, would not reveal many of the remarkable features which have now become historical in her case, and are vouched for by the testimony of so many unimpeachable witnesses; nor is this to be marveled at.

"She has lived far beyond her own, as well as the expectations of her friends. She is subject to frequent hemorrhages from her lungs, and requires the temperature in her room down almost to freezing point, and dimmest possible light. She certainly is able to see fine print, and do fine work in a light so dim, that it would be impossible for others to do the same. She is at times very clairvoyant, at others not so much so."

That, from my knowledge of the great change that had taken place in her condition, I did not believe that the investigation proposed would be at all satisfactory to the medical committee, and I advised against it on that ground.

The editor then proceeds to comment as follows:— "It is unfortunate that the friends of Miss Fancher take this attitude. Regarding the examination Judge Dailey says: 'She distinguishes color by touch; has her trances as she always had them, which serve for her the purpose that sleep does in others. She nightly goes through the various changes of personality described in my report of her case to the Psychical Congress.' Now that her sight is restored and she takes nourishment, a verification of the leading features of her present state, and the remarkable phenomena of her clairvoyant powers, as stated by Judge Dailey, by a committee of physicians, whose statements would be accepted by the scientific world, would be of the highest value to the acquisition of scientific truth, and, this now omitted, will lend additional doubt, and add to the reserve with which the medical profession receive the details of her in every way remarkable case. Judge Dailey may still be able to induce her friends and advisers to consent to the arrangement of some plan, by which the leading facts of her present state and condition may be made documentary, by the evidence of carefully selected members of the Medico-Legal Society, in some manner least objectionable to her, and leave no reasonable doubt as to the actual phenomena her case presents in the minds of the professional men."

Should Miss Fancher at this late period of her life, when some of the most remarkable features of her case have disappeared, and the most startling events of her life have become historical, submit to the desired investigation, what could this committee now investigate, that would tend to prove or disprove the most important statements concerning her? They certainly could not investigate the events of the nine years, and the phenomena which then occurred. Then, and for that long period, her clairvoyant powers were unquestionably continuous.

It has already been stated, that great physical changes have taken place in her condition, and her clairvoyant powers are not so great as formerly, and at times they are almost wholly gone. There are periods occurring with great irregularity, when her clairvoyant sight is intensely keen, and if the proposed committee was to visit her upon one of those occasions, it would unquestionably be satisfied of that one fact in her case. But these conditions are of uncertain duration, and if the gentlemen chanced to come, in what she terms one of her "dark days," when her senses are greatly blunted, she would render herself liable to their adverse criticism, and most unjustly so. That such would be the result of any investigation now, she and her friends are warranted in believing, from the language contained in the article referred to. The writer of that article assumes too much, when he says, in substance, that the scientific world would accept the statements of the committee of physicians, even as to her present condition. The statements of these learned gentlemen would only be additional testimony to what is already before the world, which would be of some value, but would be accepted as conclusive by very few.

The notoriety of her case, as has been already stated, is not of Miss Fancher's seeking. All the sensational publications concerning her have been against her wishes. She has steadfastly protested that she is in all respects a private individual, and has reluctantly consented to this publication of her case. The facts and testimonials are presented herewith, and those who read them can accept or reject them at will. I doubt not but that as private individuals, the gentlemen composing that committee, would be received by Miss Fancher, and in company with some of her friends, she may consent that they may sit at her bedside most of a night, until the nightly changes of personalities occur, should they desire to do so.

It must not be forgotten that Dr. West is published as stating, that Miss Fancher and her friends consented that a committee of scientific gentlemen, should make a through examination of her and into her case, at a time when its startling features were constant, which unfortunately was not done. Dr. West, Prof. Parkhurst, Doctors Ormiston and Speir, most of whom have known her intimately for many years, and all of whom have investigated the facts of her case, and certainly are educated and scientific men, have given their testimony which appears in this volume; and if they are not to be credited as truthful, the result of a casual investigation made now, certainly will not be. For the last twenty years or more Dr. Robert Ormiston, has, in his professional capacity, been at least a weekly visitor to Miss Fancher. His reputation is second to none as a man of integrity, and of skill and ability, as a physician. I have no authority to refer others to him for further information, as to what he knows, concerning the facts of the case of Miss Fancher, but have little doubt, that Miss Fancher will consent, that he make known much that he withholds from the public, which would be of great interest to investigators. As a scientist, while modestly disclaiming to be such, those who know him most intimately, declare him to be a gentleman of eminent attainments, and by no means a novice in psychological research. My own experience and observations in occult and unusual phenomena of a psychological character, convince me, that as a rule, every person wishes to observe and be satisfied through his own senses, and is not willing to take the statements of others as at all conclusive in such matters. That Miss Fancher should give herself up to the incessant inquisition of investigators, is unreasonable in the extreme.

The editor of the Medico-Legal Journal, when he assumes that I have said that Miss Fancher had regained her sight, is mistaken. My article reads:"And I think it is quite apparent, that with the return of other powers she has regained her eyesight to some little degree." I do not know that she can see by the use of her eyes at all, even now. At times I have been of the impression that she could, at others I have been very positive that she could not. The recent changes which have taken place in her condition, particularly in the movement of her eyes and eyelids, indicate returning sight; but I have seen the eyes of persons totally blind present a similar appearance. I doubt, considering her nervous condition, if any remarkable evidence of her clairvoyant powers could be obtained, were she to know that she was being subjected to tests to prove her clairvoyance. Once, knowing I was trying to test her powers, she was unable to tell what I had in my closed hand; but a few moments later, when her mind was diverted by conversation, she told me correctly that it was something that shone like a diamond. It was a diamond. She explained that when she knew I was going to test her, everything became dark around her, which disappeared after a few moments' conversation upon other matters.

Within the last few weeks, Miss Fancher's father died, and this event, though not unexpected, has pierced her heart with a new sorrow, though she appreciates that he is at last relieved from the great suffering which attended the closing years of his life.

In conclusion, I take this occasion to thank those who have kindly contributed articles to this work, and regret that the timidity of others, has induced them to withhold valuable testimony coming under their observation and experience.

I especially desire the public to understand, that beyond the actual cost of its publication, this book, its copyright, and proceeds of sales, are the property of Mary J. Fancher.

Brooklyn, November, 1894.

"MAD" MOLLIE

www.ingramcontent.com/pod-product-compliance
Lightning Source LLC
Chambersburg PA
CBHW062059090426
42741CB00015B/3274